By Way of Deception

*To all those who
gave their lives willingly,
though they should have
been spared*
— V.O.

*To Lydia:
My own secret
inspiration*
— C.H.

By Way of Deception

Victor Ostrovsky and Claire Hoy

St. Martin's Press
New York

Contents

Authors' Foreword

REVEALING THE FACTS as I know them from my vantage point of four years spent inside the Mossad was by no means an easy task.

Coming from an ardent Zionist background, I had been taught that the state of Israel was incapable of misconduct. That we were the David in the unending struggle against the ever-growing Goliath. That there was no one out there to protect us but ourselves — a feeling reinforced by the Holocaust survivors who lived among us.

We, the new generation of Israelites, the resurrected nation on its own land after more than two thousand years of exile, were entrusted with the fate of the nation as a whole.

The commanders of our army were called champions, not generals. Our leaders were captains at the helm of a great ship.

I was elated when I was chosen and granted the privilege to join what I considered to be the elite team of the Mossad.

But it was the twisted ideals and self-centered pragmatism that I encountered inside the Mossad, coupled with this so-called team's greed, lust, and total lack of respect for human life, that motivated me to tell this story.

It is out of love for Israel as a free and just country that I am laying my life on the line by so doing, facing up to those who took it upon themselves to turn the Zionist dream into the present-day nightmare.

The Mossad, being the intelligence body entrusted with the responsibility of plotting the course for the leaders at the helm of the nation, has betrayed that trust. Plotting on its own behalf, and for petty, self-serving reasons, it has set the nation on a collision course with all-out war.

I can not be silent any longer, nor can I risk the credibility of this book by hiding reality behind false names and obscured identities (though I have used initials for the last names of some active field personnel, to protect their lives).

Iacta alea est. The die is cast.

VICTOR OSTROVSKY, *July 1990*

* * *

In more than 25 years of journalism, I have learned that you should never say no to anyone who offers you a story, no matter how bizarre the offer sounds. Victor Ostrovsky's story sounded more bizarre than most, in the beginning.

Like most journalists, I've sat through my share of listening to people breathlessly explain why their story has been suppressed through the evil work of the Intergalactic Martian Conspiracy. On the other hand, all journalists have experienced the high of responding to a tip, only to find that the story it leads to is a dandy.

One afternoon in April 1988, I was at my usual spot in the parliamentary press gallery in Ottawa when Victor Ostrovsky phoned to say he had a story to tell me that was international in nature and might interest me. I had recently published a controversial bestseller entitled *Friends in High Places*, on the troubles of the current Canadian prime minister and his government. Victor told me he liked my approach to officialdom; that was why he had decided to offer me his story. He gave no details, but suggested meeting in a nearby coffee shop for 15 minutes so I could hear him out. Three hours later, Victor still had my attention. He did indeed have an interesting story to tell.

My first private concern, inevitably, was how do I know this man is what he says he is? Well, some private inquiries through contacts, coupled with his willingness to name names and be open himself, made it much easier over time to conclude that he is the genuine article: a former Mossad *katsa*.

Many people will not be happy with what they read in this book. It is a disturbing story, hardly a chronicle of the best that human nature has to offer. Many will see Victor as a traitor to Israel. So be it. But I see him as a man who has a deep conviction that the Mossad is a good organization gone sour; a man whose idealism was shattered by a relentless onslaught of realism; a man who believes the Mossad — or, for that matter, any government organization — needs to be publicly accountable for its actions. Even the CIA has to explain itself to an elected body. The Mossad does not.

On September 1, 1951, then prime minister David Ben-Gurion issued a directive that the Mossad be created as an intelligence organization independent of Israel's ministry of foreign affairs. To this day, although everyone knows it exists — politicians at times even boast of its successes — the Mossad remains a shadow organization in every respect. You will find no reference to it in Israeli budgets, for example. And the name of its head, while he holds that position, is never made public.

One of the main themes of this book is Victor's belief that the Mossad is out of control, that even the prime minister, although ostensibly in charge, has no real authority over its actions and is often manipulated by it into approving or taking actions that may be in the best interest of those running the Mossad, but not necessarily in the best interests of Israel.

While the nature of the intelligence business, by definition, involves considerable secrecy, certain elements of it are nevertheless open in other democratic countries. In the United States, for instance, the director and deputy directors of the CIA are first nominated by the president, subjected to public hearings by the Senate select committee on intelligence, and finally must be confirmed by a majority in the Senate.

On February 28, 1989, for example, the committee under Chairman David L. Boren met in room SH-216, Hart Senate Office Building, in Washington, to question veteran CIA official,

Richard J. Kerr, on his nomination as deputy director of Central Intelligence. Even before undergoing the public hearings, Kerr had to complete an exhaustive, 45-part questionnaire, airing everything from his biographical, academic, and employment experiences, to his finances, including what land he owned, his salary during the past five years, and the size of his mortgage, along with questions on organizations he belonged to and his general philosophy of life and intelligence.

Opening the hearing, Senator Boren acknowledged that it was a rare occasion for the committee to conduct its business in public. "While some other nations provide for legislative branch oversight of their intelligence activities, the extensive nature of the process in our country is truly unique."

Among other things, the committee conducts quarterly reviews of all presidentially mandated covert-action programs and holds special hearings whenever the president initiates a new covert action.

"While we have no power to veto proposed covert actions," he continued, "presidents have in the past heeded our advice by taking actions either to modify or cancel activities which the committee believed to be ill-conceived or which we believed posed unnecessary risks for the security interests."

In Israel, even the prime minister, although supposedly in charge of intelligence, often doesn't know about covert activities until after they've occurred. As for the public, they rarely know about them at all. And there certainly is no committee scrutiny of Mossad activities and personnel.

The importance of appropriate political guardianship of intelligence was summed up by Sir William Stephenson in the foreword to *A Man Called Intrepid*, in which he said that intelligence is a necessary condition for democracies to avoid disaster and possibly total destruction.

"Among the increasingly intricate arsenals across the world, intelligence is an essential weapon, perhaps the most important," he wrote. "But it is, being secret, the most dangerous. Safeguards to prevent its abuse must be devised, revised, and rigidly applied. But, as in all enterprise, the character and wisdom of those to whom it is entrusted will be decisive. In the integrity of that guardianship lies the hope of free people to endure and prevail."

Another legitimate question about Victor's story is how a relatively minor functionary in the Institute, as the Mossad is called, could possibly know so much about it. That's a fair question. The answer is surprisingly easy.

First of all, as an organization, the Mossad is tiny.

In his book *Games of Intelligence*, Nigel West (pseudonym of British Tory MP Rupert Allason) writes that CIA headquarters in Langley, Virginia, which "is actually signposted from the George Washington Parkway, outside Washington, DC," has about 25,000 employees, "the overwhelming majority [of whom] make no effort to conceal the nature of their work."

The entire Mossad has barely 1,200 employees, including secretaries and cleaning staff — all of whom are instructed to tell those who ask that they work for the defense department.

West also writes that "evidence accumulated from Soviet defectors indicated that the KGB's First Chief Directorate employed some 15,000 case officers" around the world, about "3,000 based at its headquarters at Teplyystan, just outside Moscow's ring road, to the southwest of the capital." That was in the 1950s. More recent figures cite the KGB's total total number of employees worldwide at more than 250,000 employees. Even the Cuban DGI intelligence service has some 2,000 trained operatives posted across the world in Cuban diplomatic missions.

The Mossad — believe it or not — has just 30 to 35 case officers, or *katsas*, operating in the world at any one time. The main reason for this extraordinarily low total, as you will read in this book, is that unlike other countries, Israel can tap the significant and loyal cadre of the worldwide Jewish community outside Israel. This is done through a unique system of *sayanim*, volunteer Jewish helpers.

Victor kept a diary of his own experiences and of many related by others. He is a rotten speller, but possesses a photographic memory for charts, plans, and other visual data so crucial to the successful operation of intelligence. And because the Mossad is such a small, tightknit organization, he had access to classified computer files and oral histories, counterparts of which would be unobtainable by a junior player in the CIA or KGB. Even as students, he and his classmates had access to the Mossad main computer, and countless hours were spent in class studying in minute detail, over and over again, dozens of actual Mossad operations — the goal being to teach the new recruits how to approach an operation and how to avoid past mistakes.

In addition, while it may be difficult to quantify, the unique historical cohesiveness of the Jewish community, their conviction that regardless of political differences they must all pull together to protect themselves from their enemies, leads to an openness among themselves that would not be found among employees of, say, the CIA or KGB. In short, among themselves, they feel free to talk in great detail. And they do.

I want to thank Victor, of course, for giving me the chance to bring this remarkable story to light. I also want to thank my wife, Lydia, for her constant support in this project, particularly since the nature of this story continues to impose more pressure than my standard political fare.

In addition, the Parliamentary Library in Ottawa was as helpful as always.

CLAIRE HOY, July 1990

Prologue:
Operation Sphinx

Butrus eben halim could be forgiven for noticing the woman. After all, she was a sultry blonde, given to wearing tight pants and low-cut blouses, revealing just enough of herself to pique any man's desire for more.

She'd been showing up at his regular bus stop in Villejuif on the southern outskirts of Paris every day for the past week. With just two buses using that stop — one local and one RATP into Paris — and usually only a few other regular passengers standing around, it was impossible to miss her. Although Halim didn't know it, that was the point.

It was August 1978. Her routine, like his, seemed constant. She was there when Halim arrived to catch his bus. Moments later, a light-skinned, blue-eyed, sharply dressed man would race up in a red Ferrari BB512 two-seater, pull in to pick up the blonde, then speed off to heaven knew where.

Halim, an Iraqi, whose wife, Samira, could no longer stand either him or their dreary life in Paris, would spend much of his lonely trip to work thinking about the woman. He certainly had the time. Halim was not inclined to speak to anyone along the way, and Iraqi security had instructed him to take a circular route to work, changing it frequently. His only constants were the bus stop near his home in Villejuif and Gare Saint-Lazare Metro station. There, Halim caught the train to Sarcelles, just north of the city, where he worked on a top-secret project that involved building a nuclear reactor for Iraq.

One day, the second bus arrived before the Ferrari. The woman first glanced down the street searching for the car, then shrugged and boarded the bus. Halim's bus had been temporarily delayed by a minor "accident" two blocks away when a Peugeot pulled out in front of it.

Moments later, the Ferrari arrived. The driver looked around for the girl, and Halim, realizing what had happened, shouted to him in French that she had taken the bus. The man, looking perplexed, replied in English, at which point Halim repeated the story for him in English.

Grateful, the man asked Halim where he was headed. Halim told him the Madeleine station, within walking distance of Saint-Lazare, and the driver, Ran S. — whom Halim would know only as Englishman Jack Donovan — said he, too, was headed that way, and offered him a lift.

Why not, Halim thought, hopping into the car and settling in for the drive.

The fish had swallowed the hook. And as luck would have it, it would prove to be a prize catch for the Mossad.

* * *

Operation Sphinx ended spectacularly on June 7, 1981, when U.S.-made Israeli fighter-bombers destroyed the Iraqi nuclear complex Tamuze 17 (or Osirak) at Tuwaitha, just outside Baghdad, in a daring raid over hostile territory. But that came only after years of international intrigue, diplomacy, sabotage, and assassinations orchestrated by the Mossad had delayed construction of the plant, though ultimately failing to stop it.

Israeli concern for the project had been high ever since France had signed an agreement to provide Iraq, then its second-largest oil supplier, with a nuclear research center in the wake of the 1973 energy crisis. The crisis had escalated interest in nuclear power as an alternative energy source, and countries that manufactured systems were drastically stepping up their international sales operations. At the time, France wanted to sell Iraq a 700-megawatt commercial nuclear reactor.

Iraq always insisted the nuclear research center was designed for peaceful purposes, basically to provide energy for Baghdad. Israel, with considerable cause, feared it would be used to manufacture nuclear bombs for use against her.

The French had agreed to supply 93-percent-enriched uranium for two reactors provided by its military enrichment plant at Pierrelatte. France agreed to sell Iraq four charges of fuel: a total of 150 pounds of enriched uranium, enough to make about four nuclear weapons. Then U.S. president, Jimmy Carter, had made opposition to nuclear proliferation his main foreign policy effort, and U.S. diplomats were actively lobbying both the French and the Iraqis to change their plans.

Even the French became wary of Iraq's intentions when that country flatly refused their offer to substitute the enriched uranium with another less potent form of fuel called "caramel," a substance that can produce nuclear energy, but not nuclear bombs.

Iraq was adamant. A deal was a deal. At a July 1980 news conference in Baghdad, Iraqi strongman Saddam Hussein mocked Israeli concerns, saying that years earlier, "Zionist circles in Europe derided the Arabs who, they said, were an uncivilized and backward people, good only for riding camels in the desert. See how today these same circles say without batting an eyelid that Iraq is on the point of producing an atomic bomb."

The fact that Iraq was fast approaching that point in the late 1970s prompted AMAN, Israel's military intelligence unit, to send a memo (labeled "black" for top secret) to Tsvy Zamir, the tall, slender, balding ex-army general who was then the Mossad head. AMAN wanted more precise inside information on the stages of development of the Iraqi project, so David Biran, head of *Tsomet*, Mossad's recruiting department, was summoned to meet with Zamir. Biran, a chubby, round-faced career Mossad man, and a noted dandy, subsequently met his department heads and ordered them to find an immediate Iraqi tie-in to the manufacturing plant at Sarcelles, France.

An exhaustive two-day search of personnel files came up empty, so Biran called the head of the Paris station, David Arbel, a white-haired multilingual career Mossad officer, giving him the necessary details for the assignment. Like all such stations, the one in Paris is located in the heavily reinforced underground of the Israeli embassy. Arbel, as head of the station, outranked even the ambassador. Mossad personnel control the diplomatic pouch (the "dip"), and all mail in and out of the embassies goes through them. They are also in charge of maintaining safe houses, known as "operational apartments"; the London station alone, for example, owns more than 100 such flats and rents another 50.

Paris also had its share of *sayanim*, Jewish volunteer helpers from all walks of life, and one of them, code-named Jacques Marcel, worked in personnel at the Sarcelles nuclear plant. Had the project been less urgent, he would not have been asked to procure an actual document. Normally, he would pass along information verbally, or even copy it onto paper. Taking a document involves the risk of getting caught and puts the sayan in danger. But in this case, they decided they needed the actual document, primarily because Arabic names are often confusing (they frequently use different names in different situations). And so, to be certain, Marcel was asked for the list of all Iraqi personnel working there.

Since he was scheduled to come into Paris for a meeting the next week anyway, Marcel was instructed to put the personnel list in the trunk of his car along with others he was legitimately bringing to the meeting. The night before, a Mossad *katsa* (gathering officer) met him, got a duplicate trunk key, and gave the man his instructions. Marcel was to make one round of a side street near the École Militaire at the appointed time: there he would see a red Peugeot with a particular sticker on the back window. The car would have been rented and left all night in front of a café to guarantee a parking spot, always a prime commodity in Paris. Marcel was told to circle the block, and when he came back, the Peugeot would be pulling out, allowing him to take that parking spot. Then he was simply told to go off to his meeting, leaving the personnel file in the trunk.

Because employees in sensitive industries are subjected to random security checks, Marcel was tailed by the Mossad, without his knowledge, on the way to his rendezvous. After again making sure there was no surveillance, a two-man Mossad squad took the file from the trunk and walked into the café. While one man ordered, the other walked into the washroom. There he produced a camera with an attached set of four small, aluminum fold-back legs, called a "clamper." This device saves setup time, since it is already in focus and uses special snap-on cartridges manufactured by the Mossad photography department that take up to 500 exposures on a single roll of film. Once the legs are shoved down, the photographer can slide the documents quickly in and out underneath it, using a rubber attachment held between his teeth to click the shutter each time. After photographing the three pages in this way, the men put the file back in Marcel's trunk and left.

The names were immediately sent by computer to the Paris desk in Tel Aviv, using the standard Mossad double coding system. Each phonetic sound has a number. If the name is Abdul, for example, then "Ab" might be assigned number seven and "dul" 21. To further complicate matters, each number has a regular code — a letter or another number — and this "sleeve" coding is changed once a week. Even then, each message tells only half the story, so that one would contain the code of the code for "Ab," while another the code of the code for "dul." Even if this transmission was intercepted, it would mean nothing to the person trying to decode it. In this way, the entire personnel list was sent to headquarters in two separate computer transmissions.

As soon as the names and positions were decoded in Tel Aviv, they were sent to the Mossad research department and to AMAN, but again, because the Iraqi personnel at Sarcelles were scientists, not previously regarded as threatening, the Mossad had little on file about them.

Word came back from the Tsomet chief to "hit it at convenience" — that is, find the easiest target. And quickly. Which is how they chanced upon Butrus Eben Halim. It would prove to be a lucky strike, but at the time, he was chosen because he was the only Iraqi scientist who had given a home address. That meant the others were either more security-minded, or lived at military quarters near the plant. Halim was also married — only half of them were — but had no children. For a 42-year-old Iraqi to have no children was unusual, not the mark of a normal, happy marriage.

Now that they had their target, the next problem was how to "recruit" him, particularly since word from Tel Aviv was that this was considered an *ain efes*, or "no miss" operation, a strong term in Hebrew.

To complete this task, two teams were called in.

The first, *yarid*, a team in charge of European security, would figure out Halim's schedule and that of his wife, Samira, see if he was under Iraqi or French surveillance, and arrange for a nearby apartment through a "real estate" sayan (one of the Paris sayanim in real estate and trusted to find an apartment in the requested neighborhood, no questions asked).

The second, *neviot*, was the team that would do any necessary break-ins, casing the target's apartment and installing listening devices — a "wood" if it had to be fitted into a table or baseboard, for example; a "glass" if it involved a telephone.

The yarid branch of the security department consists of three teams of seven to nine people each, with two teams working abroad and one backup in Israel. Calling in one of the teams for an operation usually involves considerable haggling, since everyone regards their particular operation as vital.

The neviot branch also consists of three teams of experts trained in the art of obtaining information from still objects, which means breaking in, or photographing such things as documents, entering and leaving rooms and buildings to install surveillance equipment without leaving a trace or coming into contact with anyone. Among their collection of implements, these teams have master keys for most of the major hotels in Europe and are constantly devising new methods of opening doors equipped with locks opened by card keys, code keys, and various other means. Some hotels, for example, even have locks that open using the thumbprint of the room guest.

Once the listening devices, or "bugs," were placed and operational in Halim's apartment, a *Shicklut* (listening department) employee would listen and record the conversation. The tape from the first day would be sent back to Tel Aviv headquarters, where the particular dialect would be determined and a *marats*, or listener, who best understood that dialect would be sent in from Israel as soon as possible to continue the electronic surveillance and provide immediate translations for the Paris station.

At this point in the operation, all they had was a name and an address. They did not even have a photo of the Iraqi and certainly no guarantee that he would be useful. The yarid team began by watching his apartment building from the street and spying from the nearby apartment to see just what Halim and his wife looked like.

The first actual contact was made two days later, when a young, attractive woman with short-cropped hair, introducing herself as Jacqueline, knocked on Halim's door. This was Dina, a yarid worker, whose job was simply to get a good look at the wife and identify her to the team so that surveillance could begin in earnest. Dina's cover was selling perfume, which she'd obtained in large quantities. Complete with an attaché case and printed order forms, Dina had gone from door to door offering her wares at all the other apartments in the three-story walk-up to avoid suspicion. She had made sure to arrive at Halim's apartment before he got home from work.

Samira was thrilled with the perfume offer. So were most of the women in the building. And no wonder, since the prices were much lower than in the retail stores. Customers were asked to pay half up front and the other half on delivery, with the promise of a "free gift" when the order was delivered.

Better still, Samira invited "Jacqueline" in and poured her

heart out to her about how unhappy she was, how her husband had no drive to succeed, how she had come from an affluent family and was tired of having to use her own money to live on, and — bingo — how she was going home to Iraq in two weeks because her mother was having major surgery. This would leave her husband alone and even more vulnerable.

"Jacqueline," posing as a student from a good family in southern France and selling perfume to earn extra spending money, was extremely sympathetic to Samira's plight. Although her initial task was simply to identify the woman, this particular success was indisputable. In surveillance, each minute detail is reported after each stage back to the safe house, where the team digests the information and plans the next step. This usually means hours of interrogation, of going over and over each detail, tempers often rising as various people debate the significance of a particular action or phrase. Team members chain-smoke and main-line coffee, and the atmosphere inside a safe house grows more tense as each hour passes.

And so it was decided that since Dina (Jacqueline) had struck a chord with Samira, this happy turn of events could be used to expedite matters. Her next task would be to get the woman out of the apartment twice — once so that the team could determine the best place for a listening device, the second time to install it. That meant coming in and taking photos, measurements, paint chips, everything needed to guarantee that an exact replica of an item could be produced, but with a bug implanted in it. Like all things the Mossad does, the criterion is always to minimize risk.

During the original visit, Samira had complained about her problems with finding a good local hairdresser to do something about the color of her hair. When Jacqueline returned with the merchandise two days later (this time shortly before Halim was due home, so that she could see what he looked like) she told Samira about her own fashionable Left Bank hairdresser.

"I told André about you, and he said he'd love to work on

your hair," said Jacqueline. "It will take a couple of visits. He's so particular. But I'd love to take you along with me."

Samira jumped at the chance. She and her husband had no real friends in the area, little social life, and the opportunity for a couple of afternoons in town, away from the endless drudgery of her apartment, was welcome.

As Samira's special gift for buying perfume, Jacqueline brought a fancy keyholder, complete with a little tab for each key. "Here," she said. "Give me your apartment key, and I'll show you how this works."

What Samira didn't see when she handed over the key was Jacqueline's slipping it into a hinged, two-inch box, wrapped to look like just another gift, but filled with talcum-sprinkled plasticine to prevent its sticking to the key. When the key was slipped in and the box closed tight, it left a perfect impression in the plasticine from which a duplicate could be made.

The neviot could have broken in without a key, but why take added risks of detection if you can arrange simply to walk through the front door as if you really belonged there? Once inside, they would always lock the door, then wedge a bar between the inside doorknob and the floor. That way, if anyone did manage to walk past the outside surveillance and try to unlock the door, they would probably think the lock was broken and go for assistance, giving those inside more time to get away unobserved.

Once Halim had been identified, the yarid set about the practice of "motionless following," a method to determine an individual's schedule while avoiding any chance of detection. It means watching him in stages, not actually tagging along behind him, but having a man stationed nearby to watch where he goes. After a few days of that, another man stationed at the next block would watch, and so on. In Halim's case, this was extremely easy since he went to the same bus stop every day.

Through the listening device, the team learned exactly when Samira was flying home to Iraq. They also heard Halim tell her he had to go to the Iraqi embassy for a security check, alerting the Mossad to be even more careful. But they still hadn't figured out how to recruit him, and with the top priority of this case they didn't have much time to determine whether Halim would be cooperative or not.

The use of an *oter*, an Arab paid to contact other Arabs, was ruled out by operational security as too risky in this case. This was a one-shot deal and they didn't want to mess it up. Early hopes that Dina as Jacqueline could get at Halim through his wife were soon discarded. After the second hair appointment, Samira wanted no more to do with Jacqueline. "I saw how you looked at that girl," Samira told Halim during one of her carping sessions. "Don't you get any ideas just because I'm going away. I know what you are."

Which is how they hit upon the idea of the girl at the bus stop, with katsa Ran S. as the flamboyant Englishman, Jack Donovan. They would let the rented Ferrari and Donovan's other illusory trappings of wealth do the rest.

* * *

On the first ride in the Ferrari, Halim gave nothing away about his job, claiming to be a student — a rather old one, Ran thought to himself. He did mention that his wife was going away and that he liked to eat well, but being a Muslim didn't drink.

Donovan, keeping his occupation vague to allow the greatest possible flexibility, said he dealt in international trade and suggested that maybe someday Halim would like to visit his villa in the country or join him for dinner while his wife was away. Halim did not commit himself to anything at that point.

The next morning, the blonde was back and Donovan picked her up. A day later, Donovan showed up but the girl didn't, and he again offered Halim a ride into town, this time suggesting they stop first at a local café for coffee. As for the beautiful companion, Donovan explained, "Oh, she's just some floozy I met. She was starting to make too many demands, so I ditched her. Pity in a way — she was very good, if you know what I mean. But there's never any shortage of that, old boy."

Halim did not mention his new friend to Samira. This was something he wanted to keep to himself.

After Samira left for Iraq, Donovan, who'd been picking Halim up regularly and becoming quite chummy, said he had to go to Holland on business for about 10 days. He gave Halim his business card — a front, of course, but nonetheless an actual office, complete with a sign and secretary should Halim call or come looking, at an impressive address in a renovated building near the top of the Champs Elysées.

During all this time, Ran (Donovan) was actually staying at the safe house where, after each encounter with Halim, he would meet with the head of the station or the second-in-command to plan the next move, write his reports, read the transcripts from the bugs, and go over each and every possible scenario.

Ran would do a route first to make sure he hadn't been followed. At the safe house, he'd exchange his documentation, leaving his British passport behind. Of the two reports he'd write each time, the first was an information report containing specific details of what was said at the meeting.

The second report, an operations report, would contain the five Ws: who, what, when, where, and why. It listed everything that happened during the meeting. This second report would be put into another folder and given to a *bodel*, or courier, who conveys messages between the safe houses and the embassy.

Operational and information reports are sent to Israel separately, either through computers or dips. An operational report is further broken up to avoid detection. The first might say, "I met with subject at (see separately)," and another report would contain the location, and so on. Each person has two code names, although they don't know their own codes: one information code and one operational code.

The Mossad's biggest concern is always in communications. Because they know what they can do, they figure other countries can do it, too.

* * *

With Samira gone, Halim broke from any routine, stopping

off in town after work to eat alone in a restaurant or take in a movie. One day he telephoned his friend Donovan and left a message. Three days later, Donovan called back. Halim wanted to go out, so Donovan took him to an expensive cabaret for dinner and a show. He insisted on paying for everything.

Halim was drinking now, and over the course of the long evening, Donovan outlined a deal he was working on to sell old cargo containers to African countries to use as housing units.

"They're so bloody desperate in some of these places. They just cut holes in these things for windows and a door and they live in them," said Donovan. "I've got a line on some in Toulon that I can buy for next to nothing. I'm going down there this weekend. Why don't you come along?"

"I'd probably just get in the way," said Halim. "I don't know anything about business."

"Nonsense. It's a long drive there and back, and I'd love to have the company. We'll stay over and come back Sunday. Anyway, what else are you doing this weekend?"

The plan almost failed when a local sayan got cold feet at the last moment; instead, a katsa filled in as the "businessman" selling the containers to Donovan.

As the two haggled over the price, Halim noticed that one container, which had been lifted up on a crane, had rust on the bottom (they all did — and they were hoping Halim would notice). He took Donovan aside to tell him, enabling his friend to negotiate a discount on some 1,200 containers.

That night at dinner, Donovan gave Halim $1,000 (U.S.) cash. "Go ahead. Take it," he said. "You saved me a lot more than that by spotting that rust. Not that it will matter at the other end, of course, but that bloke selling them didn't know that."

For the first time, Halim began to realize that, in addition to offering him a good time, his new-found friendship could be profitable. For the Mossad, who know that money, sex, and some type of psychological motivation — individually or in combination — can buy almost anything, their man was now really hooked. It was time to get down to some real business, or *tachless,* with Halim.

Now that he knew Halim had complete confidence in his cover story, Donovan invited the Iraqi to his luxurious hotel suite in the Sofitel-Bourbon at 32 run Saint-Dominique. He'd also invited a young hooker, Marie-Claude Magal. After ordering dinner, Donovan told his guest he had to go out on urgent business, leaving a phony telex message behind on a table for Halim to read as confirmation.

"Listen, I'm sorry about this," he said. "But you enjoy yourself, and I'll be in touch."

So Halim and the hooker did enjoy themselves. The episode was filmed, not necessarily for blackmail purposes, but just to see what was going on, what Halim would say and do. An Israeli psychiatrist was already poring over every detail of the reports on Halim for clues to the most effective approach to the man. An Israeli nuclear physicist was also on standby should his services be needed. Before too long, they would be.

Two days later, Donovan returned and called Halim. Over coffee, Halim could plainly see that his friend was upset about something.

"I've got the chance of a superb deal from a German company on some special pneumatic tubes for shipping radioactive material for medical purposes," said Donovan. "It's all very technical. There's big money involved, but I don't know the first thing about it. They've put me on to an English scientist who's agreed to inspect the tubes. The problem is he wants too much money and I'm not sure I trust him, in any case. I think he's tied in with the Germans."

"Maybe I could help," said Halim.

"Thanks, but I need a scientist to examine these tubes."

"I am a scientist," said Halim.

Donovan, looking surprised, said, "What do you mean? I thought you were a student."

"I had to tell you that at first. But I'm a scientist sent here by Iraq on a special project. I'm sure I could help."

Ran was to say later that when Halim finally admitted his

occupation it was as if somebody had drained all of Ran's blood and pumped in ice, then drained that out and pumped in boiling water. They had him! But Ran couldn't let his excitement show. He had to be calm.

"Listen, I'm supposed to meet this lot in Amsterdam this weekend. I must go a day or two early, but how be if I send my jet for you on Saturday morning?"

Halim agreed.

"You won't regret this," said Donvoan. "There's a packet of money to be made if these things are legitimate."

The jet, temporarily painted with Donovan's company logo, was a Learjet flown in from Israel for the occasion. The Amsterdam office belonged to a wealthy Jewish contractor. Ran didn't want to cross the border with Halim since he'd not be using his phony British passport but his real papers, always the preferred route to avoid possible detection at borders.

When Halim arrived at the Amsterdam office in the limousine that met him at the airport, the others were already there. The two businessmen were Itsik E., a Mossad katsa, and Benjamin Goldstein, an Israeli nuclear scientist carrying a German passport. He'd brought along one of the pneumatic tubes as the display model for Halim to examine.

After some initial discussions, Ran and Itsik left the room, supposedly to work out the financial details, leaving the two scientists together to discuss technical matters. With their common interest and expertise, the two men sensed an instant camaraderie and Goldstein asked Halim how he knew so much about the nuclear industry. It was a shot in the dark, but Halim, his defenses dropped completely, told him about his job.

Later, when Goldstein told Itsik about Halim's admission, they decided to take the unsuspecting Iraqi to dinner. Ran was to make an excuse for being unable to attend.

Over dinner, the two men outlined a plan they said they had been working on: trying to sell nuclear power plants to Third World countries — for peaceful purposes, of course.

"Your plant project would make a perfect model for us to sell to these people," said Itsik. "If you could just get us some details, the plans, that sort of thing, we would all stand to make a fortune from this.

"But it has to be kept between us. We don't want Donovan to know about this or he'd want a piece of the action. We've got the contacts and you've got the expertise. We don't really need him."

"Well, I'm not so sure," said Halim. "Donovan has been good to me. And isn't it, well, you know, kind of dangerous?"

"No. There's no danger," said Itsik. "You must have regular access to these things. We just want to use it as a model, that's all. We'd pay you well and nobody would ever know. How could they? This sort of thing is done all the time."

"I suppose so," said Halim, still hesitating, but intrigued by the prospect of big money. "But what about Donovan? I hate to go behind his back."

"Do you think he lets you in on all his deals? Come now. He won't ever know about it. You can still be friends with Donovan and do business with us. We'd certainly never tell him, because he'd want a cut."

Now they really had him. The promise of untold riches was just too much. Anyway, he felt good about Goldstein, and it wasn't as if he was helping them design a bomb. And there was no need for Donovan to ever know. So why not? he thought.

Halim had been officially recruited. And like so many recruits, he wasn't even aware of it.

Donovan paid Halim $8,000 (U.S.) for his help with the tubes, and the next day, after celebrating with an expensive brunch and a hooker in his room, the happy Iraqi was flown back to Paris on the private jet.

* * *

At this point, Donovan was supposed to get out of the picture altogether, to relieve Halim of the embarrassing position of having to hide things from him. For a time, he did disappear, although he left a London phone number with Halim just in case he wanted to get in touch. Donovan said he had a business deal in England and he wasn't sure how long he'd be gone.

Two days later, Halim met with his new business associates in Paris. Itsik, much pushier than Donovan, wanted a layout of the Iraqi plant along with details on its location, capacity, and precise construction timetable.

Halim at first complied, with no apparent problems. The two Israelis taught him how to photocopy using a "paper paper," a special paper that is simply placed on top of a document to be copied, with a book or other object left sitting on it for several hours. The image is transferred to the paper, which still looks like ordinary paper, but when it is processed, a reverse image of the copied document is obtained.

As Itsik pushed Halim for more information, paying him handsomely at each stage, the Iraqi began to show signs of what is called the "spy reaction": hot and cold flashes, rising temperatures, inability to sleep or settle down — real physical symptoms brought on by the fear of being caught. The more you do, the more you fear the consequences of your actions.

What to do? The only thing Halim could think of was to call his friend Donovan. He'd know. He knew people in high and mysterious places.

"You've got to help me," Halim pleaded, when Donovan returned his call. "I have a problem, but I can't talk about it on the telephone. I'm in trouble. I need your help."

"That's what friends are for," Donovan assured him, telling Halim he'd be flying in from London in two days and would meet him at the Sofitel suite.

"I've been tricked," Halim cried, confessing the whole "secret" deal he had made with the German company in Amsterdam. "I'm sorry. You've been such a good friend. But I was taken in by the money. My wife always wants me to earn more, to better myself. I saw the chance. I was so selfish and so stupid. Please forgive me. I need your help."

Donovan was magnanimous about it all, telling Halim, "That's business." But he went on to suggest that the Germans might, in reality, be U.S. CIA men. Halim was stunned.

"I've given them everything I have," he said, much to Ran's delight. "Still, they push me for more."

"Let me think about this," said Donovan. "I know some

people. Anyway, you're hardly the first bloke who ever got taken in by money. Let's just relax and have a good time. These things are seldom as bad as they seem once you get right down to it."

That night, Donovan and Halim went out for dinner and drinks. Later, Donovan bought him another hooker. "She'll soothe your nerves," he laughed.

Indeed, she would. Only about five months had elapsed since the operation began, a fast pace for this sort of business. But with such high stakes, speed was considered essential. Still, caution was the watchword at this stage. And with Halim so tense and frightened, he'd have to be brought along gently.

After another long heated session in the safe house, the decision was made for Ran to go back to Halim and tell him it *was* a CIA operation after all.

"They'll hang me," Halim cried. "They'll hang me."

"No, they won't," said Donovan. "It's not as if you were working for the Israelis. It's not that bad. Anyway, who will know? I've made a deal with them. They just want one more piece of information, then they'll leave you alone."

"What? What more can I give them?"

"Well, it doesn't mean anything to me, but I suppose you know about it," said Donovan, pulling a paper out of his pocket. "Oh yes, here it is. They want to know how Iraq will respond when France offers to substitute the enriched stuff with, what is it called, caramel? Tell them that and they'll never bother you again. They're not interested in harming you. They just want the information."

Halim told him Iraq wanted the enriched uranium, but in any event, Yahia El Meshad, an Egyptian-born physicist, would be arriving in a few days to inspect the project and decide these matters on behalf of Iraq.

"Will you be meeting him?" asked Donovan.

"Yes, yes. He'll be meeting all of us from the project."

"Good. Then maybe you'll be able to get that information, and your troubles will be over."

Halim, looking somewhat relieved, was suddenly in a hurry to leave. Since he now had money, he'd been hiring a hooker on his own, a friend of Marie-Claude Magal, a woman who thought she was passing information along to the local police, but in fact was tipping off the Mossad for easy money. Indeed, when Halim had told Magal he wanted to become a regular client, she had given him the name of her friend at Donovan's suggestion.

Now Donovan insisted that Halim set up a dinner meeting with the visiting Meshad at a bistro, where he would "happen" to drop in.

On the appointed evening, acting surprised, Halim introduced his friend Donovan to Meshad. The cautious Meshad, however, simply offered a polite hello and suggested Halim return to their table when he had finished chatting with his friend. Halim was far too nervous even to broach the subject of the caramel with Meshad, and the scientist showed absolutely no interest in Halim's explanation that his friend Donovan was capable of buying almost anything and might be useful to them someday.

Later that night, Halim called Donovan to tell him he'd failed to get anything out of Meshad. The next night, meeting in the suite, Donovan persuaded Halim that if he got the timetable of shipments from the Sarcelles plant to Iraq, that would satisfy the CIA and get them off his case.

By this time, the Mossad had learned from a "white" agent who worked in finance for the French government that Iraq was not receptive to the substitution of caramel for enriched uranium. Still, Meshad, as the man in charge of the entire project for Iraq, could be a valuable recruit. If only there was a way to get to him.

Samira returned from Iraq to find a changed Halim. Claiming a promotion and a raise, he was suddenly more romantic and he also began taking her out to restaurants. They even contemplated buying a car.

While Halim was a brilliant scientist, he was not wise in a worldly sense. One night, shortly after his wife's return, he proceeded to tell her about his friend Donovan and his problems with the CIA. She was furious. Twice during her rant against him, she said they were probably Israeli security, not the CIA.

"Why would the Americans care?" she screamed. "Who else except the Israelis and my mother's stupid daughter would even bother to talk to you?"

She wasn't so stupid after all.

* * *

The drivers of the other two trucks carrying engines from the Dassault Brequet plant for Mirage fighters to a hangar in the French Riviera town of La Seyne-sur-Mer near Toulon on April 5, 1979, thought nothing of it when a third truck joined them along the route.

In a modern-day twist on the Trojan Horse, the Israelis had hidden a team of five neviot saboteurs and a nuclear physicist, all dressed in regular street clothes, inside a large metal container, slipping them into the security area as part of the three-truck convoy, based on information obtained from Halim. They knew that guards were always more careful about goods being removed than about deliveries. They would probably do little more than wave the convoy on through. At least, the Israelis were banking on that. The nuclear physicist with them had been flown in from Israel to determine precisely where to plant charges on the stored nuclear-reactor cores, three years in the making, to achieve maximum damage.

One of the guards on duty was a new man, just a few days on the job, but he'd come with such impeccable credentials that no one suspected him of having taken the key to open the storage bay where the Iraqi-bound equipment was waiting to be shipped in a few more days.

On the expert advice of the physicist, the Israeli team planted five charges of plastic explosives, strategically positioned on the reactor cores.

As the guards stood at the plant gates, their attention was suddenly captured by a commotion outside on the street where it seemed a pedestrian, an attractive young woman, had been brushed by a car. She didn't appear to be badly hurt. Certainly her vocal cords weren't injured, as she screamed obscenities at the embarrassed driver.

By this time, a small crowd had gathered to watch the action, including the saboteurs, who had scaled a back fence, then walked around to the front. First checking the crowd to verify that all the French guards were out of harm's way, one of them calmly and surreptitiously detonated a sophisticated fuse with a hand-held device, destroying 60 percent of the reactor components, causing $23 million in damages, setting back Iraq's plans for several months, but amazingly, doing no harm to other equipment stored in the hangar.

When the guards heard the dull thunk behind them, they rushed immediately into the targeted hangar. As they did, the car in the "accident" drove away, while the saboteurs and the injured pedestrian, well schooled in this sort of thing, quietly disappeared down various side streets.

The mission had been a complete success, seriously delaying Iraq's plans, and embarrassing leader Saddam Hussein in the process.

An environmental organization named *Groupe des écologistes français*, unheard of before this incident, claimed credit for the blast, although French police dismissed the claim. But a police blackout on news of the investigation into the sabotage led other newspapers to print speculative stories on who was responsible. *France Soir*, for example, said the police suspected "extreme leftists" had done it, while *Le Matin* said it had been done by Palestinians working on behalf of Libya; the news weekly, *Le Point*, fingered the FBI.

Others accused the Mossad, but an Israeli government official dismissed the accusation as "anti-Semitism."

* * *

Halim and Samira arrived home well after midnight, following a leisurely dinner in a Left Bank bistro. He turned on the radio, hoping to hear some music and wind down a bit before going to bed. What he heard instead was news of the explosion. Halim panicked.

He began running around the apartment, tossing things at random, screaming a lot of nonsense.

"What's the matter with you?" Samira shouted over the din. "Have you gone mad?"

BY WAY OF DECEPTION 21

"They've blown up the reactor!" he cried. "They've blown it up! Now they'll blow me up, too!"

He phoned Donovan.

Within the hour, his friend called back. "Don't do anything foolish," he said. "Keep calm. No one can connect you to any of this. Meet me at the suite tomorrow night."

Halim was still shaking when he arrived for their meeting. He hadn't slept or shaved. He looked dreadful.

"Now the Iraqis are going to hang me," he moaned. "Then they'll give me to the French and they'll guillotine me."

"This had nothing to do with you," said Donovan. "Think about it. No one has any reason to blame you."

"This is terrible. Terrible. Is it possible the Israelis are behind this? Samira thinks it's them. Could it be?"

"Come on, man, get a grip on yourself. What are you talking about? The people I'm dealing with wouldn't do anything like that. It's probably some sort of industrial espionage. There's a lot of competition in the field. You've told me that yourself."

Halim said he was going back to Iraq. His wife wanted to go anyway, and he'd served enough time in Paris. He wanted to get away from these people. They wouldn't follow him to Baghdad.

Donovan, hoping to dismiss the notion of any Israeli involvement, pushed his theory of the industrial sabotage and told Halim that if he really wanted a new life, he could approach the Israelis. He had two reasons for suggesting this: first, to further distance himself from the Israelis; and second, to attempt a head-on recruitment.

"They'll pay. They'll give you a new identity and protect you. They'd love to know what you know about the plant."

"No, I can't," said Halim. "Not with them. I'm going home."

And he did.

* * *

Meshad was still a problem. With his stature as one of the few Arab scientists with authority in the nuclear field, and one close to senior Iraqi military and civilian authorities, the Mossad still hoped it could recruit him. Yet despite Halim's unwitting help, several key questions remained unanswered.

On June 7, 1980, Meshad made another of his frequent trips to Paris, this time to announce some final decisions about the deal. During a visit to the Sarcelles plant, he told French scientists, "We are making a change in the face of Arab world history," which is precisely what Israel was worried about. The Israelis had intercepted French telexes detailing Meshad's travel schedule and where he would stay (Room 9041 at the Meridien Hotel), making it easier to bug his room before he got there.

Meshad was born in Banham, Egypt, on January 11, 1932. He was a serious, brilliant scientist, and his thick black hair was beginning to recede noticeably. His passport listed his occupation as a lecturer in the department of atomic engineering, University of Alexandria.

In interviews later with an Egyptian newspaper, his wife, Zamuba, said the couple and their three children (two girls and a boy) had been about to leave for a Cairo vacation. In fact, she said Meshad had already bought the plane tickets when he was phoned by an official from the Sarcelles plant. She heard him say, "Why me? I can send an expert." She said that from that moment on, he was very nervous and angry and that she believed there was an Israeli agent in the French government who had set a trap for him. "There was danger, of course. He used to tell me he would continue the assignment of creating the bomb even if he had to pay for it with his life."

The official news story, released to the media by the French authorities, is that Meshad was accosted by a hooker in the elevator as he was returning to his ninth-floor room at about 7 p.m. on a stormy June 13, 1980. The Mossad already knew Meshad was heavily into kinky sex, S&M actually, and a hooker whose nickname was Marie Express had been entertaining him regularly. She was slated to show up at about 7:30 p.m. Her real name was Marie-Claude Magal, whom Ran had initially sent to Halim. Although she did considerable work for the Mossad, she never was told exactly who her employers were. And as long as they paid, she didn't care.

They also knew Meshad was a tough cookie, not as gullible as Halim. And since he would be staying only a few more days, the decision was taken to approach him directly. "If he agrees, he's recruited," explained Arbel. "If he doesn't, he's dead."

He didn't.

Yehuda Gil, an Arabic-speaking katsa, was sent to Meshad's door shortly before Magal arrived. Opening the door just enough to peek out, but leaving it chained, Meshad snapped, "Who are you? What do you want?"

"I'm from a power that will pay a lot of money for answers," Gil said.

"Get lost, you dog, or I'll call the police," Meshad replied.

So Gil left. In fact, he flew back to Israel immediately, so that he could never be connected to Meshad's destiny.

As for Meshad, he met a different fate.

The Mossad doesn't execute people unless they have blood on their hands. This man would have had the blood of Israel's children on his hands if he'd completed his project. So why wait?

Israel intelligence did at least wait until after Magal had entertained Meshad and left a couple of hours later. Might as well die happy, was the reasoning.

As Meshad slept, two men slipped quietly into the suite with a passkey and slit his throat. His blood-soaked body was found by a chambermaid the next morning. She'd come by a few times but the Do Not Disturb sign had discouraged her. Finally, she had knocked on the door and when there was no answer, walked in.

French police said at the time that it was a professional job. Nothing was taken. No money. No documents. But a towel stained with lipstick was found on the bathroom floor.

Magal was shocked to hear about the murder. After all, Meshad been alive when she left him. Partly to protect herself, and partly because she was suspicious, she went to the police and reported that Meshad had been angry when she arrived, ranting about some man approaching him earlier and wanting to buy information.

Magal confided her actions to her friend, Halim's former "regular," who in turn unknowingly passed the information on to a Mossad contact.

Late on the night of July 12, 1980, Magal was working the Boulevard St-Germain when a man in a black Mercedes pulled up to the curb and motioned for her to come around to the driver's side.

There was nothing unusual about that, but as she began talking to her potential customer, another black Mercedes pulled out from the curb and proceeded at high speed down the avenue. Just at the right moment, the driver in the parked car gave Magal a heavy shove, sending her flying backward into the path of the oncoming car. She was killed instantly. Both cars sped off into the Paris night.

* * *

While both Magal and Meshad were assassinated by the Mossad, of course the internal machinations leading up to their deaths were dramatically different.

First, Magal. Concerns about her would have become acute on the desk in Tel Aviv headquarters as the various reports from the field were received, decoded, and analyzed, and it became clear that she had gone to the police and could create serious difficulties.

These concerns would have been passed up the administrative ladder, eventually landing on the desk of the head of the Mossad, where the final decision to "take her out" would be made.

Her assassination was in the category of an operational emergency, the sort of situation that arises during operations, where decisions have to be made relatively quickly based on the precise circumstances of the case.

The decision to execute Meshad, however, emanated from an ultra-secret internal system involving a formal "execution list," and requiring the personal approval of the prime minister of Israel.

The number of names on that list varies considerably,

from just one or two up to 100 or so, depending upon the extent of anti-Israeli terrorist activities.

A request to place someone on the execution list is made by the head of the Mossad to the prime minister's office. Let's say, for example, there was a terrorist attack on an Israeli target — which doesn't necessarily mean Jewish, incidentally. It could be a bomb attack on an El Al office in Rome, for instance, that killed some Italian citizens. But that would constitute an attack on Israel, since it was designed to discourage people from using El Al, an Israeli airline.

Let's say the Mossad knew for certain that Ahmed Gibril was the culprit who ordered and/or organized the attack. At that point, it would recommend Gibril's name to the PMO, and the prime minister in turn would send it to a special judicial committee, so secret that the Israeli supreme court doesn't even know it exists.

The committee, which sits as a military court and tries accused terrorists in absentia, consists of intelligence personnel, military people, and officials from the justice department. Hearings, in a court-like setting, are held at various locations, often at someone's private residence. Both the personnel on the committee and the location of the trial are changed for each case.

Two lawyers are assigned to the case, one representing the state, or the prosecution, the other the defense, even though the accused is unaware of the whole process. The court then decides on the basis of the evidence presented whether this man — in this case, Gibril — is guilty as charged. If he is found guilty, and at this stage the accused usually are, two things can be ordered by the "court": either bring him to Israel for trial in a regular court; or, if that is too dangerous or simply impossible, execute him at the first possible opportunity.

But before the hit is carried out, the prime minister must sign the execution order. The practice differs, depending upon the prime minister. Some sign the document in advance. Others insist on first determining whether the hit would create any political difficulties at a given time.

In any event, one of the first duties of any new Israeli

prime minister is to read the execution list and decide whether or not to initial each name on it.

* * *

It was on June 7, 1981, at 4 p.m. on a bright, sunny Sunday, that a group of two dozen U.S.-built F-15s and F-16s took off from Beersheba (not from Elat, as widely reported, since that is adjacent to Jordanian radar), on a treacherous 90-minute, 650-mile journey across hostile countries to Tuwaitha, just outside Baghdad, intent on blasting the Iraqi nuclear plant to kingdom come.

Accompanying them was what looked like an Aer Lingus commercial carrier (the Irish lease their planes to Arab countries, so it wouldn't seem out of place), but in truth was an Israeli Boeing 707 refueling aircraft. The fighters kept in close formation, with the Boeing flying directly underneath, to make it appear as if there was only one aircraft, a civilian plane on a civilian route. The fighters were flying on "silent," meaning they transmitted no messages, but they did accept them from a backup Electronic Warfare & Communications plane, which also served to jam other signals, including hostile radar.

About halfway there, over Iraqi territory, the Boeing refueled the fighter aircraft. (The return flight to Israel was too long to accomplish without refueling, and they couldn't risk trying it after the attack since they might be pursued; hence the brazen refueling directly over Iraq.) The refueling complete, the Boeing peeled off from the formation, accompanied by two of the fighter aircraft for protection, cutting northwest through Syria, eventually landing in Cyprus, as if on a regular commercial route. The two fighters stayed with the Boeing only until it left hostile territory, returning to their base at Beersheba.

In the meantime, the rest of the fighters continued on their way, armed with Sidewinder missiles, iron bombs, and 2,000-pound "laser-riding" bombs (which ride a beam directly to the target).

Thanks to information originally obtained from Halim, the Israelis knew exactly where to strike to inflict the most damage. The key was bringing down the dome at the heart of the plant. An Israeli combatant was also in the area with a beacon, sending out a strong signal in short beeps on a predetermined frequency to guide the fighters to their target.

There are essentially two ways to find a target. First, you can see it with your eye. But to do that at speeds greater than 900 miles an hour you have to know the area well, especially for a relatively small target. You go by the landscape, but you have to know the terrain, recognize particular landmarks, and obviously the Israelis had not had the opportunity to practice their maneuvers over Baghdad. They had practiced over their own territory, however, on a model of the plant, before heading off to attack the real thing.

The other method of finding a target is to have a beacon, a homing device, as a guide. They had one outside the plant, but to make absolutely sure, Damien Chassepied, a French technician who had been recruited by the Mossad, was asked to deposit a briefcase containing a homing device inside the building. For reasons unknown, Chassepied lingered inside and became the only human casualty of the extraordinary assault.

At 6:30 p.m. in Iraq, the planes climbed from deck level, where they'd been flying so low (to avoid radar) that they could see the farmers in the surrounding fields, attaining a height of about 2,000 feet just before reaching the target.

So fast was their climb that it baffled the defenders' radar, and the sun setting behind the raiders blinded the Iraqis manning a ring of anti-aircraft guns. The fighters then swooped down so swiftly, one after the other, that all the Iraqis had time to do was fire some of their anti-aircraft guns harmlessly into the air. But no SAM missiles were fired, and no Iraqi aircraft were sent in pursuit as the raiders turned and headed back to Israel, flying at a higher altitude and taking a shorter route back directly over Jordan, leaving Saddam Hussein's dreams of turning Iraq into a nuclear power in tatters.

As for the plant itself, it was devastated. The huge dome cover on the reactor building was knocked clean off its foundation and the building's heavily reinforced walls were blasted apart. Two other major buildings, both vital to the plant, were badly damaged. Videotape recorded by Israeli pilots and later shown to an Israeli parliamentary committee, captured the reactor core bursting apart and tumbling into the cooling pool.

Begin had originally scheduled the strike for late April on intelligence from the Mossad that the reactor would be operating by July 1. He postponed the strike after newspaper stories saying that former defense minister Ezer Weizman told friends that Begin was "preparing an adventurous pre-election operation."

Another target date, May 10, just seven weeks before Israel's June 30 election, was also abandoned when Labor Party leader Shimon Peres sent Begin a "personal" and "top secret" note saying he should "desist" from the attack because the Mossad intelligence was "not realistic." Peres predicted the attack could isolate Israel "like a tree in the desert."

* * *

Just three hours after they'd taken off, the fighter planes arrived safely back in Israel. For two hours, Prime Minister Menachem Begin had been waiting for news in his home on Smolenskin Street, with his entire cabinet in attendance.

Shortly before 7 p.m., General Rafael Eitan, commander-in-chief of the Israeli army, phoned Begin to say the mission had been accomplished (this final stage was called Operation Babylon) and all hands were safe.

Begin is reported to have said *"Baruch hashem,"* Hebrew for "Blessed be God."

Saddam Hussein's immediate reaction was never publicly recorded.

PART I

Cadet 16

1

Recruitment

IN LATE APRIL 1979, I was just back in Tel Aviv after two days' submarine duty, when my naval commander handed me orders to attend a meeting at the Shalishut military base on the outskirts of Ramt Gan, a suburb of the city.

At the time, I was a captain, head of the weapons-system-testing branch of the Israeli navy's operations section at its Tel Aviv headquarters.

I was born in Edmonton, Alberta, on November 28, 1949, and was just a child when my parents separated. My father had served in the RCAF during World War II, flying numerous missions over Germany in his Lancaster bomber. After the war, he volunteered for Israel's War of Independence: a captain, he commanded the Sede Dov air base on Tel Aviv's northern outskirts.

My Israeli mother had also served her country during the war, driving supply trucks from Tel Aviv to Cairo for the British. Afterward, she was active in the Israeli resistance, the *Hagona*. A teacher, she moved with me to London, Ontario, then briefly to Montreal, and finally to Holon, a city near Tel Aviv, when I was six. My father had emigrated to the United States from Canada.

My mother would return to Canada again, but when I was 13, we were back in Holon. My mother would eventually return to Canada, but I remained in Holon with my maternal

grandparents, Haim and Ester Margolin, who had fled the po-
groms in Russia in 1912 with their son Rafa. Another son had
been killed in a pogrom. In Israel, they had two more children, a son Maza, and a daughter Mira, my mother. They
were real pioneers in Israel. My grandfather was an accoun-
tant, but until he could get his papers out of Russia to prove
it, he washed floors in the UJA (United Jewish Agency). He
later became their auditor-general, and was a very honorable person.

I was brought up a Zionist. My Uncle Maza had been in the
elite unit of the pre-state army, the "Wolves of Samson," and
served during the War of Independence.

My grandparents were very idealistic. My own idea of Israel as I was growing up was as the land of milk and honey.
That any hardships were worth it. I believed it was a country
that would do no wrong, would not inflict evil on others,
would set an example for all nations to see and to follow. If
there was anything wrong financially or politically in the
country, I always imagined this was at the lower echelons of
government — with the bureaucrats, who would eventually
clean up their act. Basically, I believed there were people
guarding our rights, great people like Ben-Gurion, whom I
really admired. I grew up regarding Begin as the militant I
couldn't stand. Where I grew up, political tolerance was the
main rule. Arabs were regarded as human beings. We'd had
peace with them before and eventually would again. That
was my idea of Israel.

Just before I turned 18, I joined the army for the compul-
sory three-year term, emerging as a second lieutenant in the
military police nine months later — then the youngest officer in the Israeli military.

During my term, I served at the Suez Canal, on the Golan
Heights, and along the Jordan River. I was there when Jordan
was clearing the PLO out, and we allowed the Jordanian
tanks to pass through our territory so as to surround them.
That was weird. The Jordanians were our enemy, but the
PLO was a greater enemy.

After my military term ended in November 1971, I returned

to Edmonton for five years, working at various jobs from advertising to managing the CJV carpet store at the city's Londonderry Shopping Center, missing the 1973 Yom Kippur War. But I knew that war wouldn't end for me until I gave something. I returned to Israel in May 1977 and joined the navy.

* * *

When I arrived for the meeting at the Shalishut base, I was ushered into a small office where a stranger sat at a desk, a few papers in front of him.

"We've pulled your name out of a computer," the man said. "You fit our criteria. We know you're already serving your country, but there's a way you can serve it better. Are you interested?"

"Well, yes, I'm interested. But what's involved?"

"A series of tests first, to see if you're suitable. We'll call you."

Two days later, I was summoned to an apartment in Herzlia for an 8 p.m. meeting. I was surprised when the naval base psychiatrist answered the door. They made a mistake doing that. He said he was doing this job for a security group and that I mustn't mention it on the base. I told him that was fine with me.

For the next four hours, I was given a variety of psychiatric tests: from ink blots to detailed questions on how I felt about everything imaginable.

A week later I was called to another meeting in the northern part of Tel Aviv near Bait Hahayal. I had already told my wife about it. We had this feeling it involved the Mossad. Growing up in Israel, you know these things. Anyway, who else could it be?

This would be the first of a series of meetings with a man who gave his name as Ygal, followed by long sessions in Tel Aviv's Scala Café. He kept telling me how important it was. He gave constant pep talks. I filled in hundreds of forms, questions such as: "Would you regard killing somebody for your country as something negative? Do you feel freedom is

important? Is there anything more important than freedom?"
That sort of thing. Since I was sure it was for the Mossad, I
thought the answers they wanted were fairly obvious, predictable. And I really wanted to pass.

As time went on, these meetings would be held every
three days — a process that continued for about four
months. At one point, I was given a complete medical exami-
nation at a military base. When you're in the service, normally you walk in and there are 150 guys there. It's like a
factory. But here they had 10 rooms for testing, each with a
doctor and a nurse in it, and they were waiting for me. I was
alone. Each team spent about half an hour with me as I went
from one room to the next. They did every kind of test. They
even had a dentist. Somehow that made me feel really important.

After all this, I still hadn't been given much information
about the job they were so anxious to give me. Even so, I was
keen to accept it, whatever it was.

Finally Ygal told me the job training would keep me in Israel most of the time, but not at home. I would be allowed to
see my family once every two or three weeks. Eventually, I
would be sent abroad and then I would see my family only
every other month or so. I told Ygal no, I couldn't be away
that much. It wasn't for me. Still, when he asked me to think
about it, I agreed. Then they called my wife, Bella, on the
phone. They harassed us by phone for the next eight
months.

Since I was already serving in the military, I didn't feel as if
I was neglecting my country. That compensated for it. I was
quite right-wing at the time — politically, not socially. I believed then you could separate the two, especially in Israel.
Anyway, I really *did* want that job, but I just couldn't be away
from my family that much.

I was not told at the time precisely what job I was applying
for, but later on when I actually did join the Mossad I learned
they had been grooming me for the *kidon*, the Metsada
department's assassination unit. (Metsada, now called
Komemiute, is the department in charge of combatants.) But
still I wasn't sure what I wanted to do with my life.

* * *

In 1981 I left the navy, having served in Lebanon at the start of the war. As an accomplished graphic artist, I decided to open my own business, making stained-glass windows. I made a few and tried to sell them but soon realized that stained glass wasn't all that popular in Israel, partly because it reminded people of churches. Nobody wanted to buy the windows. A number of people were interested in learning how to make them, though, so I turned my shop into a school.

In October 1982, I received a cable at home giving me a telephone number to call on Thursday between 9 a.m. and 7 p.m. I was to ask for Deborah. I phoned right away. They gave me an address on the main floor of the Hadar Dafna Building, an office tower on King Saul Boulevard, in Tel Aviv — later, I learned it was the Mossad headquarters building — one of those gray, bare concrete things popular in Israel.

I walked into the lobby. There was a bank on the right, and on the wall to the left of the entrance, a small, inconspicuous sign: Security Service Recruitment. My previous experience was still haunting me. I felt I'd really missed out on something.

Because I was so anxious, I arrived an hour early and went to the second-floor cafeteria, which is open to the public. On that side of the building, several private businesses gave the place quite a regular feeling, but Mossad headquarters was constructed as a building within a building. I had a toasted cheese sandwich — I'll never forget that. As I ate it, I was looking around the room wondering if anyone else there had been called like I had.

When the time came, I went downstairs to the designated office and eventually was shown into a small room with a large, light-colored wood desk. It was sparsely furnished. There was an in-and-out basket on the desk, a telephone, a mirror on the wall, and the photo of a man who looked familiar, though I couldn't quite place him.

The pleasant-looking fellow at the desk opened a small file, glanced at it quickly, and said, "We're looking for people. Our main goal is saving Jews all over the world. We think you might fit in. We're like a family. It's hard work and it can be dangerous, but I can't tell you any more than that until we put you through some tests." The man went on to explain that after each set of tests, they'd call. If I failed any one of them, that was it. If I passed, I'd be given details for the next test. "If you fail or drop out, you're not to contact us again. There's no appeal process. We decide and that's the end of it. Is that understood?"

"Yes."

"Fine. Two weeks from today, I want you here at 9 a.m. and we'll start the tests."

"Will this mean being away from my family a lot?"

"No, it won't."

"Good. I'll be here in two weeks."

When the day came, I was ushered into a large room. Nine other people were assembled at student desks and we were each handed a 30-page questionnaire containing personal questions, tests of all kinds, everything designed to find out who you are and what and how you think. Once we had completed the questionnaires and turned them in, we were told: "We'll call you."

A week later I was called in again for a meeting with a man who would test my English which I speak without an Israeli accent. He asked me the meanings of a lot of slang expressions, but he was slightly behind the times, with ones like "far out." He also asked me a lot about cities in Canada and the United States, who the U.S. president was, that sort of thing.

The meetings continued for about three months, but unlike my first experience, they were held in the downtown office during the day. I had another physical, but this time, I wasn't alone. I also completed two polygraph tests. The recruits were constantly reminded not to reveal anything about themselves to each other. "Keep yourself to yourself" was the watchword.

As the meetings went on I was getting more and more anxious. The man who interviewed me was called Uzi, and I got to know him better later on as Uzi Nakdimon, head of personnel recruitment. Finally, he told me I'd passed everything except the final test, but before that, they wanted to meet with Bella.

Her session lasted six hours. Uzi asked her everything imaginable, not only about me but about her own political background, her parents, her strengths and weaknesses, plus a lengthy scrutiny of her attitudes on the state of Israel and its place in the world. The office psychiatrist was also there, as a silent observer.

Afterward, Uzi called me back in and told me to show up Monday at 7 a.m. I was to bring two suitcases packed with various kinds of clothing, from jeans to a suit. This would be my final three- to four-day test. He went on to explain that the program involved two years of training and that the salary would be the equivalent of one rank higher than my present military rank. Not bad, I thought. I was then a lieutenant commander, and this would make me a colonel. I was really excited. It was finally happening. I felt I was really something special, but I found out later that thousands of men get interviewed. They hold a course once every three years or so, if they can get enough people. They end up with about 15 in the course and sometimes they all finish, sometimes none do. There is no predetermined result. They say that for every one of the 15 accepted into the course, they go through 5,000.

They pick the *right* people, not necessarily the *best* people. There's a big difference. Most of the selectors are field people and they're looking for very specific talents. But they don't reveal that. They just let you think you're something special, just being chosen for the tests.

* * *

Shortly before the appointed day, a messenger delivered a letter to my home, again stating the time and location and reminding me to bring clothes for different occasions. It also told me not to use my own name. I was to write my assumed name on an attached piece of paper, along with a short background for a new identity. I chose the name Simon Lahav. My father's name is Simon, and I'd been told that the name Ostrovsky in Polish or Russian means a sharp blade. *Lahav* is blade in Hebrew.

I listed myself as a freelance graphic designer, using my own real expertise in the field but not tying myself to anything too specific. I gave an address in Holon that I knew was an empty field.

Arriving on schedule just before 7 a.m. on a rainy day in January 1983, I found there were two women and eight other men in the group, plus three or four people I took to be instructors. After handing in the envelopes containing their new identities, the group was taken by bus to a well-known apartment-hotel resort called the Country Club, outside Tel Aviv on the road to Haifa. It boasts of having the most recreational facilities of any resort in Israel.

We were assigned in pairs to one-bedroom units, told to stow our suitcases, and then gather in Unit 1.

On a hill overlooking the Country Club sits the so-called prime minister's summer residence. In reality it is the *Midrasha*, the Mossad training academy. I looked up at the hill that first day. Everyone in Israel knows that place has something to do with the Mossad, and I wondered if after this, I'd end up there. I figured then that everyone else was there to test me. It may sound paranoid, but paranoia is a plus in this business.

Unit 1 featured a huge entrance room, with a long table set up in the middle all laid out for an elegant breakfast. There was an incredible buffet with more food on it than I'd ever seen, as well as a chef on duty waiting to take orders if anyone wanted something special.

In addition to the 10 students, a dozen or so others were milling around having breakfast. At about 10:30 the group moved into an adjoining room, also set up with a long table in the middle, where the students sat, and tables along the wall behind where the others sat. Nobody rushed us. We'd had a leisurely breakfast and there was coffee for us in the conference room — and as usual, everybody was smoking.

Uzi Nakdimon addressed the group: "Welcome to the test.

We'll be here for three days. Don't do anything you think you're expected to do. Use your own judgment in whatever circumstances arise. We're looking for the kind of people we need. You've already passed quite a few tests. Now we want to make certain you're right for us.

"Each of you will be assigned a guide/instructor," he went on. "Each of you has taken a name and a profession as a cover. You will try to keep this cover, but at the same time it's your job to try to *un*cover everybody else at this table."

I didn't know it at the time, but this was the first test group to include women. There was some political pressure to have women as katsas, so they decided to bring some in, supposedly to see if they could make it. Of course, they had no intention of allowing that to happen. It was just a gesture. There are women combatants, but they've never allowed women to be katsas. Women are more vulnerable, for one thing, but the Mossad's main target is men. Arab men. They can be lured by women, but no Arabs would work for women. So they can't be recruited by women.

We 10 recruits began by introducing ourselves and our cover stories. As each one of us did that, the other people being tested began asking questions. From time to time one of the testers sitting at the tables behind us would also ask questions.

I was fairly loose with my story. I didn't want to say I worked for such-and-such a company, because somebody there might know that company. I said I had two children, although I made them boys since I was not allowed to reveal any factual details. But I wanted to keep as close as I could to my real story. It was easy. I didn't feel pressure. It was a game, one I enjoyed.

The exercise lasted about three hours. At one point when I was asking questions, a tester leaned over with his notebook and said, "Excuse me, what's your name?" Little things like that, checking your concentration and so on. You had to be constantly on guard.

When the session ended, we were told to go back to our rooms and dress in street clothes. "You're going downtown."

We were divided into groups of three students each and

joined two instructors in a car. Once our car was in Tel Aviv, two more instructors met us at the corner of King Saul Boulevard and Ibn Gevirol. It was about 4:30 p.m. One of the instructors turned to me and said, "See that balcony on the third floor over there? I want you to stand here for three minutes and think. Then I want you to go to that building and within six minutes, I want to see you standing out on the balcony with the owner or tenant, and I want you holding a glass of water."

Now I was scared. We had no ID with us at all, and it's against the law in Israel not to have ID. We were told to use only our cover name, no matter what. In Israel, you just don't go without your papers. We were told that if we got into trouble with the police, we had to give them our cover story, too.

So what to do? My first problem was to figure out exactly which apartment it was. After what seemed a lifetime, I finally told the instructor I was ready to go.

"What, in general, are you doing?" he asked.

"In general, I'm making a movie," I replied.

Although they wanted fairly spontaneous actions, the instructors also wanted each of us to have a basic plan of action rather than an enactment of the Arabic expression, *"Ala bab Allah,"* or "Whatever will be, will be; let's just leave it to Allah."

I walked briskly into the building and up the stairs, counting the apartments from the stairwell to make sure I got the right one. A woman of about 65 answered my knock.

"Hi," I said in Hebrew. "My name is Simon. I'm from the department of transportation. You know that intersection outside has quite a few accidents." I paused to gauge her reaction.

"Yes, yes, I know," she said. (Considering the way Israelis drive, there are many accidents at most intersections, so it was quite a safe assumption for me to make.)

"We'd like to rent your balcony if we could."

"Rent my balcony?"

"Yes. We want to film the traffic at that intersection. There would be no people here. We'd just place a camera on your balcony. Could I take a look to make sure it's the right angle? If it is, would £500 a month be enough?"

"Yes, certainly," she said, ushering me toward the balcony.

"Oh, by the way, I'm sorry to trouble you, but could I have a glass of water? It's so hot today."

The two of us were soon standing side by side on the balcony looking down at the street.

I felt great. I saw everyone watching us. When the woman turned her head, I raised my glass to them. I took the woman's name and phone number, told her we still had some other places to check, and we'd let her know if we chose her balcony.

When I went back downstairs, one of the other students had gone on his assignment. He went to an automatic banking machine where he was supposed to borrow the equivalent of $10 from any stranger who was using the machine. He told a man he needed a cab because his wife was in the hospital having a baby and he had no money. He took the man's name and address and promised to send him the money. The man gave it to him.

The third student in the group wasn't quite as lucky. He was told to appear on a balcony in another apartment building, so he first gained access to the roof by saying he was checking the television antenna. Unfortunately for him, when he went to the chosen apartment with his story and asked the tenant if he could look up at the antenna from his balcony, he discovered the man was employed by the antenna company.

"What are you talking about?" the man asked. "There's nothing wrong with the antenna." The student had to make a hasty retreat when the man threatened to call the police.

After that exercise, we were driven to Hayarkon Street, a main street along the Mediterranean lined by all the major hotels. I was taken into the lobby of the Sheraton and told to sit.

"See the hotel across the road — the Basel Hotel?" one instructor said. "I want you to go in there and get me the third name from the top on their guest list."

In Israel, hotel guest books are kept underneath the counter, not on top, and like many other things there, tend to be regarded as confidential. It was just beginning to get dark as I crossed the street, still not knowing how I was going to get that name. I knew I had backing. I knew it was a game. But still, I was afraid and excited. I wanted to succeed, even though, when you think of it, the task was pretty stupid.

I decided to speak English, because right away you're treated better. They think you're a tourist. As I approached the desk to ask if there were any messages for me, I thought of the old joke about phoning somebody and asking if Dave is there. You phone several times and ask the same question, and the guy answering the phone gets angrier each time because you've got the wrong number. Then you phone and say, "Hi, this is Dave. Are there any messages for me?"

The clerk looked up at me. "Are you a guest?"

"No, I'm not," I said. "But I'm expecting to meet somebody here."

The desk clerk said there were no messages, so I sat down to wait in the lobby. After about half an hour, during which time I continually looked at my watch, I returned to the desk.

"Maybe he's already here and I've missed him," I said.

"What's his name?" asked the clerk. I mumbled a name that sounded something like "Kamalunke." The clerk reached for the guest book and began to look it over. "How do you spell that?"

"I'm not sure. Either with a C or a K," I said, leaning over the desk, ostensibly to help the clerk find the name, but in reality, reading the third name from the top.

Then, as if just realizing my mistake, I said, "Oh, this is the Basel Hotel. I thought it was the City Hotel. I'm sorry. How stupid of me."

Again, I felt great. Then I wondered how the hell my instructors would know that the name I'd got was right. But in Israel, they have access to everything.

By now, the hotel lobbies were beginning to fill up with people, so the two instructors and I walked up the street. Saying it was the day's last test, one handed me a telephone mike with two wires attached. The equipment had a letter on the back for identification purposes. I was told to enter the

Tal Hotel, go to the public wall phone in the lobby, remove its speaker, install the one I'd just been given, and return with the one I had removed, leaving the phone in working order.

There were people lined up at the phone, but I said to myself, I've got to do this thing. When my turn came, I put the token into the slot, dialed a random number, and held the receiver up by my cheek. My knees were starting to shake. People were lined up behind me now, waiting to use the phone. I unscrewed the top of the mouthpiece, then took my notebook out of my pocket, making distracting gestures as if I was going to be taking notes. I cradled the receiver between my chin and shoulder, speaking English into it.

By this time a guy behind me was standing really close, almost breathing down my neck. So I put my notebook down, turned to him, said, "Excuse me," and as he stepped back a bit, I attached the new part. Somebody had answered the random call now, and was saying, "Who is this?" But once I'd screwed the plastic part back on the mouthpiece, I hung up.

I was shaking when I put the speaker in my pocket. I had never done anything like this before — never stolen anything. I felt weak as I went over to the instructor and handed him the piece from the phone.

Soon, all five trainees were on their way back to the Country Club, saying little. After dinner we were told to complete a detailed report by the morning on every activity we had been involved in that day, omitting nothing — no matter how insignificant it might seem.

Around midnight, my roommate and I were tired and were just watching television when one of the instructors knocked on the door. He told me to get dressed in jeans and come with him. He drove me out near an orchard and told me some people were probably going to hold a meeting in this area. You could hear jackals howling in the distance, and crickets chirping constantly.

"I'll show you where," he told me. "What I want to know is how many people are at the meeting and what they say. I'll pick you up in two or three hours."

"Okay," I said.

He took me down a gravel road to a *wadi* (a stream that's dry except during periods of rainfall). There was just a trickle of water in it, and concrete piping about two and a half feet in diameter that ran under the road.

"There," he said, pointing to the pipe. "That's a good place to hide. There are some old newspapers there that you can pile up in front of you."

This was a real test for me. I'm claustrophobic and they knew it from all the psychological testing. And I hate vermin: cockroaches, worms, rats. I don't even like to swim in a lake because of all that gooey stuff on the bottom. When I looked down the pipe I couldn't see out the other end. It was the longest three hours of my life. And of course, nobody came. There wasn't any meeting. I kept trying not to fall asleep. I kept reminding myself where I was and that kept me awake.

Finally, the instructor returned. "I want a full report on the meeting," he said.

"There was nobody here," I replied.

"Are you sure?"

"Yes."

"Maybe you fell asleep."

"No, I didn't."

"Well, I passed by here," the instructor said.

"You must have passed by somewhere else. Nobody came by here."

On the way back, I was told not to talk about the incident.

The following evening, our whole group was told to dress casually. We would be taken to Tel Aviv and each given a specific building to watch. We were to take notes on everything we saw in this surveillance exercise. And we also had to create a cover story to explain what we were doing.

At about 8 p.m., I was driven into town by two men in a small car, one of them Shai Kauly, a veteran katsa with a long track record of achievement to his name.* I was dropped just one block off Dizingoff Street, Tel Aviv's main street, told to watch a five-story building and record everyone who went in: what time they arrived, what time they left, a description

* See Chapter 9: STRELLA

of them, which lights were on, which were off, and the times. They said they'd pick me up later, signaling me by flashing their headlights.

My first thought was that I should hide somewhere. But where? They told me I had to be within sight. I didn't know what to expect. Then I had an idea I would sit down and start to draw the building. In the drawing, I'd record the information I needed by hiding letters in English, written backward. My excuse for drawing at night would be that there were fewer distractions then; also, because I was drawing in black and white, I didn't need that much light.

About half an hour into the exercise, my peace and quiet was shattered by a car squealing up to the curb. A man jumped out and flashed a badge.

"Who are you?" he demanded.

"Simon Lahav."

"What are you doing here?"

"I'm drawing."

"One of the neighbors complained. He says you're watching the bank." (There was a bank on the first floor of the building.)

"No, I'm drawing. Look." I held out my work to the cop.

"Don't give me that bullshit! Get into the car."

There was a driver and another man in the front seat of the unmarked Ford Escort. They radioed in that they'd picked somebody up, while the one who'd ordered me into the car climbed into the back seat next to me. The one in the front kept asking, "What's your name?" And twice I replied, "Simon."

He asked again and as I went to answer him again, the guy next to me slapped me on the face and said, "Shut up." "He asked me a question," I said. "He didn't ask you anything," I was told.

Now I was in shock. I was wondering where my guys were. Then the one next to me asked where I was from. I said Holon, and the cop in the front punched me in the forehead and said, "I asked you your name."

When I said I was Simon from Holon, the cop in the back said, "What are you, a wiseguy?" Then he pushed my head forward and handcuffed my hands behind my back. The cop beside me was cursing his head off, calling me a dirty, scummy drug dealer.

I said I was just drawing, but he asked what my job was. I told him I was an artist.

By this time we were driving away. The cop in the front said, "We'll take you downtown now. We'll really show you." He took my drawings, crushed them all up and threw them on the floor. Then they ordered me to take my shoes off, which was hard to do handcuffed.

"Where are you keeping the drugs?" one asked.

"What do you mean? I don't have drugs. I'm an artist."

"If you don't talk now, you'll talk later," he said. In the meantime, they kept hitting me. One guy hit me so hard in the jaw, I thought I'd lost a tooth.

The man in the front passenger seat pulled me forward and yelled right into my face, threatening me, demanding to know where the drugs were, while the driver drove aimlessly around the city.

I figured this was straight harassment. They'd found a guy on the street and were going to make him pay. I'd heard about this kind of thing, so I demanded they take me to the station so I could get a lawyer. After about an hour of this, one of them asked me the name of a gallery where my art was displayed. I knew all the galleries in Tel Aviv — and also that they'd all be closed at that time of night, so I gave him a name. When we got there, I was still handcuffed, so I gestured with my head toward the gallery, and said, "My paintings are in there."

My next problem was that I had no ID. I told them I'd left it at home. Then they took my pants off because they said they wanted to check them for drugs. I felt very insecure, but eventually they became mellow and seemed to believe me. I said I wanted to go back to where they'd found me but didn't know how to get there. I told them I had no money, but that a friend would pick me up later.

So they drove me back to the area and stopped by a bus stop. The one cop took my drawings off the floor and threw them out the window. They took my cuffs off, and we sat there as the one cop filled out a report. Then a bus drove up. The guy next to me finally pulled me out onto the street, where I fell down. He threw my pants and my shoes on top of me, and they took off, warning me not to be there if they came back again.

There I was, lying on the street, with people getting off the bus, and I had no pants on. But I had to grab those papers, and when I did, it was like I'd climbed Mount Everest. What a feeling of accomplishment!

Thirty minutes later, after I had dressed and resumed my surveillance, I spotted the flashing headlights, went to the car, and was driven back to the Country Club to write my report. Much later, I met the "policemen" again.

They weren't policemen at all. It seems everybody met their "policemen" that night. It was part of the test.

One of the students had been accosted by the policemen as he stood under a tree. Asked what he was doing, he'd said he was watching owls. When the cop said he didn't see any owls, the student told him, "You guys scared them away." He, too, was taken for a ride.

One of the others was "arrested" at Kiker Hamdina, a well-known square. We used to say it represented the state of Israel. It holds the circus in the summer and it's mud in the winter. Just like Israel. Half the year mud, the other half circus. This guy was an idiot. He told them he was on a special mission. Said he was being recruited by the Mossad and this was a test. Obviously, he failed it.

Indeed, of the 10 who went through the whole of this first ordeal with me, the only one I ever saw again was one of the women. She became a lifeguard at the Mossad pool on the weekends when members' families were allowed in.

After breakfast on the third day, we were taken back into Tel Aviv. My first task was to go into a restaurant, strike up a conversation with a man who had been pointed out to me, and make an appointment to meet him that night. Watching the restaurant for a while before entering, I noticed the waiter dancing attendance on the man, so I decided he must be the manager. When I sat down at the table next to him, I saw he was reading a movie magazine.

I figured the movie trick had worked to get me on the balcony, so it might work again. I asked the waiter if I could speak to the manager, because I was making a movie and this might be a good site. Before I could finish my sentence, there he was, sitting next to me. I told him I had some other places to look at, so I had to leave, but arranged for a meeting that night. We shook hands and I left.

Later, all 10 trainees were taken to a park near Rothschild Boulevard and told a big man in a red-and-black checkered shirt would pass by. We were to follow him inconspicuously. It was hard to be inconspicuous with 10 of us doing the following and 20 more following us. It went on for two hours. We had guys looking out from balconies, others looking from behind trees, people everywhere. But the people watching us were looking for an instinct. To see how we'd react.

After that exercise ended, and we had completed our reports, we were split up again. I was driven back down Ibn Gevirol Street, but this time the car stopped in front of the Bank Hapoalim. I was told to go in and get the manager's name, private address, and as much information as possible about him.

You have to remember that Israel is a country where everyone is suspicious about everyone and everything else, all the time. I went in, wearing a suit, and asked a clerk the manager's name. The clerk told me and, on request, directed me to the second floor. I went up and asked for him, saying I'd been living for a long time in the United States but was moving back to Israel and wanted to transfer large sums of money to a new account. I asked to speak to the manager personally.

When I walked into his office I noticed a B'Nai Brith plaque on his desk. So we talked about that for a while and before I knew it, he was inviting me to his house. He was soon going to be transferred to New York where he would become an assistant manager. We exchanged addresses, and I said I would visit him. I told him I was in transit and had no phone number in Israel yet, but that I'd call him if he gave me his number. He even had coffee brought in.

I was talking $150,000 just to get settled. I told him that

when I saw how long it would take, I'd want him to transfer some more money for me. We actually got through the money part in 10 or 15 minutes, and then we started socializing. Within an hour, I knew everything about the man.

After completing that test, two other trainees and I were taken to the Tal Hotel again and told to wait until the others got back. We were there no more than 10 minutes when six men walked in. One said, "That's him," pointing directly at me.

"Come with us," said another. "You don't want to create a fuss in the hotel."

"What do you mean?" I asked. "I haven't done anything."

"Come with us," said one, flashing a badge.

They put all three of us in a van, blindfolded us, and began to drive helter skelter around the city. Eventually we were taken into a building, still blindfolded, and separated. I could hear the motion of people coming and going, but I was put into a tiny, closet-sized room and told to sit.

After two or three hours, I was taken out of the room. Apparently I'd been sitting in a little bathroom on the toilet seat. This was in the Academy (the Mossad training academy) on the second floor, although I didn't know that then. I was taken to another small room off the corridor. The window was blacked out and a massive-looking guy was sitting there. He had a small black dot in his eye: it looked like he had two pupils. He started gently, asking me questions. My name. Why I was in the hotel the other day taking the telephone apart. Was I planning a terrorist act? Where did I live?

At one point he said they'd take me to my address. I knew it was an empty lot, so I started laughing. He asked why I was laughing and I said I thought it was a funny situation. I was privately thinking of being taken there and saying, "My house! Where is my house?" I couldn't stop laughing.

"This must be some kind of joke," I said. "What do you want?"

He said he wanted my jacket. It was a Pierre Balmain blazer. So he took it. Then he took all my clothes away. I was naked when they walked me back to my bathroom, and just before they closed the door, somebody threw a bucket of water on me.

They left me, naked and shivering, for about 20 minutes, then brought me back to the burly man in the office.

"Now do you feel like laughing?" he said.

I was taken back and forth four or five times between the office and the tiny bathroom. Whenever somebody knocked on the office door, I was made to hide under the table. That happened about three times. Finally, this man said to me, "No hard feelings. There was a misunderstanding."

He returned my clothes and said they'd take me back to where they'd picked me up. They blindfolded me again and put me in the car, but just as the driver started up the engine, somebody shouted, "Wait a minute! Bring him back! We checked his address and there's nothing there."

"I don't know what you're talking about," I said, but they put me back in the bathroom.

Another 20 minutes passed, then they took me back down to the office and said, "Sorry, there's been a mistake!" They dropped me at the Country Club, apologized again, and drove away.

On the fourth morning of that first week, we were all called into a room, one at a time, for a conversation.

They asked, "What do you think? Do you think you were successful?"

I said, "I don't know. I don't know what you want of me. You told me to do the best I could and I did." Some of them were in there for 20 minutes. I was there four or five minutes. At the end they said, "Thank you. We'll call you."

Two weeks later, they did. I was ordered to report to the office early the next morning.

I was in. Now the real test was about to begin.

2

School Days

In ISRAEL, SEVERAL GROUPS of people believe the country is in constant danger. A strong army doesn't guarantee safety. I believed that then.

You know there is this immense need for security and you know there is an organization called the Mossad. It doesn't officially exist in Israel, yet everyone knows about it. It's the epitome, the top of the heap. You realize it's a very secretive organization, and once you're called in, you do what you are told because you believe that behind it is a form of super magic that will be explained to you in due course.

Growing up in Israel, this becomes ingrained. You start by going to the youth brigades. I was trained in shooting there, and at 14, finished second in Israel in target shooting. Using a sniper's Shtutser rifle, I scored 192 of a possible 200 points, four points behind the overall winner.

I'd spent quite a few years in the army, too. So I knew — or thought I knew — what I was getting into.

Not every Israeli will go blindly forward, of course, but those people who look for Mossad recruits, those who do all the psychological testing, find people who are willing, and at that stage it's assumed you will do as you're told. If you ask questions, it could bog down a whole operation later on.

At the time, I was a member of the Labor Party in Herzlia and was fairly active. My ideas were relatively liberal, so from that point on, I was in constant conflict between my beliefs and my loyalties. The whole system involves taking the proper candidates to begin with, then over time, through a well-orchestrated course of propaganda brainwashing, molding them. As they say, if ou're going to squash tomatoes, you take the ripe ones. Why take a green one? It can be squashed, but it's harder to do.

* * *

My first six weeks were uneventful. I worked at the downtown office, essentially as a gofer and filing clerk. But one chilly day in February 1984, I found myself joining 14 others on a small bus. I had never seen any of them before, but we all grew more excited as the bus eventually headed up a steep hill and through a guarded gate, stopping before the large, two-story Academy.

We cadets, 15 of us, trooped into the flat-roofed building where the spacious hall sported a Ping-Pong table in the middle. There were aerial photographs of Tel Aviv on the walls, a glass wall facing an inner garden, two long halls leading off it, and a suspended concrete staircase that appeared to float up to the second floor. The building's exterior was white brick. Inside, there were light marble floors and white brick walls.

Right away, I knew I'd been there before. As I was being dragged up to the tiny bathroom stall in the pre-training tests, I had peeped from under my blindfold and seen that staircase.

Before long, a dark-complexioned man with graying hair came in and led us out the back door and into one of four portable classrooms. The director would be with us shortly, he said.

Here again, there was lots of room, with windows on both sides, a blackboard on the front wall, and a long, T-shaped table in the middle with a viewgrapher/projector on it. This course was to be known as Cadet 16, as it was the sixteenth course of Mossad cadets.

Soon we heard swift footsteps out in the gravel parking lot, and three men walked into the room. One was short, handsome, and dark complexioned, another, whom I recognized, was older and sophisticated looking, the third a six-foot, two-inch, blond-haired man, about 50, with square, gold-rimmed glasses, casually dressed in an open shirt and sweater. He walked briskly to the head of the table while the other two sat at the back of the room.

"My name is Aharon Sherf," he said. "I am the head of the Academy. Welcome to the Mossad. Its full name is *Ha Mossad, le Modiyn ve le Tafkidim Mayuhadim* [the Institute for Intelligence and Special Operations]. Our motto is: 'By way of deception, thou shalt do war.' "

I felt like I needed oxygen. We knew it was the Mossad, but to be told at last that we were right, God, I needed air. Sherf — better known as Araleh, a nickname for Aharon — stood there leaning on the table, then straightened up, then leaned again. He seemed so stern and so strong.

"You are a team," he continued. "You have been selected out of thousands. We've sifted through endless numbers of people to come up with this group. You have the full potential to become everything we want. You have the opportunity to serve your country in a way that only a few people have.

"You have to realize there is no such thing as quotas in our organization. We'd very much love all of you to graduate and go on to fill much-needed jobs. On the other hand, we will not pass one person who is not 100 percent qualified. If that means nobody passes, that's okay. It's happened in the past.

"This is a unique academy. You will help in the teaching process by re-forming yourselves. You are just raw material for the task of security at this stage. At the other end, you will come out as the best-qualified intelligence people in the world.

"During this period, we do not have teachers. We have people from the field who are devoting a term of their time to the Academy to be your instructors. They will return to the field. They are teaching you as future partners and colleagues, not as students.

"Nothing they say is carved in stone. Everything has to be proven to work, and it varies from person to person. But their knowledge is based on experience, and it's what we want you to have. In other words, they will be trying to pass on to you the collective experience and memory of the Mossad as they know it, and as it was passed on to them through experience, trial, and error.

"The game you are stepping into is dangerous. There is much to learn. It's not a simple game. And life is not always the ultimate in this game. Always remember that in this business we have to hang on to each other — or we may hang *next* to each other.

"I'm the director of this academy and the training department. I'm here at all times. My door is always open. Good luck. I will leave you now with your instructors."

He left.

Later, I would discover the irony of a sign hanging over Sherf's door. Its quotation, attributed to former U.S. president Warren Harding, read: "Do not do an immoral thing for a moral reason" — a message that is quite the opposite of what the Academy teaches.

While Sherf had been speaking, another man had entered the room and sat down. As the director left, this heavyset man, who had a North African accent, walked to the front and introduced himself.

"My name is Eiten. I'm in charge of internal security. I'm here to tell you a few things, but I won't take up much of your time. If you have any questions, don't hesitate to stop me and ask." As we soon learned, every lecturer in the course began the lesson with that comment.

"What I want to tell you is that walls have ears. There are technological advances going on all the time that you will learn about, but there are some new ones even we don't know about yet. Be discreet. We know you all come from military backgrounds, but the kind of secrets you'll be carrying around are even more important. Please think about that all the time.

"Then, forget the word Mossad. Forget it. I don't want to hear it again. Ever. From now on, you refer to the Mossad as the office. In every conversation it's the office. I don't want to hear the word Mossad again."

"You're going to tell your friends," Eiten continued, "that you're working in the defense department and you can't talk about it. They'll see you're not working in a bank or a factory. You have to give them an answer, otherwise their curiosity will cause you problems. So that's what you tell them. As for new friends, you don't make them without approval. Is that understood?

"And you're not going to use the telephone to talk about your work. If I catch any one of you talking about the office from home, you will be severely punished. Don't ask me how I know what you're talking about on your home phone. I'm in charge of security in the office, and I know everything.

"If there's something I need to know, I will use any means at anybody's disposal to learn about it. And I want you to know that the story about me from my *Shaback* [internal security police] days — that during an investigation I accidentally pulled a guy's balls off — is not true.

"Once every three months you're going to have a lie-detector test. And later on, every time you come back from a tour abroad, a visit abroad, or any stay outside Israel, you will be required to take a test.

"You have the right to refuse this test, which gives me the right to shoot you.

"I will meet with you several times in the future, and we will go over other things. You will be receiving ID tags in a couple of days. A photographer will come to take your pictures. At that time I want you to bring in any documentation you have from abroad, be it a passport or identification card for you, your spouse, and your children. Since you're not going anywhere in the near future, we'll hold it for you."

For me, this meant turning in my and my family's Canadian passports.

With that, Eiten simply nodded and left the room. Everybody was stunned. He had a coarse, vulgar style about him. Not a pleasant person. In fact, about two months later he was out, and I never saw him again.

At this point, the dark-complexioned man went to the front and told us his name was Oren Riff, the commander of the course.

"You children are my responsibility. I'll do everything I can to make your stay here pleasant. I hope you learn as much as possible," he said, then introduced the smallest man of the group as Ran S. ("Donovan" in Operation Sphinx) — an assistant in the course. The sophisticated, well-dressed man was Shai Kauly, second-in-command of the Academy, also one of my earlier testers.

Before he began, Riff told us a little about his own background. He had worked for the office for many years. One of his first assignments had been to help the Kurds in Kurdistan fight the Iraqis in their war of independence. He had also served as liaison for Golda Meir's office, as a katsa in the Paris station, and in liaison in many other parts of the world. "As it stands right now," he said, "there are very few parts of Europe I can go to safely."*

Riff then said we would start with the two subjects that would take up most of our time over the next two or three months. The first was security, which would be taught by Shaback instructors, and the second was called NAKA, an abbreviation meaning a uniform writing system. "That means reports are to be written in one way and one way only. If you do something but don't report it, it's as if you haven't done it. On the other hand, if you didn't do something but you reported it, it would be as if you had done it," he said, laughing.

"So," he announced, "let's start learning NAKA."**

When it came to communicating messages, no variation in form was allowed. The paper was white, either square or rectangular. At the top you wrote the security clearance, underlined, in a certain way to indicate whether it was secret, top secret, or not secret.

On the righthand side of the page you wrote the recipient's name and who had to act on the message; it might be just one person, it might be two or three, but each name was underlined. Under that went the names of any other recipients who required copies but did not have to act

* See Chapter 10: CARLOS
**See APPENDIX II

on the information. The sender was usually identified as a department rather than as an individual.

The date went on the left side, along with the speed at which the message was to be delivered — cable, quick cable, regular, and so on — with an identifying number for the letter.

Underneath all this, in the middle of the page, went the subject in a one-sentence headline with a colon, and the whole thing underlined.

Under that, you wrote, for example, "in reference to your letter 3J," and the reference date. If you included people on the list of recipients who did not receive the letter referred to, you had to send them a copy of that, as well.

If there was more than one subject, they were divided by numbers, each one a single understandable reference. Every time you wrote a number, for example, "I ordered 35 rolls of toilet paper," you repeated it: "I ordered 35 x 35 rolls . . ." That way, if there was a distortion in the computer, the number would still be legible. You signed at the bottom, using your code name.

We would spend many classroom hours practicing NAKA, since the organization's main goal is gathering information and reporting it.

On the second day, a lecture on security was postponed, and we were handed stacks of newspapers, already marked up with squares around certain stories. Each of us was given a subject and, using the newspapers as resource material, told to break it down into bits of information and write reports. When all the information was exhausted, we were to write "no more information" on the report, meaning it was complete for the time being. We also learned to write the subject headline only after we had written the report.

At this point, we were still commuting to class every day. We'd now received our small white ID tag, consisting only of our photo with a barcode below it.

Toward the end of the first week, Riff announced that we would be learning about personal security. He had just begun his lecture when the classroom door was noisily kicked in and two men leapt into the room. One carried a large pistol, an Eagle, the other a machine gun, and they immediately began shooting. The cadets dove for the floor, but both Riff and Ran S. fell backward against the wall, covered in blood.

Before you could say Jack Robinson, the two guys were out the door, into a car, and gone. We were in total shock. But before we could even react, Riff stood up, pointed at Jerry S., one of the cadets, and said: "Okay, I was killed just now. I want you to give us a description of who did it, how many shots were fired, any information at all that would help us track down the killers."

As Jerry gave his description, Riff wrote it on the blackboard. He then consulted the rest of the cadets, then went outside to summon the two "killers." They didn't look anything like our description. We didn't recognize them at all.

In fact, the two men were Mousa M., head of the training department for operational security, or APAM, and his assistant, Dov L. Mousa looked a lot like Telly Savalas.

"We will explain to you what the charade was all about," said Mousa. "We do most of our work in foreign countries. For us, everything is either enemy or target. Nothing is friendly. I mean nothing.

"Yet we mustn't become paranoid. You cannot think constantly about the danger you're in or fear that you are being followed or watched. If you did, you'd be unable to do your job.

"APAM is a tool. It's short for *Avtahat Paylut Modienit*, or securing intelligence activity. It's there to give you islands of peace and security so you can do your job properly and remain in control. There's no room for mistakes in APAM. Gabriel might give you a second chance, but mistakes are fatal.

"We're going to teach you security in stages. No matter how good you are in whatever else you do, or how capable or smart you are, if you don't pass APAM to my satisfaction, you're out. It doesn't call for any particular talent, but you must be capable of learning. You have to know fear and how to handle it. You have to keep your job in mind at all times.

"The system I will teach you over the next two or three years is infallible. It's been proven. It's been perfected. It will keep being perfected. It's so logical that even if your enemies know it as well as you do, they still won't catch you."

Mousa said that Dov would be our instructor, although he would also be giving some lectures or helping out in exercises. He then took a copy of the course schedule, pointed at it and said, "See the space between the last lecture of the day and the first lecture of the next day? That's when you belong to me.

"Enjoy your last weekend as blind people, because next week we're going to start gradually opening your eyes. My door is always open. If you have any problems, don't hesitate to come to me. But if you ask my advice, I expect you to act on it."

Mousa, who was head of security for Europe the last time I had heard of him, had come from the Shaback, as had Eiten. He belonged at one time to Unit 504, a cross-border unit working for military intelligence. He was rough and he was tough. But he was still a nice person. Very ideological and dedicated. And fond of a joke, as well.*

Before leaving for the weekend, we cadets had to see Ruty Kimchy, the school secretary. Her husband at one time was head of the recruiting department and later, as deputy minister of the foreign office, was an important player in Israel's involvement in the disastrous war in Lebanon. He was also involved later in the Iran-Contra affair.

* * *

The days were usually divided into five blocks, from 8 to 10 a.m., 10 to 11, 11 to 1, 2 to 3, and 3 to 8 p.m. We had regular 20-minute breaks, while lunch was between 1 and 2 p.m. in another building farther down the hill. On the way, we passed a kiosk where we could buy cigarettes, candy, and groceries at cutrate prices. At the time, I smoked two to three packs of cigarettes a day. Almost everyone in the Academy did.

Course time was divided into four major subjects: NAKA, APAM, general military, and Cover.

* See Chapter 13: HELPING ARAFAT

Under general military, we learned all about tanks, the air force, the navy, structure of bases, neighboring countries, their political, religious, and social structures — the last usually intense lectures given by university professors.

As the days went by, we were building up more and more confidence, telling jokes in the classroom, generally in very high spirits. Three weeks into the course, a new man, Yosy C., 24, joined us. He was a friend of another cadet, Heim M., a 35-year-old, large, bald man with a huge, bulbous nose, who spoke Arabic and was always smiling slyly. Heim was married and had two children.

Yosy had worked with him in Lebanon in Unit 504, and now had just returned from Jerusalem where he'd completed a six-month course in Arabic. He was fluent in the language, though his English was appalling. He was married, and his wife was pregnant. An Orthodox Jew, Yosy always wore a knitted yarmelke, but what he really became noted for was his prowess with women. He had sex appeal. He was like a magnet to women. And he took full advantage of the fact.

At the end of school each day, if there were no more exercises, I often spent some time over coffee and cakes at Kapulsky, one of a café chain, in Ramat Hasaron on my way home to Herzlia. Later I became part of a tight clique consisting of Yosy, Heim, and Michel M., a French communications expert who had come to Israel before the Yom Kippur War and worked for a unit called 8200. He had done some work with the Mossad in Europe prior to joining as an "expert with handles." With French as his first language, he was regarded as a good candidate. Hence, he got into the course through the back door.

In our café sessions, we used to do a lot of planning, discussing strategy. Yosy would always say, "Wait for me," and he'd order cake and coffee, then leave. He'd be back 30 minutes later, saying her name was such-and-such. "I had to do her a favor," he'd say. He was constantly doing "favors." We told him he'd catch something, but he always said, "I'm young and God is on my side." It got to such an absurd point with him that we used to joke that it was like a second job.

Cover as a technique was taught mainly by katsas Shai

Kauly and Ran S. Kauly told us, "When you work in gathering intelligence, you're not a Victor or a Heim or a Yosy, you're a katsa. Most of our recruiting is done under cover. You don't walk up to a guy and say, 'Hi, I'm with Israel's intelligence and I want you to give me information for which I will give you money.'

"You work under cover. Which means you are not what you appear to be. A katsa is expected to be versatile. That is the key word — versatile. You might have three meetings in one day, and at every one, you'll be somebody else, and that means somebody else *completely*.

"What's a good cover? Something you can explain with one word. Something with the widest range of possibilities. If somebody asks what you do and you say, 'I'm a dentist,' that's a great cover. Everybody knows what a dentist is. Of course, if someone opens his mouth and asks for help, *then* you're in trouble."

We spent considerable time practicing covers, studying various cities through library files, learning to talk about a given city as if we'd lived there all our lives. We also practiced building a personality and learning a profession in one day. This included meetings with experienced katsas where cover stories would be tested, by means of casual conversation.

The exercises were staged in a room fitted with television cameras, so the other cadets could watch from the classroom.

One of the first things we learned was not to give out too much information too quickly. It's just not a natural thing to do. This was a lesson learned in short order by Tsvi G., 42, a psychologist and the first cadet to be subjected to the exercise. Tsvi faced the katsa and talked nonstop for 20 minutes, blurting out everything he knew about his cover city and profession. The katsa didn't say anything. Back in the classroom, we laughed our heads off. And when he'd finished, he came back to the class and went, "Ah, it's over." He was happy.

We were all brought up in the military where you have a sense of loyalty to your friends, so when Kauly first asked us what we thought of the exchange, I said I thought Tsvi had studied his subject well, that he knew the city. Someone else said he'd spoken clearly and his story was understandable.

Then Ran got up and said, "Hold it. You want to tell me you agree with the garbage that went on it that room? You didn't see the mistake this *putz* made? And he's a *psychologist*. Do you guys think at all? Is that a representation of this course? I want to know what you *think*. Really think. Let's start with Tsvi G."

Tsvi conceded that he'd overdone it, that he'd been too anxious. That opened the floodgates for the rest of us. Ran told us to say what we thought, because every one of us was going to be out there eventually, and we'd be crucified if we didn't do it right. "It might even save your life some day," he said.

Within 90 minutes, Tsvi had been reduced to a nonperson. Any lizard passing by the classroom would have been regarded as a smarter creature. It came to a point where we were even requesting video replays just to prove a point of stupidity. And we were all enjoying it.

That's what happens when you take a group of highly competitive people and throw away the rules of civilized behavior. You'd be surprised at the ruthlessness of it. In retrospect, it was shocking. It turned abusive. It turned into a competition over who could hit harder and hit a softer spot. Every time the abuse tapered off a bit or calmed down, Ran and Kauly would reignite it by asking another question. We had these exercises two or three times a week. It was brutal, but it certainly taught us how to structure a cover.

By now, we had been in the course for 11 weeks. Practical lectures even included wine as a topic: how to recognize good wine, how to talk about it, where it comes from. We also practiced eating in the prime minister's formal dining room at the Academy, using actual menus from major restaurants around the globe to learn how to order the appropriate food, and also how to eat it.

In one corner of the Academy's Ping-Pong room, a television set was on 24 hours a day, playing taped shows from

Canadian, British, U.S., and European television, even includ-ing reruns of series such as "I Love Lucy," and various TV soap operas, to familiarize us with U.S. shows. For instance, if we heard a theme tune, we'd know what it was from and could talk about it. Just like the new Canadian one-dollar coins. They're called loonies in Canada, but if someone asked you about them and you didn't know what he was talk-ing about, yet you were posing as a Canadian, you'd blow your cover.

Under APAM, the next thing we learned was how to follow, first in groups, then individually. How to blend in, take van-tage points, how to vanish, the difference between tailing someone in a "fast" area (busy streets where you have to fol-low more closely) and a "slow area," the concept of "space and time," which is learning to gauge the distance someone will cover in a certain time. For instance, suppose your sub-ject turns a corner on a city street, and by the time you get there, he's gone. You have to calculate if in the time you lost sight of him, he could have covered the space to the next corner. If not, then you know he's gone into a building, so you have to stop.

Once we learned how to follow, we had to learn how to tell when we were *being* followed —through a procedure called the "route routine."

We were introduced to a new room in the main building. It was on the second floor, a big room with about 20 chairs — airplane seats, the kind with fold-out tables and ashtrays in the armrests. There was a little ramp at the front of the room, a table, and a chair. Behind this was a big Plexiglas panel in front of a screen where they projected maps of Tel Aviv, sections at a time. Each of us had to explain our "route" on the map after the exercise. A route is the basis of any work that is done. Without it, we couldn't work.

Cadets were assigned various locations, told to leave them at a certain time, do a particular route, and report whether or not they were followed. If they were followed, they had to report who they saw, when, how many people, and what they looked like. Cadets who reported they were not followed had to say where and when they checked, how they checked, and why they thought they weren't followed. All of this would be drawn with special markers on the Plexiglas over the maps.

The cadets would report, usually the next morning, and after all 15 had finished, we'd be told who was and who wasn't followed.

It was just as important to know that you weren't followed as it was to know that you were. If you think you were followed, but you weren't, you can't proceed. In Europe, for example, if a katsa said he was followed, the station would cease to operate for a month or two until it could be checked out. It's dangerous to say you were followed, because it naturally raises the question of who would be following you, and why.

We were also told that the houses where we lived were safe houses. We had to make sure we were not followed when we left home in the morning or returned at night. For all intents and purposes, the Academy was a station and our own homes were the safe houses.

A route was divided into two main parts. You usually planned it on a map. You'd leave a place and act completely naturally. You'd look for vantage points — a place where you had a reason to be, and from where you could see the place you came from but nobody could see you. Suppose a dentist was on the third floor of a building. On that floor was a window overlooking the street you came from. If you'd done a little zigzag to get there, you'd notice if somebody was following you. From that window, you'd see him look and then wait.

If I was being followed by a team and I'd come out of a hotel, I'd be boxed in. So I'd walk briskly in a straight line for five minutes, to string out their box. Then I'd do a zigzag into a building, take a look from my vantage point, and watch them getting reorganized. What I had to do next was break any coincidence factor. So I'd get on a bus, ride to another section of town, and do it again. I'd do it very slowly to give them a chance to join me.

One thing you never wanted to do if you *were* being followed was to lose them. If you did, how could you verify it? So, assuming they turned up again, so that I'd know I was being followed, I'd immediately stop all planned activities. I might just go to a movie — but as far as our practices were concerned at this stage, I'd be done.

Each of us would carry a little hat in our pocket, and when we were positive we were being followed, we'd put on the hat. Then we'd walk to a phone, dial a number, say who we were, and report that we were being followed — or not — and go home. We'd often meet later at somebody's house to discuss the situation.

In the entire period of training, I made only one mistake. I once said I was being followed when I wasn't. That was because one of the other cadets copied my route plan and followed me by just five minutes. I saw the team following him and I thought they were following me. But *he* didn't see them following him.

By this time, the class had split up into several cliques, including mine. You felt the vulnerability within the course. You were always open to attack, and in the classroom, that applied to everybody. But afterward we'd start meeting in groups of three or four, offering one another advice and even starting to "recruit" the staff to help our cliques. We were practicing what we were taught on the people who were teaching us.

At this stage, the instructors were beginning to explain the application of what had been learned.

"Now that you've learned how to protect yourselves, you're learning to recruit," they told us. "You come to a place verifying you're clean, then start to recruit, and after, you write the report with the NAKA you've learned. And you know how to use information from the constant pounding of data you've received."

I remember Mousa saying, "At this point, my friends, you are starting to crack the shell of the egg."

The yolk was just around the corner.

3

Freshmen

AT THIS POINT in the course, the cadets had accumulated a fair amount of technical knowledge that now had to be given real-life application. One way we began the process was with a series of exercises called "boutiques," sometimes twice a day. The purpose of these was to teach us how to hold a follow-up meeting after successfully making the initial contact with a potential recruit.

Once again, everyone else watched each cadet's performance on television in a separate room, subjecting him to an intense, and often hostile, analysis of his efforts. The exercises lasted about 90 minutes each, and they were truly gut-wrenching and terrifying.

Our every word was scrutinized, criticized. Every move, every action. "Did you put enough hooks in? What did you mean when you said he had a nice suit? Why did you ask him this question? That question?"

A mistake in the boutique, however embarrassing, still wasn't fatal; a mistake in the real world of intelligence might well be. And we all wanted to make it to that world.

We wanted to score as many points as possible to cover for any future failures. Fear of failure was immense. Somehow, we were hooked on working in the Mossad. It seemed that there was no other life out there for you anymore. What would you do? What would set your adrenaline flowing after the Mossad?

The next major course lecture was given by Amy Yaar, department head of the Far East and Africa in Tevel (liaison). His story was so fascinating that when it was over, everybody said "How do we sign up?"

Yaar's department had people positioned throughout the Far East who did little real intelligence; instead they set the framework for future business and diplomatic ties. They had a man with a British passport living in Djakarta, for example, working under cover. That meant the Indonesian government knew he was with the Mossad. He had an escape route ready, and a gold coin belt if he needed it, among other security measures. His main task was to facilitate arms sales in the region. They also had a man in Japan, one in India, one in Africa, and occasionally, people in Sri Lanka, and in Malaysia. Yaar's annual convention for his staff was in the Seychelles. He was having a lot of fun with very little danger.

Yaar's officers in Africa were also dealing in millions of dollars in arms sales. These liaison men worked in three stages. First, they made contact to find out what the country needed, what it feared, whom it regarded as enemies — information gathered through their on-site activities. The idea was to build on those needs, create a stronger relationship, then make it known that Israel could supply the government in question with weapons and training — whatever they needed. The final step in the process, once a country's leader had been hooked on the arms, was for the Mossad man to tell him that he must take, for instance, some agricultural equipment as well. The leader was then put in the position of saying he could expand ties with Israel only if they set up formal diplomatic relations. It was essentially a way of creating those relations through the back door, although in most cases the arms deals were so lucrative, the liaison men never bothered to follow up with the next step.

They did in Sri Lanka, however. Amy Yaar made the connection, then tied the country in militarily by supplying it with substantial equipment, including PT boats for coastal patrol. At the same time, Yaar and company were supplying the warring Tamils with *anti*-PT boat equipment to use in fighting the government forces. The Israelis also trained elite forces for both sides, without either side knowing about the other,* and helped Sri Lanka cheat the World Bank and other investors out of millions of dollars to pay for all the arms they were buying from them.

The Sri Lankan government was worried about unrest among the farmers — the country has a long history of economic problems — so it wanted to split them up somewhat by moving them from one side of the island to the other. But it needed an acceptable reason to do this. That's where Amy Yaar came in. He was the one who dreamed up the great "Mahaweli Project," a massive engineering scheme to divert the Mahaweli River from its natural course to dry areas on the other side of the country. The claim was that this would double the country's hydro-electric power and open up 750,000 acres of newly irrigated land. Besides the World Bank, Sweden, Canada, Japan, Germany, the European Economic Community, and the United States all invested in the $2.5 billion (U.S.) project.

From the beginning, it was an overly ambitious project, but the World Bank and the other investors did not understand that, and as far as they are concerned, it's still going on. Originally a 30-year project, it was suddenly escalated in 1977 when Sri Lanka's president, Junius Jayawardene, discovered that with a little help from the Mossad, it could become most significant.

In order to convince the World Bank especially (with its $250 million commitment) that the project was feasible — and would also serve as a convenient excuse for moving the farmers from their land — the Mossad had two Israeli academics, one an economist from Jerusalem University, the other a professor of agriculture, write scholarly papers explaining its importance and its cost. A major Israeli construction company, Solel Bonah, was given a large contract for part of the job.

Periodically, World Bank representatives would go to Sri Lanka for spot checks, but the locals had been taught how to fool these inspectors by taking them on circuitous routes —

* See Chapter 6: THE BELGIAN TABLE

easily explained for security reasons — then back to the same, quite small area where some construction actually had been carried out for just this purpose.

Later, when I was working in Yaar's department at Mossad headquarters, I was assigned to escort Jayawardene's daughter-in-law — a woman named Penny — on a secret visit to Israel. She knew me as "Simon."

We took her wherever she wanted to go. We were talking in general terms, but she insisted on telling me about the project and how money for it was financing equipment for the army. She was complaining that they weren't really getting on with it. Ironically, the project had been *invented* to get money from the World Bank to pay for those weapons.

At that time, Israel had no diplomatic relations with Sri Lanka. In fact, they were supposedly embargoing us. But she was telling me about all these secret political meetings going on. The funny thing was that when news stories were leaked about the meetings, they claimed Israel had 150 katsas working in Sri Lanka. We didn't have that many katsas in the entire world. In fact, at that time there was only Amy and his helper, both on a short visit.

Another new world was revealed to me and the others with a lecture at Mossad headquarters on PAHA, the department of *Paylut Hablanit Oyenet*, or "hostile sabotage activities" — specifically, the PLO. The department is also sometimes called PAHA-Abroad. Its workers are essentially clerks, and theirs is one of the best research departments in the whole organization, its analysis mainly operational.

It was a shock for us. They brought us into a sixth-floor room, sat us down and told us this was where they gathered daily information on movements of the PLO and other terrorist organizations. The instructor opened his huge folding wall, about 100 feet across, and there was a massive map of the world — excluding the North Pole and Antarctica — with a series of computer consoles underneath. The wall was divided into tiny squares that lit up. If you punched "Arafat" on the computer keyboard, for example, his known location would light up on the map. If you'd asked for "Arafat, three days," it would have lit up everywhere he'd been over the past three days. The current square was always the brightest; as movements got older, the light became dimmer.

The map accommodated many people. If, for example, you wanted to know the activities of 10 key PLO people, you could punch their names in and each would show in a different color. You could also get a printout whenever you needed one. The map was particularly valuable for swift reference. For example, suppose eight of the 10 you were tracking had all been in Paris on the same day. That would probably mean they were planning something, and "steps" could be taken.

The Mossad's main computer contained more than 1.5 million names in its memory. Anyone who had been entered by the Mossad as PLO or otherwise hostile was called a "paha," after the department. The department had its own computer program, but it drew on the memory of the main computer, as well. The computer the Mossad used was a Burroughs, while the military and the rest of intelligence used IBM.

The console screens along the side also broke down into minute detail — into cities, for example. When information was fed in from any station along with the reference PLO, the computer flashed this on the screen. The man on duty would read it and take a printout (the screen also recorded the fact that a printout was taken and at what time). There was barely a move the PLO could make anywhere in the world that didn't end up on the Mossad's giant screen.

The first thing a duty person did when he came on shift was to request a complete 24-hour movement; this gave a picture of where the PLO people had been for the past 24 hours. If there was, for example, a PLO camp in northern Lebanon and an agent noted that two trucks had arrived, that information would be forwarded to the person on duty. The next step would be to find out what was on those trucks. Contact with such agents was daily, sometimes even hourly, depending on their location and the perceived threat to Israel.

Experience showed, in fact, that seemingly innocuous things often tipped off major activity. On one occasion, before the war in Lebanon, word came back from an agent that a shipment of good-quality beef had been brought into a PLO camp in Lebanon, something these camps normally didn't have. The Mossad knew the PLO had been planning an attack, but they had no idea when. The beef shipment tipped them off. It was for a celebratory dinner. Acting on this information, Israeli naval commandos made a preemptive strike, wiping out 11 PLO guerrillas as they were getting into their rubber boats.

This was another example of how important little bits of information could be — and how essential it was to report everything properly.

* * *

At the beginning of the second month, we cadets were given our own personal weapon, a .22 caliber Beretta, the official weapon of Mossad katsas, although few actually carry it in the field because it can create serious problems. In Great Britain, for example, it's illegal to carry a weapon, so it's not worth the risk of getting caught. If you do your work properly, you don't need a weapon. If you can run away or talk yourself out of something, so much the better.

However, you were taught that if your brain *does* signal your hand to draw the weapon, you go to kill. Your head has to say the guy in front of you is dead. It's him or you.

Again, use of the weapon took practice. It was like ballet — you learned one movement at a time.

The gun is kept inside the pants on the hip. Some katsas use holsters, but most don't. A Beretta is ideal because it's small. We were shown how to sew some flat lead weights inside the front lower lining of our jackets; this allows the flap to swing out of the way as you reach for your gun. The action is one of twisting and bending down at the same time to make yourself a smaller target; the time taken to open your coat first could cost you your life.

When you do have to shoot, you fire as many bullets as possible into your target. When he's on the ground you walk up to him, put your gun to his temple, and fire one more time. That way, you're sure.

Katsas normally used flat-tipped or dum-dum bullets that

are hollow or soft-nosed, expanding after firing to inflict particularly severe wounds. Our weapons training took place at a military base near Petah Tikvah, where the Israeli military also does special training for foreign governments. We practiced for hours in front of targets, as well as in a shooting gallery where cardboard targets suddenly appeared as we walked along.

There was also a facility set up to look like a hotel corridor. We would walk down it, turn right, then right again, carrying a "room key" and an attaché case. Sometimes we would get to our "rooms" without incident. At other times, a door would suddenly open and a cardboard target would pop out. We were trained to drop everything and shoot.

We were also taught how to draw a gun when sitting in a restaurant, should the need arise, either by falling back on our chair and shooting under the table or falling back, kicking the table over at the same time (I never mastered that, but some of us did), and then shooting, all in one motion.

What happens to an innocent bystander? We were taught that in a situation where there's going to be shooting, there is no such thing. A bystander will be witnessing your death or someone else's. If it's yours, do you care if he's wounded? Of course not. The idea is survival. *Your* survival. You have to forget everything you ever learned about fairness. In these situations, it's kill or be killed. Your responsibility is to protect the property of the Mossad: that's you. Once you understand that, you lose the shame of being selfish. Selfishness even seems a valuable commodity — something that's hard to shake off when you go home at the end of the day.

When we returned to the classroom after our extensive weapons training, Riff told us, "Now you know how to use a gun. So forget it. You don't need it." Here we were, the fastest guns in the West, and suddenly he was deflating us by saying we didn't need them. Still we said to ourselves, Oh sure, that's what he says, but I know I'm going to need it.

The routine at this point involved more long hours of lectures followed by practice routines in Tel Aviv, fine-tuning the ability to follow and/or be followed. One particularly boring lecture was given by a man who, at the time, was the oldest major in the Israeli army. In a low monotone, he went on for more than six hours about camouflage and detection of weapons and armaments, showing hundreds of slides of camouflaged equipment. The only move he made was to change the slide. He'd say, "This is an Egyptian tank." Then, "This is an aerial photo of four camouflaged Egyptian tanks." There's precious little to see in a photo of a desert scene with several well-camouflaged tanks. It looks pretty much like a desert with *no* tanks. We also saw Syrian jeeps, American jeeps, Egyptian jeeps, camouflaged and otherwise. It was the most tedious lecture of my life. Later, we heard that everybody gets it.

The next lecture was more to the point. It was delivered by Pinhas Aderet and had to do with documentation: passports, ID cards, credit cards, driver's licenses, and so on. The most important Mossad documents are passports, and there are four qualities: top, second, field operation, and throwaway.

Throwaway passports had either been found or stolen and were used when you needed only to flash them. They weren't used for identification. The photo would have been changed, and sometimes, the name, but the idea is to change as little as possible. But such a document would not withstand thorough scrutiny. Neviot officers (the ones who did break-ins, cased houses, and such) used them. They were also used in training exercises inside Israel, or to recruit inside Israel.

With every passport issued, there was a folio page giving the name and address, complete with a photocopy of the section of the city where that address was. The actual house was marked on the map, and there was a photograph of it and description of the neighborhood. If you happened to run into someone who knew the area, you wouldn't be caught offguard by some simple question about it.

If you were using a throwaway passport, you'd be told in the accompanying folio where it had been used before. You wouldn't use it at, say, the Hilton if someone else had recently been there with it. In addition, you had to have a story to cover all the stamps that appeared inside such a passport.

A field-operations passport was used for quick work in a foreign country. But it was not used when crossing borders. In fact, katsas rarely use false ID at all in going from one country to another, unless they are with an agent, something they always try to avoid. The *false* passport would be carried inside a diplomatic pouch sealed by a "bordero," a wax seal with a string on it, ostensibly to show it can't be opened without detection. It is used to carry papers between embassies, and recognized around the world as something that is not to be opened at border crossings. The carrier has diplomatic immunity. (The passports, of course, could also be delivered to a katsa in another country by a *bodel*, or messenger.) The wax seals were made so that these envelopes could easily be opened and closed without appearing to affect the seal.

Second-quality passports, actually perfect passports, were built on katsas' cover stories, but there were no real persons behind them.

A top-quality passport, on the other hand, had both a cover story and a person behind it who could back up the story. They would stand up completely to any official scrutiny, including a check by the country of origin.

Passports are manufactured on different types of paper. There is no way the Canadian government, for example, would sell anyone the paper it uses to make Canadian passports (still the favorite of the Mossad). But a phony passport cannot be manufactured with the wrong paper, so the Mossad had a small factory and chemical laboratory in the basement of the Academy that actually made various kinds of passport paper. Chemists analyzed the paper of genuine passports and worked out the exact formula to produce sheets of paper that duplicated what they needed.

A large storage room was kept at a precise temperature and humidity to preserve the paper. Its shelves contained passport paper for most nations. Another part of this operation was the manufacture of Jordanian dinars. These have been used successfully to trade for real dollars and also to flood Jordan with currency, exacerbating that country's inflation problems.

When I visited the factory as a trainee, I saw a large batch of blank Canadian passports. They must have been stolen. It looked like an entire shipment. There were over 1,000 of them. I don't think the shipment was ever reported missing — not in the media, anyway.

Many immigrants to Israel are also asked if they will give up their passports to save Jews. For instance, a person who had just moved to Israel from Argentina probably wouldn't mind donating his Argentine passport. It would end up in a huge, library-like room, containing many thousands of passports divided by countries, cities, and even districts, with Jewish- and non-Jewish-sounding names, also coded by ages — and all data computerized.

The Mossad also had a major collection of passport stamps and signatures that they used to stamp their own passports. These were kept in a log book. Many of them were gathered with the help of police who could hold a passport temporarily and photograph the various stamps before returning it to the owner.

Even stamping a false passport was done methodically. If, for example, my passport bore an Athens stamp on a certain day, the department would check their files for the signature and stamp from that day at the correct flight time, so that if someone should check with Athens as to which officer was on duty, that would be correct. They prided themselves on this work. Sometimes they'd fill a passport with 20 stamps. They said no operation had ever been bungled by a bad document.

In addition, I'd receive a file with my passport, which I had to memorize, then discard, with general information about the day I was supposedly in Athens: the weather, the local headlines, and the current topics of discussion, where I stayed, what I did there, and so on.

With each assignment, katsas received little reminder slips about previous work; for example, don't forget that on a certain date you were at this hotel and your name was such-and-such. These also listed all the people we met and saw, another reason to include every detail, no matter how tiny it seemed, in the reports.

If I wanted to recruit someone, the computer would search for everybody connected to me in any way: anybody I'd ever met. The same check would be run on the person being recruited. If I wanted to go to a party with that person, I wouldn't run into some friend of his I'd already recruited under another name.

* * *

For an hour or two each day during the next six weeks, the class was lectured by a Professor Arnon on the subject of Islam in daily life: a study of the various sects of Islam, its history and customs, its holidays, what its followers were permitted to do — and what they *really* did — their restrictions, everything possible to fill in a picture of the enemy and what made him tick. At the end, we had a full day to write a paper about the conflict in the Middle East.

Next we were taught about *bodlim* (*bodel* in the singular). These are people who operate as messengers between safe houses and the embassy, or between the various safe houses. A bodel's main training is in APAM, knowing whether or not he's being followed, and he carries everything in diplomatic envelopes or pouches. Carriers of the pouch have diplomatic immunity, and carry a document to this effect. Their main function is to bring passports and other documents to the katsas and to take reports back to the embassy. Katsas are not always permitted to enter the Israeli embassy, depending on the nature of their assignment.

Bodlim are usually young men in their mid-20s, who do this work for a year or two. They are often Israeli students who have been with a combat unit, as they tend to be reliable. Though it's essential that they're trained in how to avoid being followed, they can do the job while still students. They are regarded as one of the lower ranks in the station, but even so, it's not a bad job for a student.

Most stations have two or three bodlim. Another of their functions is to look after safe houses. A station's bodlim might occupy, say, six apartments, so that the neighbors don't wonder about an empty apartment next door with the mail piling up. These bodlim live rent free in the safe houses, making sure refrigerators are properly stocked with food and drink, bills are paid, and so on. If the safe house is needed, the bodel "occupier" may move to another one, or go to a hotel until the coast is clear. The bodlim can't bring friends or girlfriends to these safe-house apartments, but their individual contracts usually range between $1,000 and $1,500 a month, depending on how many apartments they're looking after. Along with no rent to pay, no food or drink bills, and no tuition — which is paid by the Mossad — it's not a bad deal.

The cadets' next subject was *Mishlasim*, or, in intelligence talk, drops and dead-letter boxes. The first rule we learned was that in the Mossad a dead-letter box was one-directional: from us to them. There was no such thing as an agent leaving you a drop, because it could very likely be a trap.

A group of people from the Mossad department that handles drops explained the basics of the art as follows:

Having established what it is you must drop, the four main considerations for success are these: you should take as little time as possible to place the item; it should look inconspicuous when being carried to the drop; it should be as simple as possible to explain its location to your contact; and when he carries it away, it should again be inconspicuous.

I made a container from a plastic soap box, matching a gray spray paint with a chip taken from a gray metal electric pole, then painting a lightning symbol in red on the box. I took four screws and nuts, also painted gray, and glued them to the plastic, then attached a magnet to the bottom. I attached the box by the magnet to the inside of the hood of my car, stopped by the electric pole as if I was having a car problem, attached the box to the inside of the leg of the pole, then drove off. Nobody would see it. And even if they did, they wouldn't touch it because it was electric. When the agent picked it up, he could put it on the side of his car engine and drive away.

We were also taught how to make a "slick," a hiding spot inside a house or apartment in a place that's easy to reach but difficult for anyone else to find. It's better than a safe. If you're in a place where you have to hide something quickly, there is no problem making slicks by using simple things you can buy in a hardware or even a variety store.

One of the simplest hiding places is a door with plywood on both sides and a frame in the middle. To hide something, you drill a hole through the top edge of the door and hang things inside it. Then there's the pipe that holds hangers in a clothes closet. There's lots of room in that. They might take your clothes off the hangers, but very few people will look at the pipe they're hanging on.

Another common way of taking a secret document or money through customs is to buy two newspapers and cut part of one out, making a little pocket inside. Then you cut out the same thing from the other paper and glue it over the spot. It's an old magicians' trick. We used to read a lot of magicians' books. You can walk right up to customs carrying the newspaper — even hand it to the officer to hold while you go through.

The next set of exercises, called "coffee," involved the trainees working in groups of three. Yosy, Arik F., a religious, six-foot-six-inch giant of a man, and I, with Shai Kauly as our instructor, went to the Hayarkon Street hotel strip, sat in the café for a while, then were taken one at a time into a hotel lobby. Each of us had a phony passport and cover story, and Kauly would walk into the lobby with us, look around, then tell us to make contact with whomever he chose. Sometimes they were plants, sometimes not, but the idea was to obtain as much information about them as possible and make another appointment.

I went up to one man who was a reporter for *Afrique-Asie* and asked him if he had a match. That led to a conversation and ultimately, I did well. He turned out to be a plant, though, a katsa who had covered a PLO convention in Tunis in the guise of a reporter for that newspaper. He actually wrote several articles for them.

As usual, after each such exercise we had to write a complete report on how we had made contact, what had been said, everything that had taken place. Back in class the next day, we critiqued each other. Oddly, sometimes you'd come to class and find your subject sitting there.

Like all exercises in the course, this one was repeated over and over again. Our schedule, already full, became hectic. We were still in training, but now we began incorporating everything, to the point that we were looking for people to hit on. It got so that we couldn't start any conversation without dropping our hooks. When you said hello, you were already planting those hooks. Normally, when recruiting, it is best to act wealthy, but you couldn't be too specific; then again, you couldn't be too vague or you might look like a crook.

The course in reality was a big school for scam — a school that taught people to be con artists for their country.

One of the problems after an exercise during which, say, I had built myself up as a rich entrepreneur, was to come back down to earth again. Suddenly I wasn't rich anymore; I was a clerk, a public servant, albeit in an interesting department, and it was time to write a report.

Sometimes things got a bit complicated in coffee. Some cadets wouldn't tell exactly what had happened, thinking that since their subjects had proven not to be insiders, they could glorify themselves a little.

One guy, Yoade Avnets, reminded us of the "oy-oy" or "ouch-ouch" bird, a bird that is not very smart but has big balls hanging below its feet, so that every time it comes in for a landing, it goes "ouch-ouch."

Every time Yoade did coffee, he'd tell this fantastic story — unless it was with an insider. He did this again and again, until one day at our morning break, Shai Kauly came in and called him by name.

"Yes?" he replied.

"Pack your bags and get out of here."

"What!" Avnets exclaimed, holding a half-eaten sandwich in his hand. "Why?"

"Remember that exercise yesterday? That was the straw that broke the camel's back."

Apparently Yoade had approached his subject and asked if he could sit down. The man had said yes, but Yoade then sat there and never opened his mouth, though he wrote a report of a lively conversation. Silence in that case was not golden, and Yoade's career came to an abrupt end.

The first half hour each day in class was now devoted to a cadet giving an exercise called *Da*, or "to know." This involved making a detailed analysis of a current news topic. It was yet another burden, but they wanted us to be very aware of what was going on. When you're into all this you can easily get disconnected from the real world, and that could be fatal — literally. It also gave us practice in public speaking and forced us to read the newspapers every day. If someone brought up a subject, we could show that we were aware of it and, maybe, if we got lucky, prove his story wrong.

Before long, we moved into what was called a "green" exercise — an activity in liaison designed to establish a particular approach to a problem. Suppose we knew there was a threat, a PAHA threat against an installation in a country. Discovering how to analyze and evaluate that threat involved a lot of discussion. Basically, if the threat was against a local installation that had nothing to do with Israel, and you could divulge it without jeopardizing your source, you would transfer the information to the relevant parties, usually through an anonymous phone call, or directly from liaison to liaison. If it was a case where you could give them the information without divulging a source, however, you could also tell them who you were, so they would owe you a favor later on.

If the target was Israeli, you had to use every means at your disposal to prevent harm, even if it meant disclosing your source. If you had to burn an agent in a target country in order to protect an installation of your own in a base country, then you would do so. That was a sacrifice you had to make. (All Arab countries are called "target countries," while anywhere the Mossad has stations is called a "base country.")

If the target was not your own and you had to endanger a source of any kind, then you just left it alone. It was not Mossad business then. The most you could do was offer a low-key warning, a vague warning that they should watch just in case something happened. That warning, of course, would likely be lost among thousands of others.*

These attitudes were engraved in our minds. We were to do what was good for us and screw everybody else, because they wouldn't be helping us. The further to the right you go in Israel, the more you hear that. In Israel, if you stay where you are politically, you're automatically shifting to the left, because now the whole country seems to be rapidly heading right. You know what Israelis say: "If they weren't burning us in World War II, they were helping, or if they weren't helping, they were ignoring it." Yet I don't remember anybody in Israel going out to demonstrate when all those people were being murdered in Cambodia. So why expect everybody to get involved just for us? Does the fact that Jews have suffered give us the right to inflict pain and misery on others?

As part of Tsomet, we were also taught how to brief an agent being sent out to a target country. The basic agent — they are quite common — is called a "warning agent." Such an agent could be a male nurse in a hospital whose assignment is to notify the Mossad if they're preparing extra beds, or opening new wings, or stockpiling extra medication — anything that looks like preparation for war. There are warning agents at the harbor who report if extra ships come in; agents at the fire department to notice if certain preparations have begun; at the library, in case half the staff is suddenly recruited because their work is non-essential.

War entails a lot of things, so you must be very specific when you brief the agent. If the Syrian president threatens war — as he often has — and nothing is happening, you don't worry too much. But if he's threatening war and all sorts of logistical things are happening, you need to know, because chances are, he means it this time.

We were also taught by David Diamond, head of *kasaht*, later called *neviot*, how to evaluate and tackle a still object, or a building. This was all talk, no practice. He gave us a simulation. Suppose your subject was on the sixth floor of a building and he had a document we needed to see. How to

* See Chapter 17: BEIRUT

go about it? He took us through watching the building, casing it, checking the traffic patterns, police movements, danger spots — not to spend too much time standing in front of a bank, for instance — how to plan a getaway, who would go in, signaling of all sorts.

Then came more lessons on secret communications, divided into sending and receiving. Sent from the Mossad, communications could be by radio, letter, telephone, dead-letter drop, or actual meetings. Each agent with a radio was given a certain time each day that his message would be broadcast over a special nonstop station that is now computerized; for example, "This is for Charlie," then a code of letters in groups of five. The message changed only once a week to give the agent a chance to hear it. Agents had a radio and a fixed antenna, usually at their home or place of business.

Another special method of communication was through what is called a floater, a little microfilm attached to the inside of an envelope. The agent would rip the envelope and tip the microfilm into a glass of water. He'd then stick it on the outside of the glass and, by using a magnifying glass, read the message.

Going the other way, agents could contact their katsas by telephone, telex, letters, special-ink letters, meetings, or burst communications, a system whereby very short bursts of information are transmitted on a specific frequency. It's difficult to track, and every time an agent uses it, he does so with a different crystal, never repeating the same frequency. Frequency changes follow a predetermined order.

The idea was to make communication as simple as possible. But the longer an agent was in a target country, the more information he had — and the more sophisticated the equipment he needed. That can be a problem, since such equipment is that much more dangerous to be caught with. The agent has to be taught how to use this equipment, and the more he's taught the more nervous he becomes.

To instill more oomph in our Zionism, the class spent one full day visiting the House of the Diaspora, at the University of Tel Aviv, a museum that contains models of synagogues from all over the world and shows the history of the Jewish nation.

Then came an important lecture by a woman named Ganit, who was in charge of the Jordanian desk, about King Hussein and the Palestinian problem. This was followed by a lecture on the operations of the Egyptian army, then nearing the end of an announced 10-year build-up. Two days of the Shaback's telling us about the methods and operations of the PAHA in Israel were rounded off by a two-hour lecture from Lipean, the Mossad historian, which marked the end of the first section of our program. This was June 1984.

So much of our training was based on forming relationships with innocent people. You'd see a likely recruit and say to yourself: "I've got to talk to him and get another meeting. He may be helpful." It built a strange sense of confidence. Suddenly everyone in the street became a tool. You'd think, hey, I can push their buttons. Suddenly it was all about telling lies; telling the truth became irrelevant. What mattered was, okay, this is a nice piece of equipment. How do I turn it on? How can I get it working for me — I mean, for my country?

I always knew what was up there on that hill. We all did. Sometimes the prime minister's summer residence is actually just that — or it's used to accommodate visiting dignitaries. Golda Meir used it a lot for that. But we knew what else it was. It's just something you hear when you're growing up in Israel — that it belongs to the Mossad.

Israel is a nation of warriors, which means that direct contact with the enemy is considered the most honorable approach to take. That makes the Mossad the ultimate Israeli status symbol. And now I was part of it. It gave a feeling of power that's hard to describe. It was worth going through *everything* I'd gone through to get there. I know that there are few people in Israel who wouldn't have traded places with me then.

4

Sophomores

THE CADETS WERE constantly told to be flexible and versatile, to build on whatever skills we had. Anything we had ever done could be turned into an asset at a later date, so we were encouraged to learn as much as we could about everything. Michel M. and Heim M., both part of my tight little clique, had, of course, entered training through the back door. The two of them were big talkers. They knew most of the lecturers and they'd go on about how they were going to recruit generals and other high-ranking officials. I had the best English of anyone in the course, apart from Jerry S., and was best in what they call operational thinking, that is, how to gauge what is going to happen and see the problems before they come up.

Because Heim and Michel seemed more worldly at the time, I looked up to them, and they, in turn, took me under their wing. We all lived in the same general area, drove to and from classes together — usually with an evening session of coffee, cake and conversation at Kapulsky's where the best Black Forest cake I've ever had was served.

We were very tight-knit. We did a lot of thinking together, a lot of attacking together. We used to try to get into the various exercises together because we could rely on each other — or so we thought. And nobody tried to prevent that.

Oren Riff, our main instructor, who had worked for Tevel, or liaison, always stressed the importance of liaison. Between 60 and 65 percent of all information collected comes from open media — radio, newspapers, television; about 25 percent from satellites, telex, telephone, and radio communications; 5 to 10 percent from liaison; and between 2 and 4 percent from *humant* — agents, or human intelligence gathering for the Tsomet department (later changed to Melucha), but that small percentage is the most important of all the intelligence gathered.

Among the lectures in this second segment of the course was a two-hour dissertation from Zave Alan, the boy wonder of liaison between the Mossad and the CIA. He spoke on the United States and Latin America. Alan explained that when you deal with a liaison person from another organization, he regards you as a link, and you regard him as a link and a source. You transfer to him the information your superiors want transferred, and vice versa. All you are is a connector. But since you are both people, chemistry is important.

For that reason, liaison people will be changed if necessary. Once the chemistry is right, you can create a personal relationship between yourself and the other side. As the relationship grows, your contact develops sympathy for you. He understands the dangers your country faces. The idea is to bring the intelligence down to such a personal level that now you're dealing with a friend. But you must remember that he's still part of a big organization. He knows a lot more than he's allowed to tell you.

Sometimes, however, you may be in a situation where you need information that he might volunteer to you as a friend, knowing it can't harm him and also knowing you won't leak it. That information is very valuable and, in terms of writing your report, is classified as "Jumbo." Alan, peering out at us through his John Lennon glasses, boasted that he got more "Jumbo" information than anyone else in the Mossad.

On the other hand, we, as Mossad officers, did not give out Jumbo. We would prepare make-believe Jumbo, information to be given on a personal level in return for personal information from the other side. But passing along real Jumbo was regarded as outright treason.

Alan told us he had many friends in U.S. intelligence. "But I always remember the most important thing," he said, pausing for effect. "When I am sitting with my friend, he's not sitting with *his* friend."

On that note, he left.

Alan's lecture was followed by one on technical cooperation between agencies, in which we learned that the Mossad had the best capability of all for cracking locks. Various lock manufacturers in Great Britain, for example, would send new mechanisms to British intelligence for security testing; they in turn sent them on to the Mossad for analysis. The procedure was for our people to analyze it, figure out how to open it, then send it back with a report that it's "impregnable."

After lunch that day, Dov L. took the class out to the parking lot where seven white Ford Escorts were parked. (In Israel, most Mossad, Shaback, and police cars are white, although the head of Mossad then drove a burgundy Lincoln Town Car.) The idea was to learn how to detect if you were being followed by a car. It's something you practice again and again. There's no such thing as you see in the movies or read in books about little hairs on the back of your neck standing up and telling you somebody is behind you. It's something you learn only by practice, and more practice.

Each night when we went home, and each day when we left home for school, it was still our responsibility to make sure we weren't being followed.

The next day Ran S. delivered a lecture on the *sayanim*, a unique and important part of the Mossad's operation. Sayanim — assistants — must be 100 percent Jewish. They live abroad, and though they are not Israeli citizens, many are reached through their relatives in Israel. An Israeli with a relative in England, for example, might be asked to write a letter saying the person bearing the letter represents an organization whose main goal is to help save Jewish people in the diaspora. Could the British relative help in any way?

There are thousands of sayanim around the world. In London alone, there are about 2,000 who are active, and another 5,000 on the list. They fulfill many different roles. A car sayan, for example, running a rental agency, could help the Mossad rent a car without having to complete the usual documentation. An apartment sayan would find accommodation without raising suspicions, a bank sayan could get you money if you needed it in the middle of the night, a doctor sayan would treat a bullet wound without reporting it to the police, and so on. The idea is to have a pool of people available when needed who can provide services but will keep quiet about them out of loyalty to the cause. They are paid only costs. Often the loyalty of sayanim is abused by katsas who take advantage of the available help for their own personal use. There is no way for the sayan to check this.

One thing you know for sure is that even if a Jewish person knows it is the Mossad, he might not agree to work with you — but he won't turn you in. You have at your disposal a nonrisk recruitment system that actually gives you a pool of millions of Jewish people to tap from outside your own borders. It's much easier to operate with what is available on the spot, and sayanim offer incredible practical support everywhere. But they are never put at risk — nor are they privy to classified information.

Suppose during an operation a katsa suddenly had to come up with an electronics store as a cover. A call to a sayan in that business could bring 50 television sets, 200 VCRs — whatever was needed — from his warehouse to your building, and in next to no time, you'd have a store with $3 or $4 million worth of stock in it.

Since most Mossad activity is in Europe, it may be preferable to have a business address in North America. So, there are address sayanim and telephone sayanim. If a katsa has to give out an address or a phone number, he can use the sayan's. And if the sayan gets a letter or a phone call, he will know immediately how to proceed. Some business sayanim have a bank of 20 operators answering phones, typing letters, faxing messages, all a front for the Mossad. The joke is that 60 percent of the business of those telephone answering companies in Europe comes from the Mossad. They'd fold otherwise.

The one problem with the system is that the Mossad does not seem to care how devastating it could be to the status of the Jewish people in the diaspora if it was known. The answer you get if you ask is: "So what's the worst that could happen to those Jews? They'd all come to Israel? Great."

Katsas in the stations are in charge of the sayanim, and most active sayanim will be visited by a katsa once every three months or so, which for the katsa usually means between two and four face-to-face meetings a day with sayanim, along with numerous telephone conversations. The system allows the Mossad to work with a skeleton staff. That's why, for example, a KGB station would employ about 100 people, while a comparable Mossad station would need only six or seven.

People make the mistake of thinking the Mossad is at a disadvantage by not having stations in obvious target countries. The United States, for example, has a station in Moscow and the Russians have stations in Washington and New York. But Israel doesn't have a station in Damascus. They don't understand that the Mossad regards the whole world outside Israel as a target, including Europe and the United States. Most of the Arab countries don't manufacture their own weapons. Most don't have high-level military colleges, for example. If you want to recruit a Syrian diplomat, you don't have to do that in Damascus. You can do it in Paris. If you want data on an Arab missile, you get that in Paris or London or the United States where it is made. You can get less information on Saudi Arabia from the Saudis themselves than you can from the Americans. What do the Saudis have? AWACs. Those are Boeing, and Boeing's American. What do you need the Saudis for? The total recruitment in Saudi Arabia during my time with the Institute was one attaché in the Japanese embassy. That was it.

And if you want to get to the senior officers, they study in England or the United States. Their pilots train in England, France, and the United States. Their commandos train in Italy and France. You can recruit them there. It's easier and it's less dangerous.

Ran S. also taught his class about "white agents," individuals being recruited, either by covert or direct means, who may or may not know they are working for Israel. They are always non-Arabs and usually more sophisticated in technical knowledge. The prejudice in Israel is that Arabs don't understand technical things. It shows itself in jokes, like the one about the man selling Arab brains for $150 a pound and Jewish brains for $2 a pound. Asked why the Arab brain was so expensive, he says, "Because it's hardly been used." A widely held perception of Arabs in Israel.

White agents are usually less risky to deal with than "black," or Arab, agents. For one thing, Arabs working abroad are very likely to be subjected to security by Arab intelligence — and if they catch you working with one as a black agent, they'll want to kill you. The worst that would happen to a Mossad katsa caught working with a white agent in France is deportation. But the white agent *himself* could be charged with treason. You do everything you can to protect him, but the main danger is to him. If you're working with an Arab, both of you are in danger.

While our classes at the Academy went on, exercises outside with cars continued apace. We learned a technique called *maulter*, the unplanned use of a car in detecting, or, improvised following. If you have to drive in an area you're unfamiliar with, and you have no pre-planned route, there's a series of procedures — turning left then right, moving, stopping, and so on — to follow, mainly to eliminate coincidence and make certain whether or not you are being followed. We were also frequently reminded that we were not "bolted" to our cars. If we thought we were being followed, but couldn't verify it completely, it might be wise to park, venture out on foot, and take it from there.

Another lecture, by a katsa named Rabitz, explained the Israel Station, or local station, which handles Cyprus, Egypt, Greece, and Turkey. Its katsas are called "hoppers" or "jumpers," because they work out of Tel Aviv headquarters. They recruit by hopping back and forth for a few days at a time, to operate the agents and the sayanim. All these countries are dangerous to operate in because their governments tend to be pro-PLO.

The Israel station is not a popular assignment for katsas. During his lecture on the subject, Ran S. dumped on it. Ironically, he was later appointed its head.

* * *

For relaxation, we began competing against 25 students from another course in the school — one for clerks, computer operators, secretaries, and other general staff. They received a basic course in how the organization works and were always far more serious than we were.

In order to keep them off the coveted Ping-Pong table, we used to hide the balls and bats, but they did compete on the basketball court. We cadets played basketball to kill. We had a guy handle the scoreboard and we'd always win. The other team would shout about it, but for a while we had a weekly game against them, every Tuesday from noon to 1 p.m.

Our lessons, meanwhile, continued thick and fast. After learning how to work a person after basic contact up to recruitment, we were taught financial guidelines. For example, before committing anything, you had to determine a recruit's financial situation. You didn't want to shower money onto a pauper, since this would immediately raise suspicions. Suppose an agent was going back to a target country, and had to be set up financially. Let's say he was on a two-year contract for which his Mossad salary was $4,000 a month. If that agent could absorb $1,000 a month without it showing or changing his lifestyle, the katsa would open a bank account for him, perhaps in England, and put a full year's salary in it. So the agent would get the $12,000 up front and have $36,000 deposited in his London account. For the second year, assuming a two-year deal, the $12,000 advance would be delivered to him and another $36,000 deposited. So, you're not only providing him day-to-day security, you're providing for his future. You are also tying him closer to you. You're protecting your own interest.

There was also a structure of bonus payments — extra per letter, for example — depending upon the quality of the information or the position of an agent. These ranged from $100 to $1,000 extra per letter on average, but a Syrian minister, say, might receive between $10,000 and $20,000 per communiqué.

Of the 30 to 35 katsas operating at any given time, each

would have at least 20 agents. Each of those 600-plus agents would average at least $3,000 a month, plus $3,000 in bonuses, and many would earn considerably more, which cost the Institute $15 million a month at least just to pay the agents. In addition, there were the costs of recruiting, safe houses, operations, vehicles, and numerous other expenses, all adding up to hundreds of millions a month.

A katsa would spend easily $200 to $300 a day on lunches and dinners, and about $1,000 a day in total expenses. That was another $30,000 to $35,000 a day just to keep the katsas in expenses. And that's not even counting the katsa's salary, which varied from $500 to $1,500 a month, depending on his rank.

Nobody said intelligence comes cheaply.

Next, Dov taught us how to build a "secure route." That means a route someone else is securing. We learned about the tie-in with the *yarid* (or "country fair") branch of operational security and watched a long training movie on the subject.

Yarid teams consisted of five to seven people. There were at this time a total of three such teams. When they were in Europe, the head of European security was their boss.

The main reason for the lesson was to show what support yarid offered katsas, but also to show them how to secure a route themselves if yarid was not available.* After I learned that, a whole new world opened up to me. I used to go into cafés in Tel Aviv, and suddenly I'd notice all this activity on the street that I'd never seen before — police following people. It happens all the time, but unless you're trained in it, you don't see it.

Next came Yehuda Gil's lecture on the subtleties of recruitment. Gil was a legendary katsa, whom Riff introduced as "a master."** He began by saying that there are three major "hooks" for recruiting people: money; emotion, be it revenge or ideology; and sex.

* See APPENDIX I
** See PROLOGUE: OPERATION SPHINX; Chapter 12: CHECKMATE; Chapter 15: OPERATION MOSES

"I want you to remember to go slowly and delicately at all times," said Gil. "Pace yourself. You'll have someone, say, from a minority in his country, who has been given a bad deal and wants revenge. He can be recruited. And when you pay him money and he takes the money, you know he's been recruited and he knows he's been recruited. Everybody understands you don't give money for nothing, and nobody expects to get money unless he's expected to give something back.

"And then there's sex. Useful, but it is not regarded as a method of payment, because most people we recruit are men. There is a saying that 'Women give and forgive, men get and forget.' That's why sex is not a method of payment. Money, people don't forget."

Even if something works, Gil said, it doesn't necessarily mean it was the right method. If it's right, it will work every time, but if it's wrong, it will still work sometimes. He told the story of an Arab worker, an *oter* (or finder) who was supposed to set up a meeting with a subject they wanted to recruit. Gil waited in a car while the oter fetched the subject. Gil's cover story was that he was a business acquaintance. The oter had been working for the Mossad for a long time, yet when he brought the recruit to see Gil in the car, he introduced Gil as Albert and the recruit as Ahmed, then said to Ahmed, "This is the Israeli intelligence guy I was telling you about. Albert, Ahmed is willing to work for you for $2,000 a month. He'll do anything you want."

Oters — always Arabs — are used because there are very few Arabic-speaking katsas, and it's much easier for one Arab to start the initial contact with another. The oter breaks the ice, as it were. After a while, katsas find out just how useful they are.

In Gil's story, the direct technique worked. Ahmed was recruited, but obviously it was not done properly. Gil taught us that life has a flow to it, and when you are recruiting, you must go with it. Things have to occur naturally. For example, suppose you know that a man you want to recruit will be at a Paris bistro on a particular evening. You know he speaks Arabic. Gil would sit beside him and the oter would be sitting a little way down the bar. Suddenly, the oter would notice Gil, say hello, and they'd begin conversing in Arabic. It wouldn't take long for this guy sitting between them to interject. They'd know his background, too, so they'd direct the conversation toward his interests.

Gil might then say to the oter, "You're meeting your girlfriend later?" The oter would reply, "Yes, but she's bringing her girlfriend along and we can't do it in front of her. Why don't you come, too?" Gil would say he couldn't, he was busy. At that point, their subject would more than likely announce that *he* was free — and so set off on the road to recruitment.

"Think of it this way," Gil went on. "If this was all happening in Hebrew in some bar in Paris, *you* might have been recruited. People are always drawn to others speaking their language in a foreign country."

The trick of making the initial contact is to make it appear so natural that if the subject looks back at it, nothing seems odd. That way, if it doesn't work, you haven't burned him. He must never be allowed to think of himself as a target. But before you ever approached him in that Paris bistro, you would have turned his file inside out, discovered everything you could about his likes and dislikes, and also about his schedule for that night — as much as you could do to remove the element of chance and, therefore, risk.

Our next major lecture was given by Yetzak Knafy, who brought along a series of charts to explain the logistical support that the Tsomet (katsa recruiting department) receives in operations. It's enormous, beginning with the sayanim, and going on through money, cars, apartments, and so on. Yet the main support is paper backup. The katsa might say he owns a company that manufactures bottles, or that he's an executive with a foreign branch of IBM. That company is a good one; it's so big that you can hide an IBM executive for years. We even had some IBM stores, offering emergency support. We had workers and an office — the whole thing — and IBM didn't know.

But setting up a business, even a phony one, is not that simple. You need business cards, letterhead, telephone, telex, and more. The Mossad had package companies ready on a shelf, complete shell companies with an address, a registered number, just waiting to come to life. They even kept some money in these companies, enough to file tax returns and avoid raising suspicions. They had hundreds of such companies around the world.

At headquarters, five rooms were filled with the paraphernalia of dummy companies, listed in alphabetical order, and set up in a pull-out box. There were eight rows of shelves, and 60 boxes per shelf, in each of the five rooms. The information included a history of each company, all its financial statements, a history of its logo, who it was registered with, anything at all that a katsa might be expected to know about the company.

* * *

About six months into the course, we had a mid-term meeting called a *bablat*, an abbreviation in Hebrew of *bilbul baitsim*, which means "mixing up the balls," or just talking and talking about everything. It lasted five hours.

Two days before that, we had undergone an exercise in which my colleague Arik F. and I were told to sit in a café on Henrietta Sold Street near Kiker Hamdina. I asked Arik if he had come there clean. He said he had. So I said, "Okay, I know I came clean and you say you did, but why is that guy over there looking at us? As far as I'm concerned, this is over. I'm leaving."

Arik said they couldn't leave; they had to wait to be picked up. "If you want to stay, fine," I told him. "I'm gone."

Arik told me I was making a mistake, but I said I'd wait for him at Kiker Hamdina.

I gave him 30 minutes. I figured when I left I would observe the café. I had the time, so I did a route, checked I was clean, came back, and went up on the roof of a building where I could watch the restaurant. Ten minutes later the man we'd been waiting for walked in, and two minutes after that, police cars surrounded the place. They dragged the two of them out and beat them senseless. I called in an emergency. I found out later that the whole episode was a joint exercise between the Mossad Academy and the undercover department of the Tel Aviv police. We were the bait.

Arik, 28 at the time, spoke English and looked a lot like kidnapped Church of England envoy Terry Waite. He'd been in military intelligence before he joined the course. He was the biggest liar on the face of the earth. If he said good morning, you had to check out the window first. Arik wasn't beaten that badly in the police incident because he was talking — lying, no doubt — but talking. Arik knew that if you talked you wouldn't be beaten.

But the other guy, Jacob, kept saying, "I don't know what you want." A big cop slapped him and his head was smashed against the wall. He suffered a hairline fracture of the skull, and was unconscious for two days and in hospital for six weeks. He received his salary for another year, but he left the course.

When we were beaten up, it was like a competition. These cops were out to prove they were better than us. It was worse than really being captured. Commanders on both sides would say, "I bet you can't break my guys." Then, "Oh yeah? How far can I go?"

We complained at the bablat that there was no point in being beaten up so severely. We were told when you fall, don't resist, talk. Your captor won't go to chemicals as long as you're talking. Every time we were on an exercise, there was the danger we'd be caught by the cops. It made us learn to take precautions.

At one point, the class schedule had a lecture from Mark Hessner* slated for the next day. It was on mutual operations, something called "Operation Ben Baker," which the Mossad had done in conjunction with French intelligence. My buddies and I decided to get a jump on things by studying the case the night before, so after class that evening, we went back to the Academy and up to Room 6, a safe room on the second floor where the files were stored. It was August 1984, a lovely Friday night, and we actually lost track of the

* See Chapter 9: STRELLA

time. It was close to midnight when we left the room and locked it up. We'd left our car in the parking lot near the dining room, and we were heading out that way when we heard a lot of noise from the pool area.

"What the hell is that?" I asked Michel.

"Let's go and see," he said.

"Wait. Wait," said Heim. "Let's go quietly."

"Better yet," I suggested, "let's just go back up to that second-floor window and see what's going on."

The noise continued as we stole back into the Academy, up the stairs, and over to the window in the little bathroom where I had once been held during my pre-course test.

I'll never forget what I saw next. There were about 25 people in and around the pool and none of them had a stitch of clothing on. The second-in-command of the Mossad — today, he is the head — was there. Hessner. Various secretaries. It was incredible. Some of the men were not a pretty sight, but most of the girls were quite impressive. I must say they looked much better than they did in uniform! Most of them were female soldiers assigned to the office, and were only 18 or 20 years old.

Some of the partiers were in the water playing, some were dancing, others were on blankets to the left and the right having a fine old time vigorously screwing each other right there. I've never seen anything like it.

"Let's make a list of who's here," I said. Heim suggested we get a camera, but Michel said, "I'm out of here. I want to stay in the office." Yosy agreed, and Heim conceded that taking photos was probably unwise.

We stayed there about 20 minutes. It was the top brass all right, and they were swapping partners. It really shook me. That's sure not what you expect. You look at these people as heroes, you look up to them, and then you see them having a sex party by the pool. Mind you, Heim and Michel didn't seem surprised.

We left quietly, went to our car, and pushed it all the way to the gate. We didn't turn it on until we were through the gate and on down the hill.

We checked up on this later and apparently these parties were going on all the time. The area around the pool is the most secure place in Israel. You don't get in there unless you're from the Mossad. What's the worst thing that could happen? A cadet sees you. So what? You can always deny it.

The next day in class, it was strange to sit there and take a lecture from Hessner after what we'd seen him doing the night before. I remember I asked him a question. I had to. "How's your back?" I said. "Why?" he replied. "You walk like you strained it," I said. Heim looked at me then, and his chin almost hit the floor.

After Hessner's rather long, dreary lecture, we sat through another about the military structure of Syria. It's hard not to fall asleep in those lectures. If you were out on the Golan Heights you'd be interested, but all that stuff about where the Syrians were deployed was rather boring, although the general picture sank in, and that was all they really wanted to happen.

* * *

Next on the course was a new subject on securing meetings in base countries. The first lecture included a Mossad-produced training film on the subject. The movie didn't have much impact on us. It had all these people sitting in restaurants. What's important is learning how to pick a restaurant or when to have a meeting. Before any meeting, you check to make sure nobody else is watching. If you're meeting an agent, you want him to enter first and sit down, so you can make sure he's clean. Every move you make in this business has rules. If you break them, you could be a dead man. If you wait for your agent in the restaurant, you're a sitting target. Even if he gets up to go to the washroom, you'd better not wait for him to come back.

That happened in Belgium once when a katsa named Tsadok Offir met an Arab agent. After they'd sat for several minutes, the Arab said he had to go and get something. When he came back, Offir was still sitting there. The agent pulled out a gun and filled Offir with lead. Offir miraculously survived, and the agent was later killed in Lebanon. Offir tells the story to anybody who will listen to show just how dangerous a simple slip can be.

We were constantly being taught how to secure ourselves. They kept saying, "What you're learning now is how to ride a bicycle, so that once you get out there, you won't have to think about it."

The idea of recruitment is like rolling a rock down a hill. We used the word *ledarder*, meaning to stand on top of a hill and push a boulder down. That's how you recruit. You take somebody and get him gradually to do something illegal or immoral. You push him down the hill. But if he's on a pedestal, he's not going to help you. You can't use him. The whole purpose is to use people. But in order to use them, you have to mold them. If you have a guy who doesn't drink, doesn't want sex, doesn't need money, has no political problems, and is happy with life, you can't recruit him. What you're doing is working with traitors. An agent is a traitor, no matter how much he rationalizes it. You're dealing with the worst kind of person. We used to say we didn't blackmail people. We didn't have to. We manipulated them.

Nobody said it was a pretty business.

5

Rookies

AT LAST, AT THE BEGINNING of March 1984, it was time to get out of the classroom.

There were still 13 in the course at this point, and we were broken into three teams, each based in a different apartment in and around Tel Aviv. My team stayed in an apartment in Givataim; another was downtown near Dizengoff Street; the third on Ben-Gurion Avenue in the northern part of the city.

Each apartment was to be both a safe house and a station. My place was a fourth-floor walk-up with a balcony off the living room, another balcony off the kitchen, two bedrooms, a bathroom, and a separate water closet. The sparsely furnished apartment belonged to a katsa who was abroad.

Shai Kauly was in charge of my safe house/station. The other rookies assigned to it were Tsvi G., the psychologist; Arik F.; Avigdor A., my buddy; and another man named Ami, a highly strung linguist who, among his other perceived faults, was a harping nonsmoker in an environment where chain-smoking was considered part of the rites of passage.

Ami, a bachelor from Haifa, had movie-star looks and was terrified that somebody would beat him up. I don't know how he ever passed the basic testing.

The five of us arrived about 9 a.m., our suitcases packed, and $300 cash in our pockets, a fair amount of money considering that a rookie salary at the time was $500 a month.

We resented having Ami with us because he was such a

wimp. And so we began chatting about what to do when the police came, how to prepare for the pain, all designed to make Ami more uncomfortable than he already was. Bastards that we were, we enjoyed that.

When a knock came at the door, Ami shot straight up, unable to hide his tension. The caller was Kauly, who was carrying a large manila envelope for each of us. Ami shrieked at him, "I don't want any more of this!" Kauly told him to go back and see Araleh Sherf, head of the Academy.

Ami was later sent to join the Dizengoff Street group, but when the police arrived there one night and kicked in the door, he stood up, said, "I've had enough of this," and just walked out, never to return.

We were down to a dozen.

Kauly's envelopes contained our assignments. My task was to make contact with a man named Mike Harari, a name that meant nothing to me at the time; I was also to gather information on a man known to his friends as "Mikey," an ex-volunteer pilot during the War of Independence in the late 1940s.

Kauly told us we'd have to help each other complete the assignments. That entailed devising a plan of operations and a routine for our apartment security. He gave each of us some documentation — I was "Simon" again — and some report forms.

First we had to devise a slick for hiding our papers, then develop a cover story to explain why we were all in the apartment, should the police raid it. The best way to do that was to invent a "chain reason." I might say I was from Holon and had come to Tel Aviv where I met Jack, the apartment owner, at a café. "Jack said I could use it because he was going abroad for two months," I'd say. "Then I met Arik in a restaurant. I'd known him from the army in Haifa, so he's staying here." Avigdor would be Arik's friend, and they would have a story, and so on, so that it would at least sound plausible. As for Kauly, we told him he'd have to invent his own cover story.

We made a slick out of our living-room table, one of those frame tables with a glass top over a wooden panel, by carefully fitting a second "false" panel. You simply lifted the glass and moved the top piece of wood. It was readily accessible, and a place where few people would think to look.

We also agreed on a special knock — the standard two knocks, then one knock, two knocks, one knock — to signal that it was one of our own at the door. Before returning to the apartment, we would call and give a coded message. Or, if nobody was home, the all-clear signal was a yellow towel hanging on a clothesline outside the kitchen balcony.

The mood was terrific. We felt as if we were walking on air. We were doing real work, even if it was still only training.

Before Kauly left that day, we had prepared our plans for approaching our subjects and gathering information about them. Since they had addresses, observation was the first step. And so, Avigdor went to watch Harari's house for me, while I went to watch Arik's assigned contact, the man who owned a company called Bukis Toys.

All I had on Harari was his name and address. He wasn't in the phone book. However, at the library, I found Harari listed in the *Who's Who* for Israel. There was little background, only that he was president of Migdal Insurance, one of the largest such firms in the country, with headquarters near a district called Hakirya. Many government buildings are located there. The entry indicated also that Harari's wife worked as a librarian at the Tel Aviv university.

I decided to apply for a job with Migdal Insurance. I was sent to their manpower department and, waiting in line, watched a man of about my own age working in a nearby office. I heard another employee call him "Yakov."

I got up, walked over to the office, and said, "Yakov?"

"Yes. Who are you?" he asked.

"I'm Simon. I remember you. We were at Tel Hashomer," I said referring to the main military recruitment base where all Israelis go.

"What year were you there?" he asked.

Instead of answering him directly, I said, "I'm a 203," the start of a serial number that represents a recruiting segment of time, rather than a specific year or month.

"I'm a 203, too," said Yakov.

"Air force?"

"No. Tanks."

"Oh, you ended up *pongos*," I said, laughing. (Pongos is a Hebrew expression that plays on the word fungus to mean people inside a tank, which is always dark and often damp.)

I said I knew Harari slightly and asked Yakov if they had any job openings.

"Oh yes, they're recruiting salesmen," Yakov told me.

"Is Harari still president?"

"No, no," he replied, naming another man.

"Oh. What's Harari doing now?"

"He's a diplomat," said Yakov. "And he also has an import-export business in the Kur Building."

That rang a bell because Avigdor had reported seeing a Mercedes with a white diplomatic plate at Harari's house. At the time, I was puzzled. For a person with a Hebrew name to associate with foreign diplomats in Israel was very suspicious. All diplomats in this country are considered spies. That's why an Israeli soldier who is hitchhiking can't accept a ride from someone with diplomatic plates; he'd be court-martialed if he did. And when Avigdor saw the Mercedes at Harari's house, we didn't know it was his car. We thought it belonged to a visitor.

Yakov and I chatted for a few more minutes until a woman came over and told me it was my turn for the job interview. Not wanting to raise any suspicions, I went in to the interview but deliberately flubbed it.

So far, I knew where Harari's wife worked — at Tel Aviv University — and that Harari himself was a diplomat. But where? And for whom? I could tail his car, but if Harari was a diplomat, he'd probably had intelligence training; I didn't want to get burned on my first exercise.

On the second day, I told Kauly that I planned to complete my exercises one at a time. First I'd make contact with Harari; then I'd find out who Mikey was.

Every time we walked out of the apartment, it was possible we were being followed. If that happened, you had to

warn the others in the safe house that it wasn't safe anymore. Of course, each of us knew where the others were
going because we filed our reports to Shai Kauly.

At that point, I could do APAM in my sleep. On the fourth
day, as I was heading to the Kur Building, I noticed I'd been
picked up by someone near the Hakirya district. My regular
security route was to take the bus from Givataim, go to
Derah Petha Tikvah, and get off at the corner of Kaplan
Street, which cuts right through the Hakirya.

That day I got off the bus, did a circle — having done the
same thing before boarding it in Givataim — looked to the
right, and saw nothing. Glancing left, however, I noticed
some men in a car in a parking lot. They just looked out of
place, so I thought to myself, okay, I'll play them and make
them eat dirt.

I headed south on Derah Petha Tikvah, a major artery with
three lanes in both directions, which meant the car in the
parking lot would have to get ahead of me or they would lose
me.

I reached a point where a bridge crosses over Petha
Tikvah to the Kalka Building. It was about 11:45 a.m., and
traffic was badly jammed. I walked up onto the bridge,
stopped, and could see the driver of the car looking up at
me, not expecting me to be looking down. There was another
man behind me, but he couldn't approach me without my
noticing him. On the other side of the bridge, there was yet
another man ready to follow me if I turned north, and a third
man ready to follow if I went south. From my vantage point
on the bridge, I could see all of this clearly.

There was an area under the bridge where cars could
make U-turns. Instead of crossing the bridge, I made a big
display of slapping my head, as if I'd forgotten something,
then turned around and walked back to Kaplan Street —
slowly for them to catch up. I chuckled to myself when I
heard cars honking from under the bridge as the tailing car
tried to negotiate a U-turn in heavy traffic.

On Kaplan, all they could do was follow me in a line. I went
halfway up the street to a military post in front of the "Victor

Gate" (named after my one-time sergeant major), then crossed through the traffic to a kiosk where I bought a Danish and gazoz, flavored soda water.

Standing there, I could see the car slowly approaching. Suddenly I realized that the driver was Dov L. Finishing my snack, I walked up to the car — by now hopelessly stalled in traffic — and used its hood to hoist myself up onto the sidewalk before walking away. I could hear Dov behind me honking in a beep-beep, pattern as if to say, "All right. One for you. You got me."

I was elated. It was really fun. Dov said to me later that nobody had ever nailed him so hard, and he was frankly embarrassed.

After making sure I was clean, I took a cab to another part of Tel Aviv where I would do a route and be sure that it hadn't all been a trick just to make me relax. Then I went back to the Kur Building, and at the information desk said I had an appointment with Mike Harari. I was directed to the fourth floor, where a small sign read something like Import/Export Shipping.

I had decided to go during the lunch break, because in Israel, management rarely stays in for lunch. All I wanted at this stage was to talk to a secretary and get a phone number, plus a bit of information. If Harari was there, I'd have to play it by ear.

Fortunately, there was only the secretary. She told me that the firm handled its own products, mainly South American, but it sometimes took hitchhikers, or partial shipments from others, to complete a cargo.

I told her I'd heard from the insurance company that Harari worked there.

"No, no," she said. "He's a partner, but he doesn't work here. He's the ambassador for Panama."

"Excuse me," I said (a bad response, but I'd been caught off guard), "I thought he was Israeli?"

"He is," she said. "He's also the honorary ambassador for Panama."

And so I left, did my route, and wrote a complete report about the day's activities.

When Kauly arrived and asked me what I had, he wanted to know how I planned to make contact.

"I'm going to go to the Panamanian embassy."

"Why?" said Kauly.

I had already devised a plan. The Pearl Archipelago off Panama used to house a rich industry in cultured pearls. In Israel, the Red Sea is very conducive to growing pearls. It is quiet, has the appropriate salt content, and across the way in the Persian Gulf there are pearl oysters in abundance. I had learned all about this — particularly the process for creating cultured pearls — at the library. I would go to the embassy, ostensibly as a partner of a wealthy American businessman who wanted to start a pearl farm in Eilat. Because of the high quality of Panamanian pearls, they'd want to bring a whole container of pearl oysters to Israel to start the farm. The plan would indicate that the people involved had a lot of money and were serious — not looking for a quick scam — since there'd be no return for at least three years.

Kauly approved it.

Now I had to get an appointment with Harari, rather than the *official* Panamanian ambassador. When I phoned, I identified myself as Simon Lahav. I said I wanted to propose an investment in Panama. The secretary suggested I meet with an attaché. But I said, "No, I need someone with business experience," to which she replied, "Perhaps you could meet with Mr. Harari." We made an appointment for the next day.

I told her I could be reached with specific details at the Sheraton. I had been registered there under the Mossad arrangement with security at various hotels: officers are registered and assigned a room number for messages.

Later that day, a message was left for me to meet Harari at the embassy the next evening at 6 p.m. That seemed weird, because everything closes at five.

Panama's embassy is on the beach south of the Sede Dov Airport, in an apartment building on the first floor above ground level. I arrived smartly dressed in a suit and ready to do business. I had requested a passport because I was not appearing as an Israeli, but as a businessman from British

Columbia, Canada. I had already telephoned the mayor of Eilat, Rafi Hochman, whom I'd known when I lived in Eilat for a year. We had been in the same high school class. Of course, I didn't tell Hochman who I was, but I did discuss the proposal with him in case Harari decided to follow it up.

Unfortunately, Kauly didn't get the passport I needed, so I went without it. I figured what the hell, if he asked, I'd tell him I'm a Canadian, that I don't normally carry my passport around, it was in the hotel.

I arrived at the embassy to find Harari the only one there. We sat facing each other in a lavish office, Harari behind his large desk, listening to me describe my plan.

His first question was, "Are you bank-backed, or is it individual investors?"

I said it was venture capital, regarded as high-risk. Harari smiled. I was ready to go into great detail about oysters, but Harari asked, "How much money are you talking about?"

"Whatever it takes, up to $15 million. But we have a lot of leeway. We estimate the operating costs for three years won't exceed $3.5 million."

"So why such a high ceiling if you have such a low cost?" asked Harari.

"Because the potential returns are very high and my partner is good at raising money."

Now I was anxious to get into the technical aspects of the plan, to throw in the name of the mayor of Eilat, the lot. But Harari cut right through that, leaned across the desk, and said, "For the right price, you can get just about anything you want in Panama."

This presented me with a real problem. I was going in to talk to a guy and start his roll down the hill, get him dirty slowly. I went in playing the clean guy, but before I could open my mouth, he was already rolling *me* down the hill. I was in an embassy talking to the honorary ambassador. He didn't even know me and already we were talking about bribes.

And so, I replied, "What do you mean?"

"Panama is a funny country," Harari said. "It's not really a country. It's more like a business. I know the right people or

—to put it another way—the storekeeper. One hand washes the other in Panama. Today, you might need to negotiate for your pearl business. We might need something else from you tomorrow. It's a business agreement, but we like to deal in long terms."

Harari paused and said, "But before we go any further, can I see your identification?"

"What sort of identification?"

"Well, your Canadian passport."

"I don't carry my passport around."

"In Israel you should always carry your ID with you. Call me when you have it, and we'll talk," he said. "Now, as you know, the embassy is closed."

And he got up and walked me to the door without saying another word.

I had done badly when Harari asked for my passport. I had hesitated, almost stammered. I probably lit up his security lights and he became wary. Suddenly he'd looked very dangerous.

I went back to the apartment, following the usual security procedures, and finished my report about 10 p.m., at which point Kauly came in specifically to read it.

Kauly left, and hadn't been gone long when the police arrived. They kicked in the door of the apartment and the entire frame buckled with it. We rookies were all taken to the police station in Ramat Gan and put in separate cells for interrogation. This was once again to instill in us that, when working in a station, our biggest enemy could be the local authorities. If you were being followed, for example, you had to state in your report if you thought it was the locals or not.

We were held overnight, but when we got back to the apartment, the door had already been fixed. About 10 minutes later, the phone rang. It was Araleh Sherf, head of the school. He said, "Victor? Drop everything you're doing. I want you here. Now."

I took a cab to the corner near the Country Club, then got out and walked up to the school. Something wasn't right, I knew. Maybe they'd already found out the toy manufacturer was ex-Mossad, for example, as was Avigdor's contact, the owner of a booze factory.

Sherf said, "Let me put it to you straight. Mike Harari used to be head of Metsada. His only fuckup was in Lillehammer when he was the commander.

"Shai Kauly was very proud of you. He passed your report on to me, but according to you, Harari doesn't sound too good. He sounds like a crook. So I called him last night and asked him for his response. I read him your report. He told me that everything you said is wrong." Sherf then proceeded to tell me Harari's account.

According to him, I had arrived, waited 20 minutes until Harari was ready to see me, then started talking in a bad English accent. He said he spotted me for a phony and kicked me out. He said he didn't know anything about the pearl story and accused me of making the whole thing up.

"Harari was my commander," said Sherf. "You want me to believe you, a rookie, or him?"

I felt the blood rushing to my head. I was getting angry.

My memory for names is imperfect, but my reports were always damn near perfect. I had turned on the tape recorder inside my attaché case before beginning the meeting with Harari, and now I handed the tape to Sherf. "Here's the conversation. You tell me who you believe. I copied it word for word from the tape."

With that, Sherf took the tape and left the office. He returned 15 minutes later.

"Do you want a drive back to the apartment?" he said. "There was obviously a misunderstanding here. Now, here's the money for your team in these envelopes."

"Can I have the tape?" I said. "There are some things on it from another operation."

"What tape?" said Sherf.

"The one I just gave you."

"Look," he said. "I know it was a hard night for you at the police station. I'm sorry I had to drag you all the way up here just to get the money for your team. But that's the way it is sometimes."

In a later conversation, Kauly told me he was happy to

hear I'd made a tape. "Otherwise," he said, "you'd be out on your ass and probably out of the course."

I never saw or heard the tape again, but I learned my lesson well. That put a little blotch on my vision of the Mossad. Here's the big hero. I'd heard a lot about Harari's exploits before, but only by his code name, "Cobra." Then I found out what he really was.

When the United States invaded General Manuel Noriega's Panama shortly after midnight on December 20, 1989, early reports said that Harari had been captured, too. He was described in wire service news stories as a "shadowy former officer of Israel's Mossad intelligence service who became one of Noriega's most influential advisers." An official for the new, American-installed government expressed his delight, saying that next to Noriega, Harari was "the most important person in Panama." The celebration was premature, however. They caught Noriega, but Harari disappeared, showing up again shortly afterward in Israel where he remains.

* * *

I still had my other project to complete, the gathering of information on the former flyer named "Mikey." My father, Syd Osten (he'd anglicized Ostrovsky), who now lives in Omaha, Nebraska, had been a captain in Israel's volunteer air force, so I was familiar with their flamboyant escapades and heroism during the independence war. They'd been mainly flyers for the U.S., British, and Canadian air forces during World War II who'd later volunteered to fight for Israel.

Many of them were based at the Sede Dov Airport, where my father had been base commander. I got many of their names from the archives, but I could find no reference to a man named "Mikey."

Next, I called security chief Mousa M. for a registration at the Hilton Hotel. I then got some cardboard and tripods for signs, and called the liaison office of the air force to say I was a Canadian film-maker wanting to make a documentary on the volunteers who had helped establish the state of Israel. I said I would be at the Hilton for two days and would like to meet as many of the men as possible.

Only a month before, the air force had had an awards ceremony, so their address list was up-to-date. The liaison man confirmed that he'd reached 23 of them and about 15 had promised to show up at the Hilton. If I needed anything else, I was to call.

I took the cardboard and made signs that read Blazing Skies: The Story of the War of Independence. Above that, I wrote, Canadian Documentary Film Board.

On the Friday at 10 a.m., Avigdor and I walked into the Hilton. Avigdor was wearing coveralls and carrying the signs. I was wearing a business suit. Avigdor set up one of the signs at the front entrance, telling which room the meeting was in, then another down the hallway. Nobody from the hotel even asked us what we were doing.

I met with the men for about five hours, a tape recorder on the table. One of them — without realizing it — was even telling me stories about my father.

At one point, with two or three conversations going on simultaneously, I said, "Mikey? Who is Mikey?", even though nobody had mentioned his name.

"Oh, that's Jake Cohen," said one of the men. "He was a doctor in South Africa."

They then proceeded to talk for a while about "Mikey," who now spent half his time in Israel, the other half in the United States. Soon, I thanked the men and said I had to go.

I didn't give out a single business card. I didn't make any promises. I got everybody's names. They all invited me to lunch. It was like jelly in a mold. You could do anything you wanted with it. But that was all I did.

I then went back to the apartment, wrote my report, and said to Kauly, "If there's something in this tape you don't want me to write, tell me now."

Kauly laughed.

* * *

As we were completing this portion of the course in March 1984, Araleh Sherf volunteered our services to put on a stage show directed by acclaimed Israeli movie producer Amos

Etinger at the Museum of Man Concert Hall in Tel Aviv for the annual Mossad convention, which was to be held in another day and a half. Tamar Avidar, Etinger's wife, is a well-known newspaper columnist who was also Israel's cultural attaché to Washington at one time.

The event was one of those rare occasions when the Mossad actually did something publicly involving outside people, although these outsiders were perhaps more like its extended family — mainly politicians, military intelligence, old-timers and several newspaper editors.

We were exhausted. We still had reports to do for Kauly, and we'd had very little sleep the night before, because we were rehearsing for the big show. Yosy had suggested our group go to his house to grab some sleep because we had to stay together. Then Yosy said there was a woman down the street he'd promised to visit. So he didn't get any sleep at all.

I said to him, "You're quite newly married. You're just about to have a baby. Why did you get married? You never rest. You're like a fish in water. At least part of you is always swimming."

He explained that his in-laws had a store in Kiker Hamdina Square (now similar to New York's posh Fifth Avenue), so money was no problem. Also, he was Orthodox, so his parents expected a grandchild. "Does that answer your question?" Yosy asked.

"In part," I replied. "Don't you love your wife?"

"At least twice a week," he said.

The only one competing with Yosy for sexual prowess was Heim. He was a wonder. Yosy was very smart, but not Heim. I never understood how the Mossad recruited somebody as stupid as Heim. He had a lot of street smarts, but that was about it. All he wanted to do was out-screw Yosy. And Jimmy Durante would have beaten Heim in a beauty contest. He had this incredibly big schnozzle. But he went for quantity, not quality.

Many people, when they know you work for the Mossad, are impressed. It shows you have a lot of power. These guys were doing their thing by using their Mossad connection to impress women. That was dangerous. That was breaking all the rules. But that was their game. They were always boasting about their conquests.

Heim was married, and he and his wife often came to our house for parties. His wife told Bella, my wife, once that she wasn't worried about Heim because he was "the most faithful person in the world." I was astonished to hear that.

To me, Yosy's most shocking conquest occurred in the fourteenth floor "silent room," at headquarters in Tel Aviv, the room used to call agents. The phone system had a bypass setup whereby a katsa could call his agent in, say, Lebanon, but for anyone tracing the call, it would appear to have originated in London, Paris, or some other European capital.

When the room was in use, a red light was turned on — rather appropriately for this occasion — and no one could enter. Yosy brought a secretary to the room, a serious breach of the rules, and seduced her while he was actually speaking with his agent in Lebanon. To prove he'd done it, he told Heim he would leave the woman's panties under a monitor in the room. Later, Heim went in, and sure enough, found the panties. He took them to the woman and said, "Are these yours?"

Embarrassed, she said no, but Heim tossed them onto her desk and left, saying, "Don't get cold."

Everyone in the building knew about it. By being straight, I missed out on a lot of contacts. There was a bond developed between men who screwed around. What disappointed me was that I'd thought I was entering Israel's Olympus, but actually found myself in Sodom and Gomorrah. It carried through the entire work. Virtually everyone was tied to everyone else through sex. It was a whole system of favors. I owe you. You owe me. You help me. I'll help you. That was how katsas advanced, by screwing their way to the top.

Most of the secretaries in the building were very pretty. That's how they were selected. But it got to the point where they were hand-me-downs; it went with the job. Nobody screwed his own secretary, though. That wasn't good for work. You had combatants who were away for two, three, even four years. The katsas who ran them in Metsada were the only link between them and their families. There was weekly contact with the wives, and after a while the contact became more than conversation, and they ended up having sex with the wives.

This was the guy you trusted with your life, but you'd better not trust him with your wife. You'd be in an Arab country, and he'd be seducing her. It was so common that if you asked to work for Metsada they used to say the question was, "Why, are you horny?"

The rookies' stage show was called "The Shadows," and it was a spy story played completely behind three large screens, with lights shining through to cast everything in silhouette. Because we were to go on to become katsas, our faces couldn't be revealed to a general audience.

The play opened with a belly dancer and the appropriate Turkish music, with a man carrying an attaché case passing by on the screen. That was an inside joke. They say you can tell a katsa by the three S's: Samsonite luggage, Seven Star (a leather-bound diary), and a Seiko watch.

The next scene showed a recruitment operation. Then there was a skit about opening the diplomatic pouches, after which the scene shifted to a London apartment with a man sitting in one room talking and in the next room (or, in this case, the next screen) a second man with earphones listening in on the conversation.

That was followed by the depiction of a London party, with Arabs in their headdresses shown in silhouette. They were all drinking and becoming more and more friendly. On the next screen, a katsa was meeting with Arabs on the street. They were exchanging Samsonite cases.

At the end, the entire cast walked up to the screens, joined hands, and sang the Hebrew song "Waiting for the Other Day," the musical equivalent of the old saying "Next year in Jerusalem," a traditional wish from Jews before the formation of Israel.

Two days later we held a graduation party barbecue in the open garden area of an inner court at the school, right next to the Ping-Pong room. Our wives, instructors, everyone directly involved was there.

We had finally made it.

It was March 1984, and we were one course down, two to go.

PART II

Inside and Out

6

The Belgian Table

In APRIL 1984, the members of my group weren't katsas yet, but we were no longer cadets, either. Essentially, we were junior katsas or trainees, still facing a stint in headquarters and then the second intelligence course before being able to call ourselves katsas.

I was assigned to research. As Shai Kauly explained the next morning, the trainees would spend the next year or so rotating from one department to another every couple of months, learning the whole operation to prepare for our second course.

After a long discussion, punctuated by the usual joking, smoking, and coffee guzzling, Kauly announced that Aharon Shahar, the head of *Komemiute* (formerly called Metsada, but changed along with the other departmental names when a code book was lost in the London station in July 1984), wanted to speak to us. He chose two of us to join his department: Tsvi G., the psychologist; and Amiram, a quiet, likable man who had joined the office directly from the army as a lieutenant colonel. These two men were to become case officers for combatants.

Komemiute, which translates as "independence with head erect," operates almost like a Mossad within the Mossad, a highly secretive department that handles the combatants, the real "spies," who are Israelis sent to Arab countries under deep cover. There is a small internal unit within this department called *kidon* or "bayonet," divided into three teams of about 12 men each. They are the assassins, euphemistically called "the long arm of Israeli justice." Normally, there are two such teams training in Israel and one out on an operation abroad. They know nothing about the rest of the Mossad and don't even know each other's real names.

The combatants, on the other hand, work closely together in pairs. One is a target-country combatant, his partner a base-country combatant. They do not do any spying inside friendly countries like England, but they might operate a business together there. When needed, the target-country combatant goes into a target country, using the company as his cover, while his partner, the base-country combatant, acts as his lifeline and gives whatever support is needed.

Their role has changed over the years as Israel itself has evolved. At one time, the Mossad had people working for long periods of time in Arab countries, but often they were there too long and got burned. They used to rely on "Arabists" for that, Israelis who could speak and pose as Arabs. In the early days of the country, when many Jews from Arab countries were coming to Israel, there was no shortage of Arabists. This is no longer true, and Arabic learned in school is not considered good enough for deep cover.

Now, most combatants pose as Europeans. They sign up for a four-year stint. It is crucial for cover that they have an actual business that will allow them to travel at any time on short notice. The Mossad sets them up with a partner — the base-country combatant. They actually run the business. It is not just a cover story, but a real one — usually dealing in import/export sales.

About 70 percent of the base-country businesses are in Canada. The combatants' only contact with the office is through their case officer. Each case officer operates four or five sets of combatants, no more.

There is a branch in Komemiute where a group of about 20 business experts work. They analyze each company and each market, passing this information to the case officer who, in turn, advises the combatants how to operate the business.

Combatants are recruited from the general Israeli public. They are people from all walks of life — doctors, lawyers, engineers, academics — people who are willing to give four years of their lives to serve their country. Their families are paid an average Israeli salary as compensation, but a bonus for overseas work is put in a separate account for the combatant. At the end of four years, they'll have $20,000 to $30,000 in this account.

Combatants do not gather direct intelligence — actual physical observations, such as movement of arms or the readiness of hospitals for war — but they do gather "fiber" intelligence, which means the observation of economics, rumors, feelings, morale, and such. They can come and go easily and observe these things without any real risk to themselves. They do not broadcast reports from a target country, but they sometimes deliver things there — money, messages. Many bridges in Arab countries had bombs planted in the concrete by combatants during their construction — all combatants are trained in demolition techniques. In the case of war, these bridges could be easily demolished by a combatant sent in to detonate the explosives.

In any event, after Tsvi and Amiram had been assigned to Komemiute, Shai Kauly had a message for the rest of us. It had to do with our promised holiday.

"As you know," he said, "every plan is a base for change. I know you are all anxious for your holiday, but before you go on it you have something else to do. You'll be the first course to receive intensive training on the total use of the office computer. That will take no more than three weeks, and after that you can have what is left of your holiday."

We learned to expect this in the Mossad. There were times a holiday would be coming up and we'd be told we could leave Friday at noon. Then noon would come and somebody would say they needed us, but just for the next 24 hours. Then we'd have 20 minutes to phone home and everybody would rush to the phone.

For full-fledged katsas, there was a message system that would kick in on request, conveying something brief, such as "Hi, I'm from the office. Your husband won't be coming home as planned. He'll contact you as soon as he can. If you should have any problems in the interim, please call Jakob."

It was done deliberately. You can't imagine the importance sex plays in the life of a katsa. The whole uncertainty factor meant total freedom. If a katsa ran into a soldier girl and wanted to spend the weekend with her, well, his wife was quite used to the fact that he might not be home. That kind of freedom was openly desired. But the real joke was that you couldn't be a katsa if you weren't married. You couldn't go abroad. They said that someone who wasn't married would be running around and might meet a girl who had been planted. On the other hand, everybody else was screwing around, making a real case for blackmail, and they knew it. It was always a total mystery to me.

For the computer course, one of the rooms on the second floor of the Academy had been cleared out and tables arranged in a C-shape with consoles for everyone to work at. The instructor projected images on the wall screen for all to see: we learned first how to fill in the personnel data file of a subject according to the "carrot page," an orange page containing a series of questions that had to be answered before you could access the computer system. These training consoles were the real thing, tied in directly with headquarters, giving us access to real files, teaching us how to operate the existing program, finding and retrieving data according to different cuts of interest.

One memorable episode during the course involved a system called *ksharim* ("knots"), which means the records of an individual's contacts. Arik F. sat down at the instructor's console one day when she was not there and keyed in "Arafat," and then "ksharim." Because Arafat was PLO, he had priority on the computer. The higher the priority of the person you were asking about, the more quickly you'd be answered.

Priorities don't come much higher than Arafat, but the real problem was his hundreds of thousands of ties, so when the computer began running vast lists of names on the screen, the system became so overloaded that everyone else's computers stopped. There was so much data for the computer to find that it could do nothing else. Arik effectively shut down the Mossad computer for eight hours; at the time the system had no way to stop or override commands.

Since then, the system has been changed so that a limit of 300 listings is placed on any single request, and requests must be more specific. Rather than just asking for all of Arafat's contact listings, for example, you'd have to ask just for his Syrian contacts.

* * *

After the computer course and what was left of my vacation — three days — my first assignment was research, at the Saudi Arabian desk, under a woman named Aerna, which was near the Jordanian desk headed by Ganit. Neither was regarded as an important desk. The Mossad then had a single source in Saudi Arabia, a man in the Japanese embassy. Everything else for the region came from newspapers, magazines and other media, plus extensive communications interference orchestrated by Unit 8200.

Aerna was busy putting together a book on the family tree of the Saudi Arabian royal family. She was also gathering information on a proposed second oil pipeline across the country which the Iraqis wanted to patch into when it was built, so that they could pump out their oil and sell it to pay for their war effort against Iran. Because of the war, it was extremely difficult to transport the oil safely by ship through the Persian Gulf. We saw interesting reports about Saudi Arabia from British Intelligence. They wrote extremely good reports, which were really political analyses of a situation, never real intelligence. The British were very bad as far as sharing intelligence went. One of their reports said that the Saudis felt the oil situation was going to get better; therefore they should build this second pipeline. But the Brits were saying there was going to be a glut, and the Saudi economy would suffer once they ran out of cash to support their extensive free hospitalization and education systems.

We took the Brits seriously, but everyone in the building

used to say they were probably deluded because of "the Bitch." That's what they always called Margaret Thatcher inside the Mossad. They had her tagged as an anti-Semite. There was one simple question asked when anything happened: "Is it good for the Jews or not?" Forget about policies, or anything else. That was the only thing that counted, and depending on the answer, people were called anti-Semites, whether deservedly or not.

We used to receive long sheets of paper that resembled white carbon paper, with conversations from tapped phone calls typed on them, conversations between the Saudi king and his relatives, already translated. We'd get calls where a prince was talking to a relative in Europe. He'd say he was out of cash and was putting someone else on the line to work something out. The next one would explain that there was a ship headed for Amsterdam carrying millions of gallons of oil, and he would instruct the relative to change the registration to the prince and put the money in his Swiss account. It was unbelievable how much money the Saudis were shifting around so casually.

In one memorable conversation, Arafat called to solicit the king's help because he couldn't get through to Assad in Syria. So the king called Assad, flattering him with terms such as "Father of all Arabs," and "Son of the Holy Sword." While Assad took the Saudi king's call, he still wouldn't agree to accept Arafat's.

One man I ran into at this time was named Efraim (Effy for short), a former liaison man to the CIA when he was stationed in Washington for the Mossad. Efraim used to boast that it was he who had brought down Yitzhak Rabin in 1977, after only three years as the country's Labor prime minister. The Mossad did not like Rabin. The former Israeli ambassador to the United States, he had left that job in 1974 and come back to take over the party and succeed Golda Meir as prime minister. Rabin demanded raw data from intelligence, rather than the distilled version normally offered, making it much more difficult for Mossad to use their information to set the agenda the way they wanted.

In December 1976, Rabin and his cabinet resigned after he

had forced the three ministers of the National Religious Party out of the government following their abstinence on a Knesset vote of confidence. After that, Rabin remained prime minister in an interim government until the national Knesset elections in May 1977, when Menachem Begin became prime minister, much to the delight of the Mossad. What had really finished Rabin, however, was a "scandal" reported by well-known Israeli journalist Dan Margalit, shortly before the elections.

It was against the law for an Israeli citizen to hold a bank account in a foreign country. Rabin's wife had an account in New York with less than $10,000 in it; she used it when they traveled there even though she was entitled, as the prime minister's wife, to have all her expenses paid by the government. Still, the Mossad knew about the bank account, and Rabin knew they knew, but he didn't take it seriously. He should have.

When the time was right, Margalit was tipped off that Rabin had a foreign account. According to Efraim, when Margalit flew to the United states to check out the story, he had supplied him with all the necessary documentation on the account. The subsequent story, and scandal, were instrumental in helping Begin defeat Rabin. Rabin was an honest man, but the Mossad didn't like him. So they got him. Efraim bragged constantly about being the man who brought him down. I have never heard anyone contradict him.

During the first course, students were taken on a tour of Israeli Aeronautical Industries (IAI). Through the Saudi desk, I learned that the Israelis were selling IAI reserve fuel tank pilons through a third country (I don't know which one) to Saudi Arabia, allowing their fighter jets to carry enough extra fuel for extended flights, should the need arise. Israel also had a contract to supply the same reserve tanks to the United States.

The Saudis, figuring they were paying too much under this arrangement, turned to the Americans and asked if they could buy the pilons from them. Israel stood on its hind legs and hollered no! The whole Jewish lobby swung into action to oppose it because it would have given the Saudi F-16s the capability of attacking Israel. Yet we knew how dishonest this was because they were being sold under a civilian cover for much more than the Americans would have charged. A lot of things were being sold to the Saudis in that way. They're a big market.

The research department was located in the basement and on the ground floor in the headquarters building. The space accommodated the head of research, his second-in-command, the library, computer room, typing pool, and liaison for other research. Most of the staff worked at one of the 15 research desks: United States, South America, general desk (which included Canada and Western Europe), the Atom desk (jokingly referred to as the "kaput" desk), Egypt, Syria, Iran, Iraq, Jordan, Saudi Arabia and the United Arab Emirates, Libya, Morocco/Algiers/Tunis (known as the MAGREB), Africa, the Soviet Union, and China.

Research produced short daily reports that were available to everyone on their computer first thing in the morning. They did a more extensive, four-page weekly report on light green paper with highlights in the Arab world, and a monthly, 15- to 20-page report with considerable detail, including maps and charts.

I prepared one map of the proposed new oil pipeline route, complete with specifications, and another chart calculating the chances of an oil tanker's getting safely through the Gulf. At the time, I gave it a 30 percent chance. The policy was that if it was over 48 percent, the Mossad would begin notifying each side of the whereabouts of the other's ships. We had a man in London who was calling the Iraqi and Iranian embassies, posing as a patriot in both cases, giving them information. They wanted to meet and pay him, because his information was so good. But he always said he was doing it out of patriotism, not for money. We would allow so many Iraqi and Iranian ships to pass, but anything beyond that and we'd make sure the other side was notified and the ship targeted. That way we could keep the war hot. And if they were busy fighting each other, they couldn't fight us.

* * *

After several months in research, I was transferred to what was to me the most exciting department in the building, *Kaisarut*, or liaison. I was in the section called *Dardasim*, or "Smerfs," which handled the Far East and Africa. I worked under Amy Yaar.

It was like a train station, sort of a mini foreign office to countries Israel has no formal ties with. Ex-generals and various former security people would be sauntering in and out all the time, wearing visitors' tags and using their former Mossad contacts to arrange deals for their private companies — usually selling arms. Because these "consultants" couldn't go to certain countries as Israelis, liaison would facilitate the sales by providing false passports and other items for them.

It wasn't right, but nobody would ever say anything. Everyone felt that one day he'd be a has-been, too, and likely doing the same thing.

Amy told me that if I received any unusual requests, I was not to ask why, but simply to bring such things to his attention. One day a man came in and asked me to have a contract signed that had to be approved by the prime minister. The contract was for the sale of between 20 and 30 U.S.-made Skyhawk fighters to Indonesia, something that contravened Israel's armament agreement with the United States. They were not supposed to resell such armaments without U.S. approval.

"Okay," I said, "if you don't mind coming tomorrow, or leaving me your phone number. I'll call you once it's taken care of."

"No, I'll wait," he said.

During my trip to IAI, I had seen about 30 of these Skyhawk fighter jets sitting on runway completely wrapped in bright yellow plastic, and ready for shipping. When we asked about it, they just said they were for shipment overseas, but they wouldn't tell us where they were going. I was quite sure there was no way the Americans would approve of the sale of these planes to Indonesia. It would change the balance of power in the area. But it wasn't up to me. So when he said he'd wait for Prime Minister Peres's approval, I opened my drawer, looked in, and said, "Shimon, Shimon." I turned to him and said, "Sorry, Mr. Peres is not here right now."

The guy got really mad and told me to go see Amy. I hadn't even bothered asking who he was. When I told Amy about it, he got quite excited. "Where is he? Where is he?"

"Out in the hall."

"Well, send him in with the contract," said Amy.

About 20 minutes later the man left Yaar's office and walked by mine. Holding the contract under his chin for me to see, and grinning from ear to ear, he said, "Apparently Mr. Peres was in, after all."

Peres, in reality, was probably in Jerusalem, and would certainly have known nothing about his signature being put on these documents. The paper involved was known as an "ass-cover," for internal use only, just to show the shipper or whoever else was involved that they were covered financially because the prime minister had approved the deal.

Officially, of course, Mossad employees work for the prime minister's office. The PM would be aware of money transactions, but he often did not know about actual deals. And many times that was fine with him. It was sometimes better not to know. If he knew, he'd have to make decisions. This way, if, say, the Americans found out, he could say he didn't know and it would be what the Americans call a "plausible deniability."

The Asia Building, owned by wealthy Israeli industrialist Saul Eisenberg, was right next to headquarters. Because of Eisenberg's connections to the Far East, he was the Mossad's tie-in with China. He and his people were doing considerable armament dealing with various places. Many of the sales were of leftover equipment, Russian-made materiel captured from the Egyptians and Syrians during the wars. When Israel ran out of Russian-built AK-47s to sell, it began manufacturing its own — a cross between the AK-47 assault rifle and the American M-16, called the Galil. It was sold all over the world.

It was like working in a department store servicing all these private consultants. They were supposed to be tools used by us, but the tools got out of hand. They had more experience than any of us, so that in fact they were using us.

One of my assignments, in mid-July 1984, was to escort a group of Indian nuclear scientists who were worried about the threat of the Islamic bomb (Pakistan's bomb) and had come on a secret mission to Israel to meet with Israeli nuclear experts and exchange information. As it turned out, the Israelis were happy to accept information from the Indians, but reluctant to return the favor.

The day after they left, I was picking up my regular paperwork when Amy called me into the office for two assignments. The first was to help get the gear and staff for a group of Israelis going to South Africa to help train that country's secret-police units. After that, I was to go to an African embassy and pick up a man who was supposed to fly back to his home country. He was to be taken to his home in Herzlia Pituah, then driven to the airport and ushered through security.

"I'll meet you at the airport," Amy said, "because we have a group of people coming from Sri Lanka to train here."

Amy was waiting for the Sri Lankans' flight from London when I joined him. "When these guys arrive," he said, "don't make a face. Don't do anything."

"What do you mean?" I asked

"Well, these guys are monkeylike. They come from a place that's not developed. They're not long out of the trees. So don't expect much."

Amy and I escorted the nine Sri Lankans through a back door of the airport into an air-conditioned van. These were the first arrivals from a group that would finally total nearly 50. They would then be divided into three smaller groups:

- An anti-terror group training at the military base near Petha Tikvah, called Kfar Sirkin, learning how to overtake hijacked buses and airplanes, or deal with hijackers in a building, how to descend from helicopters on a rope, and other anti-terrorist tactics. And, of course, they would be buying Uzis and other Israeli-made equipment, including bulletproof vests, special grenades, and more.

- A purchasing team, in Israel to buy weapons on a larger scale. They bought seven or eight large PT boats, for example, called *Devora*, which they would use mainly to patrol their northern shores against Tamils.
- A group of high-ranking officers who wanted to purchase radar and other naval equipment to counter the Tamils who were still getting through from India and mining Sri Lankan waters.

I was to squire Penny,* President Jayawardene's daughter-in-law, around to the usual tourist spots for two days, and then she would be looked after by someone else from the office. Penny was a pleasant woman, physically an Indian version of Corazon Aquino. She was a Buddhist because her husband was, but she was somehow still a Christian, so she wanted to see all the Christian holy places. On the second day, I took her to Vered Haglil, or the Rose of Galilee, a horse-ranch-restaurant on the mountain with a nice view and good food. We had an account there.

Next I was assigned to the high-ranking officers who were looking for radar equipment. I was told to take them to a manufacturer in Ashdod named Alta that could do the work. But when he saw their specifications, the Alta representative said, "They're just going through the motions. They're not going to buy our radar."

"Why?" I said.

"These specs were not written by these monkeys," the man said. "They were written by a British radar manufacturer called Deca, so these guys already know what they're going to buy. Give them a banana and send them home. You're wasting your time."

"Okay, but how about a brochure or something to make them happy?"

This conversation was going on in Hebrew while we all sat together eating cookies, and drinking tea and coffee. The

* See Chapter 3 : FRESHMEN

Alta rep said he didn't mind giving them a lecture to make it look as if they weren't being brushed off, "but if we're going to do that, let's have some fun."

With that, he went into another office for a set of big transparencies of a large vacuum-cleaner system that is used to clean harbors after oil spills. He had a series of colorful schematic drawings. Everything was written in Hebrew, but he lectured in English on this "high capability radar equipment." I found it difficult not to laugh. He laid it on so thick, claiming this radar could locate a guy swimming in the water and practically tell his shoe size, his name and address, and his blood type. When he'd finished, the Sri Lankans thanked him, said they were surprised at this technological advancement, but that it wouldn't fit their ships. Here they were telling us about their ships. Well, we knew about their ships. We built them!

After dropping me off at the hotel, I told Amy the Sri Lankans weren't buying the radar. "Yes, we knew that," he replied.

Amy then told me to go to Kfar Sirkin where the Sri Lankan special-forces group was training, get them whatever they needed, then take them into Tel Aviv for the evening. But he cautioned me to make sure it was all coordinated with Yosy, who had just been transferred to the same department that week.

Yosy was also looking after a group being trained by the Israelis. But they weren't supposed to meet my people. They were Tamils, bitter enemies of my Sinhalese group. Tamils, who are mostly Hindu, argue that since Sri Lanka won independence from Great Britain in 1948 (as Ceylon), they have been discriminated against by the island's predominantly Buddhist Sinhalese majority. Of the 16 million or so Sri Lankans, about 74 percent are Sinhalese, and just 20 percent are Tamil, largely centered in the northern section of the country. Around 1983, a group of Tamil guerrilla factions, collectively known as the Tamil Tigers, began an armed struggle to create a Tamil homeland in the north called Eelam — an ongoing battle that has claimed thousands of lives on both sides.

Sympathy for the Tamils runs high in the southern Indian state of Tamil Nadu, where 40 million Tamils live. Many Sri Lankan Tamils, escaping the bloodshed, have sought refuge there, and the Sri Lankan government has accused Indian officials of arming and training the Tamils. They should be accusing the Mossad.

The Tamils were training at the commando naval base, learning penetration techniques, mining landings, communications, and how to sabotage ships similar to the Devora. There were about 28 men in each group, so it was decided that Yosy should take the Tamils to Haifa that night while I took the Sinhalese to Tel Aviv, thus avoiding any chance encounters.

The real problem started about two weeks into the courses, when both the Tamils and Sinhalese — unknown to each other, of course — were training at Kfar Sirkin. It is a fairly large base, but even so, on one occasion the two groups passed within a few yards of each other while they were out jogging. After their basic training routine at Kfar Sirkin, the Sinhalese were taken to the naval base to be taught essentially how to deal with all the techniques the Israelis had just taught the Tamils. It was pretty hectic. We had to dream up punishments or night training exercises just to keep them busy, so that both groups wouldn't be in Tel Aviv at the same time. The actions of this one man (Amy) could have jeopardized the political situation in Israel if these groups had met. I'm sure Peres wouldn't have slept at night if he'd known this was going on. But, of course, he didn't know.

When the three weeks were just about up and the Sinhalese were preparing to go to Atlit, the top-secret naval commando base, Amy told me he wouldn't be going with them. The *Sayret Matcal* would take over their training. This was the top intelligence reconnaissance group, the one that carried out the famous Entebbe raid. (The naval commandos are the equivalent of the American Seals.)

"Look, we have a problem," said Amy. "We have a group of 27 SWAT team guys from India coming in."

"My God," I said   "What *is* this? We've got Sinhalese, Tamils, and now Indians. Who's next?"

The SWAT team was supposed to train at the same base where Yosy had the Tamils, a tricky and potentially volatile situation. And I still had my regular office work to do, along with the daily reports. In the evenings, I took the SWAT team to dinner, again making sure none of the groups ended up in the same place. Every day I had an envelope brought to me with about $300 in Israeli currency to spend on them.

At the same time, I was meeting with a Taiwanese air-force general named Key, the representative of their intelligence community in Israel. He worked out of the Japanese embassy, and he wanted to buy weapons. I was told to show him around, but not to sell to him, since the Taiwanese would replicate in two days anything they bought, and end up competing with Israel on the market. I took him to the Sultan factory in the Galil, where mortars and mortar shells were made. He was impressed, but the manufacturer told me he couldn't sell him anything, anyway: first, because he was from Taiwan, and second, because everything he had was pre-ordered. I told him I had no idea we were training so hard with mortars. He said, "We aren't, but the Iranians are sure using a lot of them." That was keeping the company in business.

At one point they made arrangements to bring in a whole group of Taiwanese for training. It was a compromise of sorts. They had asked the Mossad to give them combatants in China, but they wouldn't; instead, they trained a unit similar to the neviot, capable of gathering information from inanimate objects.

At this time, the department also had a series of Africans coming and going and being offered various services. I stayed with the department two months longer than I was supposed to, at Amy's specific request — both a compliment and a useful addition to my personnel record.

They used to tell the story of the "kerplunk machine" to illustrate some of the weird and useless things the Africans would spend their money on. Someone asked an African leader if he had a kerplunk machine. He didn't, so they offered to build him one for $25 million. When a huge arm, nearly 1,000 feet long and over 600 feet high, hovering over the water, was complete, its creator went back to the leader and said he'd need another $5 million to finish it. He then devised an elevator apparatus under the arm that held a huge stainless steel ball more than 60 feet in diameter. All the leader's subjects and visiting dignitaries from other African countries gathered at the river bank on "launch" day to see the wonderful machine in action. When it was turned on, the elevator moved slowly along to the end of the arm, it opened, and the giant ball fell into the water and went "kerplunk."

It's just a joke, but it's not so far from the truth.

I never saw so much money changing hands so quickly and among so many people as during my time with Amy. The Mossad regarded all these contracts as initial contact with various places that someday would bring diplomatic relations, so money was no object. And the businessmen, of course, were looking at it from a profit point of view. They were all getting their healthy percentages.

My last assignment with Amy was a four-day trip around Israel with a man and a woman from Communist China who wanted to buy electronic equipment.

They were angry at being shown equipment of lesser quality than they already had. They complained saying, "What are they trying to sell us, socks?", which I found really funny, because I used to say that if we could sell socks to the Chinese army, we'd be economically sound. Everybody would be knitting.

But the Chinese couple were badly treated, and that was because Amy thought they weren't high-ranking enough. He was making foreign-affairs decisions by himself, without asking anyone. It was astonishing. All his life Amy worked for government at a government salary, yet he lived on this acreage north of Tel Aviv in a huge villa with a small forest of his own. We'd stop there sometimes for a drink when we were working on the weekends and there were always businessmen wandering around the lawns, and a barbecue going. I once said to him, "How can you manage all this?" and he said, "You work hard, you save, and you can manage." Yeah, sure.

* * *

I was next assigned to the Tsomet (or Meluckah) department and put on the Benelux desk, where part of my job was approving Danish visa applications.

In Tsomet, the desk is there to service the station, not to instruct it. The head of a station in Tsomet is the boss and, in most cases, equals the rank of the head of the branch he's under. (This is the opposite of Kaisarut, where I had just been working. There, decisions are taken at the desk and the branches, so that the liaison station head in London, for example, is the direct subordinate of the head of the London desk in Tel Aviv, which has total control.)

The first branch of Tsomet had several desks. One, called the Benelux desk, handled Belgium, The Netherlands, Luxembourg, and also Scandinavia (with stations in Brussels and Copenhagen); then there were the French and the British desks, with stations in London, Paris, and Marseille.

There was also a second major branch with the Italian desk, and stations in Rome and Milan; the German and Austrian desk, then with a station in Hamburg (changed later to Berlin); and a jumper desk, called the Israeli station, in Tel Aviv, with katsas jumping to Greece, Turkey, Egypt, and Spain, when needed.

The head of a station had the rank of the head of a branch and could overrule him if need be, then go directly to the head of department. The structure was flawed, because if his case failed with the head of department, he could still turn to the head of Europe, in Brussels. As a field command, that would override even the head of department. It became a constant struggle, and with every change in personnel there, the power base shifted.

There was no such thing as orders in the Mossad. It was nicer that way. First, they didn't want to make anybody angry, and then, nobody really had to do what you asked them to do. Most people had a horse or two in the system —

an open horse and a secret horse — one to help push you up and a secret one to get you out of shit. So there was a constant battle trying to guess who had whom and why.

When information came in on the computer from an agent, who was then assistant air attaché at the Syrian embassy in Paris, that the head of the Syrian air force (who was also head of their intelligence) would be coming to Europe to buy some expensive furniture, headquarters thought immediately of creating something that could "talk," because of communications equipment planted inside it.

The computer was asked to find all available furniture sayanim. A plan would be devised to create a speaking table for the renovated offices at Syrian air-force headquarters. A katsa from the London station was sent to Paris to run the show, though the Mossad knew the general would be buying his furniture in Belgium, not France. (They did not know why.)

Prior to the general's arrival, the London katsa was set up in business as someone who could get you any piece of furniture you wanted, but cheaper. We knew the general himself was not looking for bargains. He was rich and, anyway, would get cash through the embassy, and so pay in cash. The idea was not to get to him, but to the aide who would actually do the purchasing. We had less than three weeks to accomplish it.

We contacted a well-known interior designer, a sayan, and obtained photos of his work, putting together in a couple of days a brochure for a company that delivered quality furniture at good prices. We would use a three-point plan to approach the general's aide. First, we would try to reach him directly. Give him the brochure, see if he'd bite and buy the furniture directly from the Mossad. If that didn't work, we would find out where he bought the furniture and arrange to handle the delivery. The next step, if all else failed, was to hijack the furniture.

We knew what hotel the general was staying at in Brussels and that he'd be at the hotel with his bodyguards for three days before going off to Paris. We followed the general and his aide from store to store, watching the aide making notes.

At that point, the katsa thought he'd blown it. We didn't know what to do. The day was over and the general went back to his hotel. Our guy at the Syrian embassy notified us that the general was going back to Paris the next day, but one ticket had been canceled. We figured it had to be the aide staying behind to complete the purchase.

It was. The next morning, the aide was tailed from the hotel to a very exclusive furniture store. He had a long conversation with the salespeople, and the katsa decided that this was the best opportunity to make his move. So he went into the store and started looking around. A sayan came in then, walked up to the katsa and thanked him loudly, and with conviction, for getting him the furniture he'd wanted and saving him thousands of dollars.

After the sayan left, the general's aide glanced curiously in his direction.

"Buying furniture?" the katsa asked.

"Yes."

"Here, look at this," he said, handing him the special brochure.

"Do you work in the store?" the aide asked, appearing puzzled.

"No, no. I purchase for my clients," the katsa told him. "I buy in large quantities at excellent discounts. I handle the shipping and make payment easier than most."

"What do you mean?"

"I have customers all over. They come in and pick the style they want and I purchase it from the source. Then I ship it to them and they pay on arrival. That way they don't have to worry if something is broken. There's no hassle. They don't have to get involved in trying to get a refund or something."

"How do you know they'll pay you?"

"That's never a problem."

By now, all the lights were going on in the aide's head. He saw a chance to make some real money. It took the katsa about three hours, but he got a list of everything the general needed. The furniture alone came to $180,000, not counting shipping and crating, and the katsa "sold" it to him for $105,000, so right off the top, the aide could pocket $75,000.

The funny thing was, the aide gave the shipping address as the harbor in Litakia, but he gave a false name for himself and the general. The only thing that wasn't false was where to pick it up. He said if we needed verification, we could call the Syrian embassy in Paris. Half an hour after he left our katsa, the aide phoned our man inside the embassy and told him that if anyone called to verify that name and address, he was to do so because it was a top-priority operation.

Two days later, an ornate Belgian table was shipped to Israel. It was gutted, and $50,000 worth of listening and broadcasting equipment was installed in it, including a special battery that would last three to four years. The equipment was sealed up in such a way that no one would find it unless they took the top off the table and sawed it in two. The table was then shipped back to Belgium and put into the furniture shipment for Syria.

The Mossad are still waiting to hear from the table. They've already had combatants going around with listening devices trying to pick it up, and they can't find a thing. It would have been a dream, had it worked out. Of course, it might have been put into a bunker office in Damascus. The Russians made some there, and they're frequency-proof. But if they'd discovered it, they surely would have used it.

My work in the department was otherwise quite monotonous. I was filing, watching schedules, and most of all, covering up for bosses when their wives called asking where they were — I had to say they were on assignment.

Like everybody else, I was working in the whorehouse.

7

Hairpiece

I<small>T WAS</small> OCTOBER 27, 1984. My colleagues and I had just finished our term as junior katsas, or trainees, in the headquarters building, and were about to enter the operational intelligence officers' course back at the Academy. This time, we would be working in a large room on the second floor of the main building. The original group of 15 had dropped to 12, but went back up again with the addition of three men left over from previous courses, where too few trainees had been left to make finishing the course worthwhile. Our three new colleagues were Oded L., Pinhas M., and Yegal A.

There were other changes, too. Araleh Sherf had left as head of the Academy to take over the *Tsafririm*, or "morning breeze," department and had been replaced by David Arbel, former head of the Paris office but late of the infamous Lillehammer affair — the one who had told all to local authorities. Shai Kauly was still there, but Oren Riff had been transferred to the office of the head of the Mossad. Our new course leader was Itsik E.,* another katsa with a less than distinguished career — one of the two men overheard by the PLO speaking Hebrew at Orly airport after loading a valuable agent on a flight to Rome.

Arbel, a white-haired, short, timid, and bespectacled man,

---

* See PROLOGUE: OPERATION SPHINX

did not exude or inspire confidence. Itsik, on the other hand, played to the gallery as a capable, straight-from-the-field katsa who had just finished a tour as second-in-command at the Paris station. He was fluent in French, English, and Greek, and immediately took a shine to French-born Michel M. The two men, always speaking to each other in French, developed an instant camaraderie that only added to the dislike the others had begun to feel for Michel. My clique had once been close to him, but we had been growing apart — mainly because he was using his language to ingratiate himself with Itsik and malign the others, including me.

We used to call Michel "frog," though not to his face. When somebody saw him coming, they'd make a hand signal of a frog jumping across their palm. Michel could never stop talking about how great French food was, French wine, French everything. We had one joke we liked about the Israeli going into a French restaurant. "Do you have frogs' legs?" he'd ask. "Yes, sir, but of course." "Then do me a favor and hop into the kitchen and get me a hummus."

By this time, Michel was no longer in my clique, though Yosy and Heim still were. We were a leaner and meaner group then, a bunch of real bastards. We thought we knew all the tricks of the game. The idea now, they said, was to teach us the *essence* of intelligence. Until now, we had studied behavior and information-gathering at a lower level. Now we had to get down to the nuts and bolts of gathering.

The first thing we were shown, by security man Nahaman Lavy and a man named Tal, was another Mossad Productions movie entitled "All Because of a Little Nail," the famous story of how an army lost a war because of a nail that was missing from the commander's horse's shoe, the point being that no detail is too small. No matter how insignificant it seems, a detail left unchecked can unravel a whole operation. This was part of a four-hour session that also included a lecture on secured behavior, security, and reliability.

After that, we spent an hour with Ury Dinure, our new instructor on NAKA. Next we began an extensive course in international business, learning how a business is run, how to do mail purchasing, managerial structures, the relationships between executives and shareholders, the duties of a board chairman, how the stock exchanges work, preparing overseas contracts, shipping goods C.O.D. or F.O.B., everything we needed to understand how a company works when we were using it as a cover for operations. This business course ran the entire length of our last term, with two-hour lectures at least twice a week, as well as numerous tests and papers to be completed.

By now, Itsik had embarked on a new exercise teaching us how to operate an agent down to the last detail. In a new twist, one exercise showed us how to assassinate an agent who had gone astray, if we were in a situation where we could not rely on Metsada to send in the kidon unit for the job. We were divided into three teams of five each. Each team had a different "subject" on whom to gather data and devise a plan for elimination.

My team took three days to gather the necessary information. The only consistent thing our subject did was to buy two packs of cigarettes from his local grocery store every day at 5:30 p.m. You could set your watch by it. That was obviously the best place to pick him up. We had a driver; another man and I sat in the back seat. When I called out to the agent, he recognized his katsa and readily joined us in the back. We drove out of town and, at a planned spot, effected putting an ether mask over his face to knock him out. The whole thing was, of course, a simulation exercise.

The rest of the plan was to make the "hit" look like an accident. We would have hidden his car near a cliff, then put our unconscious man in it; then we would have poured vodka (which burns well) down his throat through a newspaper funnel, waited a little while for the alcohol to be absorbed into his bloodstream should anyone check later, put him behind the wheel, pour the rest of the vodka on the seats, and put a lighter and a cigarette butt beside him. That would be seen as the "cause" of the fire. As the car burned, the idea was to shove it off the cliff.

One of the other teams found their man liked to go to a club every evening. They took a more direct approach, walking up to him on the street near the club. Using blanks, they "shot" him five times, got back into their car, and simply drove away.

In the meantime, we were working more and more on our covers, learning how to use various passports. We could be walking down the street with one identity and be arrested, back up our story under interrogation, be let out, meet a bodel with a new passport, and bingo, a different cop would arrest us and we'd have to back up the new identity.

We were now also learning about Tsafririm and the "frames" set up as a defense mechanism by Jews around the world. In this area we had a problem, or at least some of us did. I just couldn't agree with this concept of having guard groups everywhere. I thought frames in England, for example, where kids learn how to build slicks for their weapons to protect their synagogues, were more dangerous than beneficial to the Jewish community. I brought up the argument that even if a group of people had been oppressed, with attempts made to exterminate them — as with the Jews — they had no right to act obstructively in democratic countries. I could understand this happening in Chile or Argentina, or any other country where people disappear off the streets, but not in England or France or Belgium.

The fact that there are anti-Semitic groups, whether real or imaginary, is definitely not an excuse, because if you look into Israel's own backyard, you'll see anti-Palestinian groups. Did this mean we thought the Palestinians therefore had the right to store weapons and organize vigilante groups? Or would we call them terrorists?

Of course, any talk of this sort within the Mossad was not regarded as smart, especially within the context of the Holocaust. I know the Holocaust was one of the gravest things ever to happen to Jews: Bella's father, for one, spent four years in Auschwitz and most of her family was eliminated by the Germans. But remember that close to 50 million other people died, too. Germans tried to eliminate Gypsies, various religious groups, Russians, and Poles. The Holocaust could have been, and I think should have been, a source for unity with other nations rather than a tool for separation.

But that was just my opinion, and it didn't help much to express it.

Our weekly "sports" program also changed dramatically, to include a new sport potentially hazardous to our health. We would go to a building in a military camp near Herzlia and run up and down the stairs firing live bullets and being shot at by a machine with wooden bullets that hurt if they hit you at close range. The idea was to practice ducking and shooting, getting used to your gun and exercising your body at the same time.

We also practiced rappelling — coming down the side of a building by rope, pushing yourself off, dropping a bit, pushing off again, all the way to the ground. And we practiced descending from a helicopter by rope, plus other commando-style exercises such as the "jump and shoot" technique of firing at a hijacker inside a bus.

Another segment of the course was called "recruiting an agent with a friendly agency," that is, mutual recruitment, say with the CIA. The lecturer began by saying that was the purpose of the lecture. "How is it done?" he would ask, then quickly reply, "It's not. We don't do that. We will assist them if they have a subject and make it look like it's mutual, but if we can do it alone, we will."

He taught us how to steal an agent from a friendly agency by starting him off as a mutual operation, then eventually changing his country of operation, giving him separate instructions and notifying the friendly agency of a loss of contact with the mutual agent. It was a simple procedure. I'd meet him and, if he was perceived as worth it, whisk him off and double his pay. Then he'd be *our* agent, what we called "blue and white," the colors of Israel's flag.

One particularly intriguing aspect of the course was a movie called, "A President on the Crosshairs," a detailed study of the November 22, 1963, assassination of John F. Kennedy. The Mossad theory was that the killers — Mafiosa hit men, not Lee Harvey Oswald — actually wanted to murder then Texas governor John Connally, who was in the car with JFK but was only wounded. Oswald was seen as a dupe in

the whole thing and Connally as the target of mobsters trying to muscle their way into the oil business. The Mossad believed that the official version of the assassination was pure,
unadulterated hokum. To test their theory, they did a simulation exercise of the presidential cavalcade to see if expert
marksmen with far better equipment than Oswald's could hit
a moving target from the recorded distance of 88 yards. They
couldn't.

It would have been the perfect cover. If Connally had been
killed, everyone would have assumed it was an attempt on
JFK. If they'd wanted to get Kennedy, they could have got
him anywhere. A single bullet is supposed to have gone
through the back of Kennedy's head, out his chest, and into
Connally. If you look at the film, you'll see those points were
not aligned. If ever a bullet could do the Waltzing Matilda,
that was it.

The Mossad had every film taken of the Dallas assassination, pictures of the area, the topography, aerial photographs, everything. Using mannequins, they duplicated the
presidential cavalcade over and over again. Professionals
will do a job in the same way. If I'm going to use a high-
powered rifle, there are very few places I'd work from, and
ideally I'd want a place where I held the target for the longest
possible time, where I could get closest to it, but still create
the least disturbance. Based on that, we picked a few likely
places, and we had more than one person doing the shooting
from more than one angle.

Oswald had used a mail-order, bolt-action, clip-fed 6.5 mm
Mannlicher-Carcano rifle, with a four-power telescopic sight.
He'd bought it through a catalogue for $21.45. He also had a
.38 Smith & Wesson revolver. It was never determined
whether he had fired two rounds or three, but he used regular military full-jacketed cartridges with a muzzle velocity of
2,165 feet per second.

During the simulation exercise, the Mossad, using better,
more powerful equipment, would aim their rifles, which were
set up on tripods, and when the moment came they'd say
"bang" over the loudspeakers and a laser direction-finder
would show where the people in the car would have been

hit, and the bullet exits. According to what we found, the rifle was probably aimed at the back of Connally's head, and JFK gestured or moved just at the wrong moment — or possibly the assassin hesitated.

It was just an exercise. But it showed that it was impossible to do what Oswald was supposed to have done. He wasn't even a professional. Look at the distance, from the sixth-floor window of a building, the kind of equipment he had. He didn't even reinforce the bullets. The guy had just bought the rifle. Anyone knows it takes time and skill to adjust the telescopic sights on a new rifle. The official version just isn't believable.

* * *

Someone we did believe, however, was a man who arrived one morning at the end of the first month of this final term. Only about five foot six and squarely built, the man began with, "My name is irrelevant, but I'm going to tell you all about something I participated in, along with a gentleman named Amikan. I was, for a time, with a unit called kidon and my team received instructions to take out the head of the PLO station in Athens and his assistant. I mention Amikan because he was a religious man, a big man, about six foot six, solid like me. He looked like a door."

The speaker was Dan Drory, and the event he described was called Operation PASAT, a successful Mossad operation in the mid-70s in Athens.

Drory, who obviously loved his work, then opened an attaché case and said, "I like this one," pulling out a Parabellum, a German pistol similar to a Luger, and placing it on the table. "I like this, too, but they won't let me carry it," and he put an Eagle on the table, an Israeli-made magnum with an air-cooling system. But I can use this, too," he said, pulling out a Beretta high-powered .22 caliber. "The advantage of this is that you don't need a silencer."

He paused, then said, "But this is my favorite of all." He brandished a stiletto, the deadly dagger with a narrow blade that widens near the end, then narrows again into a point. "You can stick it in and pull it out and there's no external bleeding. When you pull it out, the flesh closes back. The advantage of this is you can stick it between the ribs, and then when it's inside, you can twist it so that it tends to rip everything apart. Then you just pull it out."

Finally, he took out a claw with a special glove that held one blade along the thumb and another along the index finger. He put it on, attached the two blades — one could be compacted like a Swiss army knife, the other looked like a carpet knife — and he attached the claw, saying, "This is what Amikan likes to use. You catch the guy on his throat and just close your hand. It's like scissors. It cuts everything. It keeps the guy quiet. It's total, yet it's not immediate, which makes Amikan happy. It will take the guy a while to die. But to use this, you have to be a very strong person — like Amikan."

I knew immediately I didn't want to meet this guy Amikan. He was a very hands-on person.

Amikan, as a deeply religious man, insisted on always wearing his yarmelke. Since his work was undercover, and normally in unfriendly places, Amikan could hardly wear a traditional yarmelke without attracting some unwelcome attention. So he shaved a bald spot on the top of his head at the back and wove in a yarmelke made of hair — a hairpiece that served as his undercover yarmelke.

When their instructions came to get the two PLO men, Drory, Amikan, and the rest of their team went to Athens. The two targets were located. Both men had apartments in the city, and while they held regular strategy meetings, they did not socialize with each other.

Because the Institute was still hurting at the time from the embarrassing publicity of the Lillehammer debacle, where the wrong man had been killed, the new head of Mossad, Yitzhak Hofi, wanted personally to verify the hits and give final approval on site. He wanted to see the victims before they were shot.

For simplicity's sake, I'll call the station chief Abdul, and his assistant Said. After the situation was studied, it was decided the job could not be done at Abdul's apartment. However, the two held their meetings at a hotel on a fairly major street — usually every Tuesday and Thursday, along with a few other PLO officials. The two men were tailed for nearly a month before any decisions were made.

Both men were repeatedly photographed and their files checked and rechecked to make sure there was no mistake. Indeed, as a young man, Abdul had been arrested in East Jerusalem by Jordanian police, and after the Israeli occupation, his file had been kept. So, they even obtained a glass Abdul had used in the hotel in order to check his fingerprints against that old file. It was him all right.

After the meetings, Abdul always left the hotel and drove to the house of one of his girlfriends. Said went his separate way. He would arrive for the meetings in casual clothing, then afterward drive the 20 minutes to his apartment in an upper-class suburb and change into more formal clothes before going out for the evening. He lived on the second floor of a two-story, four-apartment building. There were four parking stalls off a driveway underneath the building at the side. He parked in the second stall from the end, then walked back down the driveway and in the front door. There was a lamppost directly across from the parking stalls and also lights on the walls where the cars parked.

While Abdul was the more political and had little personal security, Said was involved in the military arm. He shared his apartment with three other PLO members, at least two of them his armed bodyguards. It was a kind of PLO safe house.

The road in front of the hotel had two lanes in each direction with a median in the middle. It was not a particularly busy area, with few pedestrians. There was parking lot at the side for people using the restaurant, which was where Abdul and Said both parked, and one at the back for hotel guests.

After considering all the factors, Drory and Amikan decided to take the men out after a particular Thursday-evening meeting.

There was a pay phone across the street and down half a block from the hotel, and also one within sight of Said's apartment. Since Said always left the hotel meeting before

Abdul, the idea was to take Abdul out at the hotel, then signal the man waiting on the phone near Said's apartment that he should be hit when he returned home.

Amikan was in charge of the unit responsible for Said. He was instructed to use a 9 mm pistol and his commander double-checked to make sure the bullets he used were not dum-dums. The Mossad is known to use them, and they wanted to pin this double hit on one of the PLO factions rather than take the blame — or credit — themselves.

On the appointed night, a small van was parked directly across from the hotel facing up the street on the other side of the median. One man was sitting in the lobby while Drory was to approach the front door from the side parking lot, closely followed by Yitzhak Hofi. Drory and Hofi were to wait in their car until being signaled over small walkie-talkies — by a series of clicks — that it was time to move.

For some reason, however, both Abdul and Said came out at the same time that Thursday — the first time they had — so nobody moved. The would-be assassins just watched the two men get in their cars and leave.

On the following Tuesday the team set up again. This time, Said left the meeting at about 9 p.m. and headed for his car. The Mossad men moved their car forward a bit, as if we had just arrived and were parking it, as Said started up and drove away.

About two minutes later they heard the telltale clicks from their man inside the lobby: Abdul was on his way out. The hotel had a revolving door at the front with a standard door beside it. To make sure Abdul used the revolving door, we had jammed the other one shut.

The Mossad man planted in the lobby came through the revolving door directly behind Abdul, stopping on the outside and holding the door so that no one else could turn it. Another man was at the pay phone down the street, on the line with his counterpart near Said's apartment.

Abdul walked down the steps and turned left toward the parking lot, just as Drory came up to him, with Hofi directly behind. Hofi said, "Abdul?" As he replied yes, Drory fired two bullets into his chest and one through his head, leaving him dead on the sidewalk. Hofi was already on his way across the street to the van, which had started to move slowly forward, and the man on the phone down the street said, "It's done," signaling his party that the Said phase of the operation was now on.

For his part, Drory simply turned and walked back into the side parking lot where he got into his car and drove off. The man who had been stationed in the lobby went back in through the revolving doors, crossed the lobby, and left by the back door, where he, too, had a car waiting. The whole thing took only about 10 seconds; if anyone had been watching from the lobby, it would simply have looked as if the man had gone out the revolving door, forgotten something, and come back into the hotel. It was almost 10 minutes before Abdul's body was found in the parking lot.

When Said pulled up to his parking stall at his apartment, Amikan was waiting in the bushes between the two apartment houses. The lamp across from the stalls was burned out, but through the back window and against the lights on the wall of the stalls, Amikan could see that Said had picked someone up on the way home. His problem, of course, was that he couldn't tell from there which of the two was Said, so he took the view that his enemy's friend must be his enemy, too. He walked up to the back of the car and, using an extended magazine on his 9 mm pistol, fired 11 rounds through their heads, pumping quickly back and forth from one man to the other.

Then he stepped around the driver's side of the car to make sure both were dead. Because he had fired from behind, neither man had a front to his head anymore.

The shooting was quick, but fairly noisy. Though Amikan had used a silencer, the crash of glass and thud of bullets hitting the wall attracted Said's bodyguards. They came out on the second-floor balcony, the light from the apartment at their backs, peering down into the darkness and shouting Said's name. Another member of Amikan's team, who had been staked out in front of the apartment building as a backup if needed, shouted to them in Arabic, "Get down! Get down!" and they did. In the meantime, both he and Amikan ran across the street, got into the car with the man who had been on the phone, and drove off into the night.

I remember best the way Drory described the operation. It was the way you'd describe a good meal, when you've really enjoyed yourself at a good place. Like a superb dinner. I'll never forget the way Drory described the hit part. He lifted his hands in front of him as if he had a gun and then shot it. It was scary. I've been shot at and seen a lot of things. But the face Drory made at that moment is something I'll never forget. He was so excited he was grinding his teeth.

During a short question period later, Drory was asked how it felt to shoot someone when it wasn't self-defense or on a battlefield. "This was national self-defense," he replied. "He wasn't shooting at me, but he was figuratively holding a gun at my nation. Feeling has nothing to do with this. Besides, I wasn't feeling that badly."

Asked what his colleague Amikan might have been thinking as he lurked in the bushes waiting for his prey to come home, Drory explained that he said he'd kept looking at his watch because it was getting late and he was hungry. He wanted to get it over with and get out of there and grab something to eat — just like anyone else whose job was keeping them from dinner.

We didn't ask him many questions after that.

* * *

We were soon to begin an extensive course in photography, learning the use of various cameras, and how to develop film, including a method of using two chemical tablets to make a solution with lukewarm water and soak a film for 90 seconds so that it is not fully developed — that can be done later — but can be checked to make sure the required image is there. We also experimented with various lenses and with taking photographs from various hidden devices, such as side bags.

Pinhas Maidan, one of the three newcomers who had joined the group for this final term, decided to turn his photography lessons into a handsome profit.

There is an area along the beach north of Tel Aviv called Tel Barbach, not far from the Country Club, where all the hookers hang out waiting for men to come along in their cars, pick them up, go behind the sand dunes, do their thing, and drive off. Pinhas decided to take his night photography equipment and set up on a hill by the sand dunes, photographing men in their cars with the hookers, and thereby collecting some explicit photos, thanks to the high-quality equipment and powerful telescopic lenses. We had already been taught how to invade the police computer — plugging into it without police knowledge or permission — so Maidan simply ran the car license plates through the computer to find the owners' names and addresses, and began blackmailing them. He'd phone, say he had some compromising photos, and ask for money.

He boasted that he was making quite a bit. He didn't say how much, but eventually someone complained and he was reprimanded. I thought he'd be kicked out. But apparently somebody regarded this as showing initiative. I guess when you're rolling so deep in the shit, you don't notice when something smells bad.

Of course, to the Mossad's way of thinking, the production of such photos could sometimes be a powerful persuader in recruiting — and sometimes not. A story was told of one senior Saudi Arabian official who was photographed in bed with a hooker who had been given instructions to situate herself and her bedmate in such a way that the camera recorded both his face and the actual penetration. Later, the Mossad confronted him with the evidence of his sexual escapades, spreading the photos on a table and saying, "You might want to cooperate with us." But instead of recoiling in shock and horror, the Saudi was thrilled with the photos. "This is wonderful," he said. "I'll take two of those, three of that," adding he wanted to show them to all his friends. Needless to say, that particular recruiting effort failed.

The course went on to deal with intelligence units in the various Arab countries, and the trainee katsas also spent some time talking to security officers in hotels, learning about their point of view. Because we operated a lot in hotels, we had to know what to avoid in terms of drawing the attention of security — those *little* things. For example, if a maid knocks on the door, comes in, and everybody stops talking while she's there, she'll probably tell security there's something going on in that room. But if everyone just goes on talking as if she wasn't there, no suspicions would be raised.

We also sat through a series of lectures on all the European police, force by force, analyzing them, understanding them, learning their strengths and weaknesses. We studied the Islamic bomb and visited various military bases, as well as the nuclear plant at the Dimona research center in the Negev, about 40 miles northeast of Beersheba. It was initially disguised as a textile factory, then a "pumping station," until the CIA obtained photographic evidence from a U-2 flight in December 1960 that it housed a nuclear reactor. There was also a much smaller reactor called KAMG (the abbreviation for *Kure Garny Le Machkar*, or Nuclear Research Facility) in Nahal Sorek, inside an air-force base just south of Tel Aviv. I visited both plants.

After its secret got out in 1960, David Ben-Gurion formally announced Israel's "peaceful" atomic project, though much of it remains anything but peaceful.

In 1986, a Moroccan-born Israeli named Mordechai Vanunu who had worked at Dimona from 1976 to 1985 before moving to Australia revealed that he had smuggled a camera into the establishment and had 57 photographs of the top-secret processing plant, located several levels below the surface, which at that time had stockpiled enough weapons-grade plutonium to arm 150 nuclear and thermo-nuclear devices. He also confirmed that the Israelis had helped South Africa detonate a nuclear device in September 1979 in the southern end of the Indian Ocean over the uninhabited islands of Prince Edward and Marion.

For his trouble, Vanunu ended up being sentenced to 18 years in jail for espionage after a closed-door trial in Jerusalem. He was captured by the Mossad after being enticed by a beautiful agent to a yacht in the Mediterranean off Rome. The London *Sunday Times* had been preparing to publish his story and the photos, but Vanunu was drugged, smuggled aboard an Israeli ship, swiftly tried, and jailed.

In fact, the kidnapping was a sloppy job. Vanunu wasn't exactly a pro or a danger, yet because of the way the job was handled, the public knew about it. The operation got Vanunu back to Israel, but the Mossad couldn't have been very proud of it.

From my personal observation of the Dimona plant, Vanunu's description was very accurate. Not only that, his interpretation was also accurate. He said they were building those bombs and they'd use them if needed. That's true. It was no secret, either, within the Institute that we helped South Africa with its nuclear program. We supplied them with most of their military equipment. We trained their special units. We worked hand in hand with them for years. These are two countries that regarded themselves as needing the doomsday machine and were prepared to use it.

While security at Dimona was extremely tight, it was also ringed with Hawk and Chapparal surface-to-air missiles. The joke when we visited the Hawk sites was that the missiles were just rotting away. They wouldn't have protected anything. Yet they were sold to Iran later. We laughed about that a lot.

The junior katsas also learned about an international communications system, particularly the Mediterranean cable that emerged at Palermo, Sicily, where it tied into satellites transmitting most of the Arab communications. Israel was linked into that through Unit 8200 and got access to almost everything the Arabs sent.

The other regular feature of our course was a "sociometric" paper written every couple of weeks, whereby each of us would list everyone else in the course in order of preference in various categories: operations, trustworthiness, reliability, friendliness, cordiality, and so on. I didn't do badly in that, but it wasn't honest. You weren't supposed to know the results, but we did. If you didn't like somebody, you naturally put him at the bottom. And since we were all a bit short on trust, Yosy, Heim, and I checked each other's lists just to be on the safe side.

Now we were ready for the final exercise. In just two weeks, we would be full-fledged katsas.

8

Hail and Farewell

ONE DAY BEFORE the beginning of the final two-week exercise, I got a call from my colleague Jerry S. At the time, I could not have imagined the profound significance of this seemingly innocent phone call.

Jerry, then 32, was an American citizen. He had a beard, mustache, and grayish hair. He was slim and had been a lawyer in the private law office of Cyrus Vance, U.S. president Jimmy Carter's secretary of state. At the time, Jerry and I were friends, though I was certainly aware of rumors that he was homosexual. At one point, he had told everyone he had a girlfriend who had flown over from the States and was staying at his place, but she had to go back because she was married. Since no one ever met her, the rumors persisted. Jerry had been at my house many times, and vice versa. I often helped him build his cover. Apart from the odd minor disagreement, we got along well. So there was nothing unusual about his asking me over to his apartment. He said he just wanted to talk to me and show me something. I said, fine, why not?

When I arrived, he made us his favorite drink, a concoction of vodka, ice, and strawberries, crushed and mixed in a blender. Before he sat down, he put on a video cassette.

"I've got something I want to show you," he said, "but before I do, I want to tell you that I have an inside source, and from now on, before an exercise, I will know if we're being followed. I'll be able to tell you when or where. We don't need that kind of hassle anymore."

"I'll be honest with you, Jerry," I told him. "I'm not worried about being followed. Actually, I quite like it. It's exciting."

"Listen," he said. "I told Ran H. [another classmate, who had serious problems with APAM], and he was happy."

"I'm not surprised. But who do you think you're doing a favor?"

"Well, you still have to find out *how* they're following you," said Jerry, getting edgy.

"Okay, Jerry, you do your thing," I told him. "I don't care. If you think that's going to help you, fine. But I *am* curious. How do you get that kind of information?"

"Well, there's this woman that Itsik is screwing," he said. "She's the famous number four. I'm having a small affair with her myself, and she's giving me all this data."

"You're kidding me."

"I knew you wouldn't believe me, so why don't you sit there and relax, and let me show you the video?"

Some time earlier, Jerry had dropped by Itsik's house and happened to see a woman leaving. She was attractive, with tanned skin, light brown hair, and a magnificent body. Jerry watched her leave, waited a while, then went to see Itsik, whose wife was not at home. He didn't say anything about the woman.

Yarid, the team that handled European security, naturally practiced its techniques in Israel. One of the best ways to practice was to test their skills tailing the junior katsas. These teams used numbers, not names, and the katsas weren't supposed to know who they were. The yarid team was told the day before whom they would be following, the time, the starting point, and they were shown a picture of the subject. This particular woman was called number four.

Jerry had spotted her during an earlier exercise, and although he didn't know who she was at the time, had put it in his report. Then when he saw her leaving Itsik's house, he'd put two and two together. After she left, he watched her get into her car, wrote down the plate number, and checked it later through the police computer, getting her name and address.

He wanted to take advantage of his knowledge. For one thing, he knew what people were saying about him and wanted to quash the rumors. He also wanted to get to know who was going to be followed any given day of the exercise so he wouldn't have to continually worry about APAM. He wasn't good at the exercise, so he wanted to short-circuit it because it was so important to the course. A katsa can't go abroad without passing APAM.

His apartment, which had every electronic device imaginable, also featured a large exercise machine called a Soloflex, which has a bench and a bar suspended from a frame. One of the exercises is to wrap hard rubber attachments around your ankles, then hook them onto the bar, and pull yourself up and down, exercising your stomach muscles while hanging upside down from the bar.

Another vital piece of equipment was a small audio-visual camera unit built right into an attaché case — a camera they used in many exercises. It could be borrowed from the Academy as needed. Not only were the stars of these movies unaware of their status, the high quality of the equipment resulted in broadcast-quality pictures.

The movie began with a wide-angle shot of the room. The curtains were drawn, but there was a lot of light. There was a pale wooden wall cabinet and a dining-room table to the side, but the Soloflex dominated the center of the room.

At first, Jerry and number four were talking. Then they began kissing and fondling each other. "Let's exercise," he said, and started putting the rubber straps around her ankles, once she'd taken off her sweatpants. Then he attached her upside down to the bar.

I couldn't believe it. I thought, my God, this can't be true. But it was.

As she hung there suspended, Jerry stepped back, spread his arms, as if for the camera, and said, "Ta-da!"

Naturally, her shirt had fallen over her head and her breasts were still hanging free. Jerry pulled her shirt off, bent over, held her up, and the two began kissing each other. Then he put his hand under her panties and began to fondle her. After doing that for a while, Jerry took his own clothes off, and the last few minutes of the film showed her hanging upside down giving him a blow job as he sat nude on the bench.

"Jerry, you didn't need to make a movie to get her to cooperate," I told him after it was over.

"Maybe not. But I figured if she wouldn't cooperate, I'd show her the movie and then she would. It's arousing, isn't it?"

"Yes, in a way," I replied cautiously.

"You know what they've been saying about me in the office?"

"What, that you're a homo?"

"Yes."

"That's your problem, not mine. I'm not here to judge you."

At that point, he sat down next to me. Close. "Look, you saw I'm not a homo."

"Jerry, why are you telling me this?" I asked him, now getting a little nervous.

"Listen, I like going both ways," he said. "I think we could have more fun that you can imagine."

"Jerry, do I understand what you're telling me?"

"I hope so."

I was befuddled, but getting angry. I got up from the couch and walked to the door. Jerry put his hand on my shoulder to stop me. At this point, I saw red. I threw his hand off my shoulder and hit him. I'd never punched anybody that hard in the stomach before. I ran downstairs and out into the street to get air. I ran for about 40 minutes all the way to the Academy — probably four or five miles. I wasn't in the best of shape. I was coughing, but I kept going.

Inside the Academy, I ran into Itsik. "Itsik, I've got to tell you something," I said. "This has to stop."

"Come into my office."

I told him the entire story. I can't say I gave him a completely coherent version, for I was babbling. But it was clear enough. I told him Jerry had a video of himself fucking his girlfriend, and that he'd made a sexual advance toward me.

"Calm down, calm down," Itsik said. "Let me give you a ride home."

I thanked him, but told him my bike was there at the Academy and I wanted to ride it home.

"Look," said Itsik. "You told me. Now forget it."

"What do you mean, forget it?"

"I mean forget it. I don't want to hear about it anymore."

"What kind of horse [inside booster] does this guy have?" I said. "The Trojan horse?"

"*Forget* it."

There was little I could do. For Itsik to tell me to forget it right off the bat, without checking the story, was incredible. Then he added, "And I don't want to hear this repeated through anybody. Don't tell Heim or Yosy or anybody else. Understand?"

"Okay, I'll forget it. But I'm going to give it to you in writing, and I want a copy-to-file."

"Fine, do that."

A copy-to-file meant that a copy of a letter sent to someone for his eyes only could be placed in a sealed envelope and sent to a computer file, where it remained sealed. But the recipient had to sign to indicate that he had read it, and the date was registered. Suppose a katsa told his superiors that the Syrians were going to attack the following week, but his warning was ignored. Then when they did attack, people would ask why they hadn't been notified. If the katsa had a copy-to-file, he'd simply produce it to show that he *had* tipped them off.

On the way home, I stopped by security chief Mousa M.'s house and told him the whole story. "You should change the program and take the girl off," I said.

"Did you tell Itsik?"

"Yes."

"What did he say?"

"He said forget it."

"I guess I can't take the girl off," Mousa said, "because then Itsik will know you told me."

* * *

The first order of business the next day, when the final three-week exercise began in mid-October 1985, was for the three teams of five each to settle into our apartments. One team was in Haifa, another in Jerusalem, and mine was on the third floor of a building near the Mugraby movie theater near Allenby and Ben Yehuda streets, in the south-center of Tel Aviv — a slightly grotty section where the hookers hang out.

Besides Jerry, my team consisted of Arik, Oded L., and Michel. After we had built our slick in a cupboard and prepared all the other necessary security work for our safe house/station, we were given passports, taken to the airport, and told to go through customs and security as if we were just arriving in Israel. I had a Canadian passport.

After that, I took a cab from the airport to the apartment, scouted the area, learned where the public telephones were, and so on, arriving in plenty of time for the 1 p.m. briefing. (From time to time, we were allowed to go home from this assignment, but it was on a rotation system because someone always had to be at the apartment at night.) When I got back to the apartment, it was as if nothing had happened between Jerry and me, except now I knew that I could neither "touch" him nor protect myself from him. His horse was too powerful.

The first field exercise was to go to the Grand Beach Hotel, at the corner of Dizengoff Street and Ben-Gurion Avenue, across the street from what used to be the Sheraton. The old Sheraton was handed over to the Americans who were building airfields in the Negev as part of the Camp David peace deal when Israel gave up airfields in the Sinai. I rented a room at the Grand Beach by phone, while Jerry was supposed to meet a contact in the lobby of that hotel. The contact had documents in an attaché case in his car trunk, and the idea was to get the case, take pictures of the documents, and return it to the trunk with no one noticing.

We already had the car key, and the vehicle was supposed to have been parked six stalls down from the former Sheraton Hotel entrance. As it turned out, it was only three stalls away, in clear view of the old Sheraton's doorman.

Jerry's assignment was to talk to the contact in the upper lobby at the Grand Beach, while sitting in a position where he could see me enter with the attaché case and carry it across the lobby to the elevators. When photos of the documents had been taken in the hotel room, everything was to be returned, the case wiped clean of fingerprints, and I would take it back out to the car. Once the case was back in the trunk, I would signal Arik who in turn would signal Jerry, and he could then let the man go. All this activity was going on without the contact's knowledge.

The only hitch in the whole exercise was that the car was too visible to the doorman. And so, I asked Arik if he had a wallet, told him to take everything out of it, except some cash which he could leave sticking out, then go up and tell the doorman he'd found it and wanted it taken to the lost and found. That way, he'd be elsewhere while I removed the case from the car trunk.

By the time I came back downstairs, Arik already knew the doorman's name, so he made an urgent phone call to him. While the doorman went inside to take his call, I put the case back into the trunk.

Two hours later we all met back in the apartment. Everyone was quiet, but there didn't seem to be a problem. Soon Itsik and Shai Kauly entered. We all gave a full description of what had happened, but when everyone had finished, Jerry turned to Itsik and said, "I want to file a complaint about Vic's behavior."

I was dumbfounded. I had exceeded what was expected of me, and here was this little twit filing a complaint.

But Jerry continued. "When Victor was working for the Smerfs in Kaisarut, he hosted some Africans in this hotel. By doing this exercise in a hotel where he's known, he has endangered the entire operation."

"Wait a minute," I said. "We've done exercises in every bloody hotel in town. Anyway, hypothetically, for purposes of this exercise we are now in Paris, and I'm not known in *any* hotels in Paris."

No matter, Itsik listened, then wrote in his book: "A point well taken."

I turned to Kauly. "Shai —"

"Look," Kauly replied, "don't involve me in this."

* * *

The next day, I asked to start my second assignment right away. It would give me the opportunity to be outside the safe house for several days. I was already sick of being in the same place as Jerry.

What I had to do was make contact with a British diplomat who was in charge of maintaining all our military graveyards (mainly from World War I) in Israel. He had an office in Ramlah, just east of Tel Aviv, site of a large cemetery, and an office in the British embassy in Tel Aviv. The man had been spotted several times by the Shaback stopping his car on the highway, taking pictures of military installations, then driving off. We suspected he was either in intelligence himself or working for someone else. As a result, the Shaback had sent in a request to have him checked out.

My first order of business was to concoct a reason to meet this man. Why not a movie again? After booking a room at the Carleton Hotel, just across from the Marina in Tel Aviv's Hayarkon Street, I went to a monument near the spot where British general Allenby's troops had crossed the Yarkon River during World War I, ending four centuries of Ottoman rule over the Holy Land. With the dates of the battles in mind, and the names of the brigades that had fought, I then headed for another large British cemetery outside Haifa, searching tombstones until I found one with the name of a soldier (McPhee) who had fought and died at that time.

Posing as a Canadian from Toronto, complete with business cards, I said that I would be doing a movie about a family that had moved to Canada from London, but had one member who'd died in the battle to free the Holy Land. First I called the office in Ramlah and told the story to a Christian Arab woman there. She gave me the target's phone number at the embassy, so I called him, told him the story, gave him McPhee's name (saying I didn't know where he was buried), said I was staying at the Carleton Hotel, and wanted a meeting. No problem.

Sure enough, the Britisher showed up along with another man, and the three of us talked for two and a half hours. The diplomat was a landscaper by profession and really anxious to help me. He came with the name and exact directions for where to find the grave. He'd just assumed it was all legitimate and we even began discussing hiring him to stage the big battle scenes I supposedly wanted to make. I told him I would be leaving shortly, but that I'd contact him within a month. My instructions had been not to carry it beyond making contact and opening a door.

My next assignment was to contact a man in East Jerusalem who had a souvenir shop on Salaha Adin Street. I scoured the area, took pictures with a hidden camera, and became really friendly with the guy, a PLO, which was why they wanted to know more about him.

On another assignment, Itsik took me to an apartment building in Tel Aviv and said there was a man in the third-floor apartment who had a guest with him and that I had 20 minutes to strike up a conversation with the guest.

"This is chutzpah," I said.

"Define chutzpah," said Itsik.

"You shit in front of the guy's door, then you knock on his door and ask for toilet paper. That's chutzpah."

I went to a nearby store and bought two bottles of Mouton Cadet claret. I went into the building and checked the names on the board, pressed one buzzer, and said I had a parcel to deliver for a woman.

"Oh, you're probably looking for Dina," said the voice.

"Is Dina married?" I asked.

"No," came the response.

I buzzed Dina's apartment, but happily, she wasn't home. I got into the building and started walking up the stairs: it was one of those buildings where you pass every door on the way up. When I got to the third floor, where my targets were, I took one the wine bottles, held it up high, then dropped it, making a loud crash right in front of the designated apartment. I knocked on the door.

"I'm really sorry," I said when the door was opened. "I went upstairs to meet Dina, but she wasn't in. Now I've dropped this bottle. Do you have something I can clean it up with?"

The man and his guest both helped. I suggested we might as well share the other bottle, and I stayed there for two hours, getting to know both their life histories. Mission accomplished.

In the meantime, the team in the Haifa apartment was concentrating on the UN peacekeeping troops, particularly the Canadians. Canadians were a great target. They were friendly. They tended to be nice people. They felt in Israel as if they were in a Western country, so they were quite comfortable — a lot more so than in an Arab country. I mean, if you're going to have fun, where would you go, Damascus?

There were several Canadian *duvshanim* (literally honey pies, UN peacekeeping forces paid to transport messages and packages) transferring packages back and forth over the borders for us. Two exercises involved breaking into police stations, once at the headquarters of Mador on Dizengoff Street in Tel Aviv, the other time at the special investigative police headquarters in Jerusalem. A man named Zigel headed a large, special fraud investigative unit there. One of the cases he was working on at the time was called the "Peach File" (*Tik Afarsek* in Hebrew).

When we broke into the headquarters, we brought along an "expert with handles" who told us which files to take. The Peach File turned out to be about an investigation involving a veteran religious cabinet minister called Yosef Burg, one of the oldest members of parliament in Israel. Burg had been around so long we used to tell a joke about three archaeologists, an American, a Brit, and an Israeli, who stumbled across a 3,000-year-old Egyptian mummy. When they opened the tomb, the mummy woke up and said to the American, "Where are you from?"

"America. It's a great country across the oceans. The most powerful country in the world."

"I've never heard of it," the mummy said, turning to the British archaeologist and going through the same routine.

Finally he turned to the Israeli. "Where are you from?"

"Israel," came the reply.

"Oh yes, Israel. I've heard of that. By the way, is Burg still a cabinet minister?"

I don't know what was in the File or what the investigation was about, but I do know the Peach File was taken after a request from the prime minister's office, and the whole investigation collapsed because of lack of documentation. Whether it was Begin, Peres, or Shamir, it didn't matter. Once you got a tool that you could use, you would use it. And the Mossad always did.

While the junior katsas did only a few exercises of that nature, the men training for neviot were doing them on a regular basis. When you want an exercise against a secure place, you choose one. And a police station is a secure place.

I was upset about this practice and asked why we did such things when they were against our own regulations. We were supposed to work outside the country, not inside.

Oren Riff, who I'd thought was a friend, replied, "When you look for something, you look where it is lost, not under the light," a reference to the story of the man who lost something in the dark but went looking for it under the light. When asked why he was looking there instead of where he'd lost it, he said he couldn't see in the dark, but he could see under the light.

"You'd better just shut up and do your job," Riff said, "because it's none of your business." Riff then told me the story of the man who came from the desert and was standing on the railroad tracks. He heard the whistle of an oncoming train, but didn't know what it was. Gradually he could see this large thing coming at him, but he didn't know what a train was, either, so he stayed there and got hit. Somehow he survived, and after a long stay in the hospital, he was taken home and his friends had a party for him. Somebody put on a kettle to make some tea, but when he heard the whistle from the boiling kettle he jumped up, grabbed an ax, ran into the kitchen, and smashed the kettle. When asked why he did that, he said, "Let me tell you something. You have to kill these things when they're small!"

Oren then said to me, "Now, you listen to me. Stop whistling now. You can whistle when you're bigger than the guys you're whistling about."

Furious, I replied, "Kiss my ass!" and stormed out of the office. I thought I was right. When I was talking to the other guys in the office, small potatoes like me, they would all agree with me. But nobody wanted to open his mouth because everybody was in line to go abroad, and that's all anyone cared about. With that kind of attitude you're going to fuck up. You can't make it work.

* * *

When we finished the course in mid-November 1985 and finally became katsas — it had taken three years in all — the atmosphere was so bad that we didn't even have a party. Oded didn't graduate, but became a communications expert for the office in Europe. Avigdor didn't graduate, either. He was lent as a hit man through Mike Harari to some people in South America. Michel went to Belgium and Agasy Y. went to be in liaison in Cairo. Jerry went to Tsafririm to work with Araleh Sherf. The last I heard of him, he was planning to start an operation in Yemen to see if he could bring some Jews into Israel. Heim, Yosy, and I were all assigned to the Israel station.

I had done well in the course, but had made some powerful enemies. Efraim Halevy, for example, the head of liaison, called me "a pain in the ass."

Still, I was scheduled to go to Belgium, a great honor for a rookie, to join the attack katsa pool. That annoyed Itsik. After all, there weren't that many openings. When I went, I would be locked in for three to five years.

In the meantime, I was in the jumper pool under Ran, until he had to go to Egypt on a recruiting mission. Egyptian television had shown a movie critical of the Mossad called "The Man with the Teasing Eyes," containing a lot of inside information. But instead of offending everybody, it had brought a flood of volunteers to the embassy wanting to work for the Mossad.

Two weeks after I joined the Israel station, I was told to

transfer a parcel that had arrived on an El Al flight from the Far East to an address in Panama provided by Mike Harari. I drove over for it in a Suburu, but when I got to the airport I was astounded to find a large, 6½ x 10 x 5-foot parcel all wrapped in plastic, with many small packages inside — far too large for the car. So I called for a truck to collect it, take it to the office for repackaging, and send it to Panama.

I asked Amy Yaar what was in the packages.

"It's none of your business," said Yaar. "Just get on with it."

At the airport, the parcel wasn't loaded on a Panamanian plane, as I had been told it would, but on an Israeli air force plane. I said there must be some mistake. They said, "No, no. The plane is on loan to Panama."

It was a Hercules transport carrier. When I returned to the office I complained. I knew what we were sending. I wasn't that stupid. We weren't middlemen for weapons from the Far East. It couldn't have been anything else but drugs. So I asked why we had to use an Israeli airplane, and was told that the guy running the Panamanian air force was Harari, so what was the problem?

I was heard talking at lunch and in the office, complaining about why we were supporting Harari in this sort of activity. There was a complaint-box system inside the office where you could complain by computer and it would go to internal security. I complained formally. The problem with the system is that if you file a complaint, high-ranking officials had access to it; so Harari would have found out about it.

It was the straw that broke the camel's back. My action hit a weak spot with Harari. He didn't like me to begin with, because we had a history.

* * *

At the time there was a case unfolding that resulted in my being sent to Cyprus. I wasn't really supposed to go, but Itsik wanted me to. I was as surprised that he wanted me to go abroad as I was excited.

My task was to pose as the middleman in an operation that was already in motion. I knew little about the details, but was supposed to meet a man and set up a system whereby he would receive assorted explosives equipment in Europe. I didn't even know the contact's name. He was European and in Cyprus liaising with the PLO and making arms deals at the same time. The idea was to nip all this in the bud. The man's buyers were arms dealers and we figured if we could get them, they'd think the militant PLO factions had turned them in.

I had to make sure the men involved would come to a certain rendezvous point in Brussels to receive the goods. The deal was set for Brussels because the explosives and detonators were sent from Mossad headquarters in Tel Aviv to European headquarters in Brussels through the diplomatic pouch. Because of its status, Brussels' diplomatic pouch was frequently very large.

The buyers were equipment merchants from Belgium and Holland. The idea was to tie them in, get an investigation going by the police in their own countries, and let them take it from there. Naturally, the police wanted proof. The Mossad, unknown to the police, were supplying the proof.

Part of the scheme involved using Michel, because of his perfect French, to phone in tips to the police over a period of time, building up to the point where the deliveries would actually be made.

I was staying at the Sun Hall Hotel overlooking the harbor in Larnaca. The equipment was to be transferred to Belgium and placed in a car. I had a set of keys to give to one of the men in Cyprus, telling them they'd be notified exactly when and where to pick up the car. They wanted to meet me on Butterfly Hill, but I insisted on handing over the keys at my hotel.

The men were caught red-handed by Belgian police as they approached the car, including the man I had given the keys to, on February 2, 1986. More than 200 pounds of plastic explosives and 200 or 300 detonators were confiscated.

After that, I was ready to go home. I didn't realize I had actually been sent to Cyprus for another purpose — as part of an operation I was slightly familiar with from working on the office computer.

My new orders were to stay put in my hotel and wait for a phone call from a Metsada combatant who was watching the airport in Tripoli, Libya. The magic message was: "The chickens have flown the coop." Once I received that, I was to turn on a beeper every 15 seconds, constantly repeating, "The chickens have flown the coop." This would be picked up by a nearby missile boat and passed to the Israeli air force, which would have airplanes in the air waiting to force a Libyan Gulfstream 11 executive jet to land in Israel.

The "chickens" in question were some of the toughest, most wanted PLO terrorists in the world, specifically: Abu Khaled Amli, Abu Ali Mustafa, Abdul Fatah Ghamen, and Arabi Awad Ahmed Jibril of the PFLP general command. Jibril did the *Achille Lauro* hijacking and was the one who so worried U.S. Colonel Oliver North that he bought an expensive security system to guard his home.

Libyan strongman Moamer al Kadhafi had called a three-day meeting in Tripoli of what he called the Allied Leadership of the Revolutionary Forces of the Arab Nation, with representatives of 22 Palestinian and other Arab organizations at his stronghold, the Bab al Azizia barracks. Kadhafi was reacting to U.S. naval maneuvers off the Libyan coast, and the delegates approved creation of suicide squads for commando attacks against U.S. targets in America and elsewhere if the U.S. should dare to launch an aggression against Libya or any other Arab country.

Naturally, the Mossad was monitoring the event. Just as naturally, the Palestinians assumed they would be. And so word was leaked that the senior PLO officials planned to leave early on their jet and fly over the southeastern coast of Cyprus to Damascus. The Mossad had two combatants, who didn't know each other — which is quite normal — waiting on a phone line. One watched the airport. He was supposed to see the men board the plane and take off, then tell the other combatant, who in turn would notify me by phone. Then I would pass the message via beeper to the missile boat.

I had entered Cyprus under the name Jason Burton. Taken

halfway by an Israeli PT boat, then picked up by a private yacht from the harbor, I had my entrance visa stamped as if I had come in through the airport.

It was cold and windy, and there weren't many tourists around. There were, however, a number of Palestinians staying in my hotel. After I'd finished my first assignment and was simply waiting for the phone call, I had nothing much to do. I could leave my room but not the hotel, so I simply told the desk to pass on any calls to wherever I was in the hotel.

It was the evening of February 3, 1986, when I spotted the man in the lobby. He was very well dressed, wore gold-rimmed glasses, and three large rings on his right hand. He had a small goatee and mustache, and looked about 45. His black hair was beginning to turn white. He wore expensive leather shoes and a well-tailored wool suit of high quality.

He was sitting in the lobby looking at an Arabic magazine, but I could see he had a copy of *Playboy* tucked inside it. I knew he was an Arab and I could tell he felt he was important. I thought, what the hell, I have nothing else to do, so I made contact.

The contact was direct. I simply walked up to him and said in English, "Do you mind if I look at the centerfold?"

"I beg your pardon?" the man replied, his English heavily accented.

"You know, the chick. The girl in the middle."

He laughed, then showed it to me. I described myself as a British businessman who had lived most of my life in Canada. We had a very friendly conversation and after a while decided to have dinner together. The man was a Palestinian who lived in Aman and, like my "cover person," was in the import/export business. He loved to drink, so after dinner we adjourned to the bar where he began to get drunk.

In the meantime, I expressed strong sympathy for the Palestinian cause. I even mentioned losing a lot of money in a shipment to Beirut because of the war. "Those bloody Israelis," I said.

The man kept talking about business deals he was doing in Libya, and eventually, spurred on by the booze and my apparent friendliness, he said, "We're going to make the Israelis eat shit tomorrow."

"Great, great. How are you going to do that?"

"We heard from a source that Israel is following this PLO meeting with Kadhafi. We're going to do a trick at the airport. The Israelis think all these top PLO men are going to get on a plane together, but they're not."

I was fighting to keep calm. I was not supposed to initiate contact but I had to do something. Finally, at about 1 a.m., I left my "friend" and went back to my room to call an emergency number. I asked for Itsik.

"He can't be reached. He's busy."

"I've got to talk to him. It's an emergency. I'll talk to the head of Tsomet."

"Sorry, he's busy, too."

I had already identified myself as a katsa by my code name, but incredibly, they wouldn't put me through. So I called Araleh Sherf at home, but he wasn't there. Then I called a friend in naval intelligence and asked to be patched through to where all his bosses were, a war room set up by Unit 8200 in an air-force base in the Galil.

Sure enough, Itsik came on the phone. "Why are you calling me here?"

"Listen, the whole thing is a trick. Those guys are not going to be on the plane."

"How do you know?"

I told him the story, but Itsik said, "This sounds like LAP [psychological warfare]. Besides, you weren't authorized to make contact."

"That's not your call to make," I said. By now we were yelling at each other. "This is ridiculous!"

"Look, we know what has to be done. You just do your job. Do you remember what you have to do?"

"Yes, I do. But for the record, I want you to know what I said."

"Okay. Now do your job."

I didn't sleep all night, but about noon the next day, the message finally came. "The chickens have flown the coop."

Unfortunately for the Mossad, they hadn't. Still, I passed the message on, then immediately left the hotel, walked down to the harbor, boarded the private yacht, and was taken to a standby PT boat for the trip back to Israel.

* * *

That day, February 4, the Israelis forced the private jet to land at the Ramat David air-force base near Haifa. But rather than the big-name PLOs, the nine passengers were minor Syrian and Lebanese officials, a major international embarrassment for both the Mossad and Israel. Four hours later they let them go, but not before Jibril held a press conference, announcing: "Tell the world not to board American or Israeli planes. From this day onward, we will not respect civilians who take such planes."

In Damascus, Syrian Foreign Minister Farouk al Shara'a demanded an emergency meeting of the UN Security Council. It was held that week, but the United States vetoed a resolution condemning Israel. In Syria, Major General Hikmat Shehabi, the army's chief of staff, said, "We will answer this crime by teaching those who committed it a lesson they will not forget. We will choose the method, the time, and the place." Kadhafi then announced he had ordered his air force to intercept Israeli civilian airliners over the Mediterranean, force them to land in Libya, and search them for "Israeli terrorists." Libya blamed the U.S. Sixth Fleet, as well, for taking part in the operation.

An embarrassed Prime Minister Shimon Peres told the Knesset Defense and Foreign Affairs Committee that because there was information that a high-ranking Palestinian was aboard, "we decided we had to verify whether he was on the plane. The nature of the information was such that it gave us a solid basis for our decision to intercept . . . It turned out to be a mistake."

Defense Minister Yitzhak Rabin said, "We did not find what we had hoped to find."

While all this was going on, I was still on the PT boat headed for home. I soon learned the Mossad officials were blaming me for the debacle, and to make sure I wouldn't be there to defend myself, the captain of the PT boat, a man I knew from my own days in the navy, was ordered to develop "engine trouble" about 11 miles off Haifa.

When the boat stopped, I had been drinking coffee. I asked the captain what he was doing.

"I've been notified I have engine trouble," he said.

We sat there for two days. I was not authorized to use the radio communications, either. In fact, the captain was actually the commander of a small flotilla of 11 PT boats, but had been sent specifically for this job. I guess they thought I could intimidate a young guy.

Not much frightened this captain. He had made his name years earlier on a foggy night when he saw a "skunk" on his radar screen. It seemed his radio wasn't working properly. He could send but not receive. As the shadow got closer and closer, he warned over his PA system, "Stop or I'll shoot." Just about the time he was ready to blast away with the small, anti-aircraft cannon at the stern of his boat, a mammoth Nimitz class aircraft carrier came out of the fog and turned its floodlights on him. He was ready to open fire. The anchor on the Nimitz was bigger than his PT boat. People used to really laugh about that.

Nobody was laughing about the intercept embarrassment, however — except the Arabs and Palestinians — and when I finally was allowed back on shore, Oren Riff said to me, "You blew it this time."

I started to explain to him what had happened, but he said, "I don't want to hear it."

I kept trying to talk to Nahum Admony, the head of Mossad, but he wouldn't talk to me. Then I was told by manpower head Amiram Arnon that I was going to be let go. He recommended I resign. I said I wasn't leaving and Arnon said, "Okay, so you get your pay."

I went to Riff and said I still wanted to speak with Admony. Riff said, "Not only does he not want to talk to you, he doesn't want you to stop him in the corridors or on the elevator. And if you try to stop him outside the building, he'll regard that as a personal attack." Which meant that his bodyguards would shoot.

I talked to Sherf, who said there was nothing he could do, either.

"But this is a setup," I said.

"It doesn't matter" Sherf replied. "There is nothing you can do."

So I quit. It was the last week in March 1986.

The next day a friend of mine from the navy called to ask why my file had been taken from the special holding place where they are kept so that Mossad officers won't be called up for the reserves. (Most people in Israel serve 30, 60, or 90 days a year in the reserves. That includes unmarried women and all men up to age 55. The higher the rank, the longer the service.)

Normally, if you left the Mossad, your file was put back in the regular reserve file, but with the order that this person was not to be assigned to front-line activities. That was because they knew too much. And so, my friend, blissfully unaware of the internal problems, wondered why the file had been transferred. He assumed it was something I had requested myself, because it usually took five or six months after leaving the Mossad for the file transfer. I had been gone one day. Worse, the file carried a request to transfer me to liaison with the Southern Lebanese army, as good as a death warrant for an ex-Mossad man.

I figured this had gone too far. So I talked to Bella, packed my things, took a Tower Air charter flight to London, then TWA to New York. After a couple of days there, I flew to see my father in Omaha.

The day after I left, a recruiting order was hand-delivered to my house in Tel Aviv. Normally that process would take about 60 days, with another 30 days to prepare.

Bella accepted the order. But the next day, the phone started ringing, with officials demanding to know where I was. Why I hadn't shown up for service yet. She said I was out of the country.

"How could that be?" the official said. "He didn't get a release from the army."

Actually, I did. Well, not exactly from the army. I made my own release, stamped it myself, and then flew the coop.

I went to Washington for a few days, in an attempt to contact Mossad liaison. But I wasn't successful. Nobody would come on the line, and I didn't want to say where I was. Then Bella flew to Washington, while our two daughters flew to Montreal. We settled finally in Ottawa.

* * *

I'm not sure my entire problem was only talking. They would have used me as a scapegoat and left me, anyway. It's one of those things.

But remember that Palestinian in Cyprus who told me about the trick? He said something else even more shocking. He said he had two friends who spoke Hebrew like Israelis, Arabs who grew up in Israel, who were setting up a security company in Europe as if they were Israeli security types, and recruiting Israelis to help write manuals on how to train clandestine groups. It was all a fake. All they were doing was getting information — getting Israelis to talk freely, as they do when there is no one else around. When I mentioned this to several people in the office, they told me I was crazy, that it couldn't be, and that this couldn't get out because it would cause havoc. I asked them what they were talking about. We should warn people, I said. But they were adamant.

The Palestinian probably opened up to me because he knew it was late the night before the operation; we were in a hotel bar in Larnaca, and what was I going to do, anyway? Incidentally, the combatant in Tripoli did see the PLO heavyweights board the private jet. What he did not see was them getting off, with the plane being reloaded behind a hangar en route to its take-off position.

They should have let me pursue a whole operation with that Arab. Obviously he knew things. But I never got the chance. If this had been a normal situation, since I was a katsa, after my phone call they shouldn't have let personal information interfere. We could have saved ourselves some embarrassment and even double-tricked the other side.

We should have seen it coming. These were the men who were scared shitless of us. Yet we thought five of them would board a plane together? These were men who normally hid under rocks. They were sophisticated, experienced. We should have known it was a trick. The Mossad didn't need some middleman in Cyprus to pass a message, either. What they needed was a scapegoat. And that's what I turned out to be.

My problems had begun when I was a cadet, but the instructors apparently hoped I would grow out of it and adapt better to the system. I was good at the job and they had made a big investment in me. Not everyone was against me, either, so it took some time to reach the stage where it was finally decided that I was more trouble than I was worth. My problems with Jerry are likely what brought matters to a head. Obviously he had a powerful horse working for him. And against me.

Clearly the Mossad does not appreciate people who question the system, or those who operate it. They prefer people who obediently accept it as is and even use it to their own advantage. As long as they don't rock the boat, no one seems to care.

Even so, I learned enough during my extensive training period and brief career as a katsa to keep a diary and collect extensive information on numerous Mossad operations.

Many of the training courses were taught by those who had carried out various Mossad operations. The trainees studied these operations in minute detail, reenacting them, having every detail explained. In addition, my open access to the Mossad computer allowed me to build up a vast knowledge of the organization and its activities, many of which you are now going to read about, and much of it for the first time.

PART III

By Way of Deception

9

Strella

On NOVEMBER 28, 1971, four terrorists brazenly assassinated Jordanian Premier Wasfi Tell as he entered the Cairo-Sheraton Hotel. Tell, a pro-Western Arab intent on negotiating with Israel, thus became the first target of a murderous band of Palestinians called Black September, or *Ailul al Aswad* in Arabic, which took its name from the month in 1970 when Jordan's King Hussein crushed the Palestinian guerrillas in his country.

Easily the bloodiest and most extreme of the *fedayeen* — an Arabic word for guerrilla fighter — Black September quickly followed up Tell's assassination by murdering five Jordanians living in West Germany whom they accused of spying for Israel. They attempted to assassinate Jordan's ambassador to London and they set off damaging explosives in a Hamburg plant making electronic components for sale to Israel, and in a refinery in Trieste that they claimed was processing oil for "pro-Zionist interests" in Germany and Austria.

On May 8, 1972, a team of two men and two women seized a Sabena jet with 90 passengers and 10 crewmen at Tel Aviv's Lod International Airport, trying to force the release of 117 fedayeen imprisoned in Israel. Next day, the two male terrorists were shot dead by Israeli commandos, the women captured and sentenced to life in prison. On May 30, three machine-gun-toting Japanese radicals, paid by the fedayeen, opened fire in Lod Airport, killing 26 tourists and wounding another 85.

Then on September 5, 1972, at the height of the XX Olympiad in Munich, a Black September team stormed the Israeli compound in the Olympic Village, murdering 11 Israeli athletes and coaches. The resulting standoff with German police was televised live around the world. The group already had members working in Germany, and the week before the Olympics began, several Black September members had headed for Munich, traveling separately, bringing with them an arsenal of Russian-built Kalashnikov assault rifles, pistols, and hand grenades.

Three days later, Israel had reacted to the atrocity by ordering about 75 planes — the heaviest raids since the 1967 war — to bomb what Israel said were guerrilla bases in Syria and Lebanon, leaving 66 dead and scores wounded. Israeli jets even shot down three Syrian planes over the Golan Heights, while Syria downed two Israeli jets. Israel sent ground troops into Lebanon to fight Palestinian terrorists who had been mining Israeli roads, and the Syrian army massed on that country's borders in case the hostilities turned into all-out war.

Israelis, already deeply disturbed by outside actions against them, were literally dumbfounded when on December 7 the country's internal intelligence agency, Shin Bet, arrested 46 people for either spying for Syria's Deuxième Bureau (G-2) or knowing about the spy ring and not reporting it. What really shocked them was that four of those arrested were Jews and two of them, including the leader, were *sabras*, native-born Israelis, caught spying for an Arab country.

Right after Munich, Prime Minister Golda Meir ordered retribution. Then a grandmother in her mid-70s, Meir had mourned the Munich Olympics massacre by publicly promising a war of revenge in which Israel would fight "with assiduity and skill [on a] far-flung, dangerous and vital front line." Translated, that meant the Mossad would get them, or as they say: "No one will escape the long arm of Israeli justice." Meir signed death warrants for about 35 known Black September terrorists, including their Beirut-based leader Mohammed Yusif Najjar, known as Abu Yusuf, a former senior intelligence officer with Yassar Arafat's Al Fatah. The group also included the colorful but brutal Ali Hassan Salameh, whom the Mossad called "the Red Prince" and who had masterminded the Munich massacre and was then operating from East Germany. He eventually met his fate in a 1979 car bombing in Beirut.

Because Meir had given the Mossad orders to track down the Black September killers and take them out as they found them, she herself became the terrorists' number one target. For the Mossad, that meant unleashing Metsada's assassination unit, the kidon.

Their first post-Munich visit was paid to the PLO's Rome representative, Abdel Wa'il Zwaiter, 38, who was waiting for the elevator in his apartment building on October 16, 1972, when he was shot 12 times at close range.

On December 8, Mahmoud Hamchari, 34, the PLO's principal representative in France, answered a telephone call to his Paris apartment.

"Hello."

"Is this Hamchari?"

"Yes."

Boom! The Mossad team had installed an explosive device in his telephone; when he lifted the receiver to his head and identified himself, it was set off by remote control. Hamchari was badly maimed and died a month after the explosion.

In late January 1973, Hussein Al Bashir, 33, described as head of Palmyra Enterprises and traveling on a Syrian passport, went to bed in his second-floor room in Nicosia's Olympic Hotel. Moments later, an explosion demolished both the room and Bashir, Al Fatah's representative in Cyprus. The killer had simply watched until Bashir turned the lights off in his room, then by remote control detonated the explosive device he had planted under the bed.

In eulogizing his dead comrade, Arafat swore to seek revenge himself, but "not on Cyprus, not in Israel, and not in the occupied territories," a clear warning that he planned an international escalation of the battle of terrorists. Altogether, the Mossad killed about a dozen Black September members in Meir's war of revenge.

To further make its point, the Mossad began running obituaries in local Arab newspapers of suspected terrorists who were still alive. Others received anonymous letters detailing intimate knowledge of their private lives, especially sex-related activities, advising them to leave town. In addition, many Arabs were injured in Europe and the Middle East when they opened Mossad-made letter bombs. Although the Mossad would have it otherwise, many innocent bystanders were also hurt in this campaign of revenge.

But the PLO, also, had been mailing letter bombs: to Israeli officials around the world and to prominent Jewish figures, the letters bearing Amsterdam postmarks. On September 19, 1972, Ami Shachori, 44, an agricultural counselor in Israel's London embassy, died instantly when he opened one. A number of widely reported hits on Mossad men at the time were actually what is called "white noise": the chaff that gets into the newspapers, much of it planted by the Mossad itself to add confusion to the public record. A classic example occurred on January 26, 1973, when Israeli businessman Moshe Hanan Yshai (later reported to be Mossad katsa Baruch Cohen, 37) was gunned down in Madrid's busiest street, the Gran Via, by a Black September terrorist he was supposedly tracking. He was not, in fact, tracking anyone. That was merely what the Mossad wanted people to think.

Another example was the November 1972 death of Syrian journalist Khodr Kanou, 36, said to be a double agent, shot dead in his apartment doorway in Paris because Black September believed he was passing on information about their activities to the Mossad. He wasn't. But that's the way his murder was reported in the media. While much is written about double agents, very few actually exist. Those who do have to be in a stable bureaucratic environment in order to function in such a role.

* * *

In that fall of 1972, Meir was looking for a way to turn Israeli minds from the horrors of international terrorism and the country's growing isolation since the Six Day War. Politically, at least, she needed a diversion. There had been a standing request from Israel for an audience with Pope Paul VI in Rome. And so in November, after receiving a message from the Vatican agreeing to the request, Meir asked her officials to make the arrangements.

However, she told them, "I don't want to go to Canossa," a common saying in Israel that refers to the castle in Italy where Emperor Henry IV of the Holy Roman Empire humiliated himself by going as a simple penitent before Pope Gregory VII in 1077. Because he was deliberately kept waiting outside for three days before being granted absolution, the visit has come to symbolize an act of submission.

It was decided that Meir would visit Paris to attend an unofficial international socialist conference on January 13-14 — a conference that French President Georges Pompidou strongly criticized — then drop by the Vatican on January 15 for one day, followed by two days with Ivory Coast President Felix Houphouet-Boigny before returning home to Israel.

Within a week of her request, the papal audience was formalized, although it was not announced to the public.

Because about three percent of Israel's population, or about 100,000 people, are Christian Arabs, the PLO is well connected inside the Vatican, with sources privy to internal discussions. That was how Abu Yusuf quickly got the news of Meir's plan to visit the pope. He immediately sent a message to Ali Hassan Salameh in East Germany, telling him: "Let's get the one who is spilling our blood all over Europe." (That message, and much of the material appearing in this chapter, was unknown to the Israelis until after they seized a mountain of PLO documents in the 1982 Lebanon war.)

Just how Meir would be killed, and precisely when, was left to the Red Prince, but the decision had been made to strike, and he was determined to bring it off. Quite apart from the fact that Meir was their most visible enemy, Yusuf also saw the strike as a spectacular opportunity to show the world that Black September was still a potent force to be reckoned with.

* * *

In late November 1972, the Mossad's London station received an unexpected telephone call from a man named Akbar, a Palestinian student who used to pick up loose change selling information to the Mossad but hadn't been heard from in a long time.

Even though he was a "stale agent," Akbar had PLO connections and he indicated that he wanted a meeting. Because he had not been active for so long, he would not have had a direct link to a specific katsa, and although his calling names would identify him, he would still have to leave a phone number where his call could be returned. His message would have been something like: "Tell Robert it's Isaac calling," plus the phone number and city, as this could be someone normally working in Paris but now calling from London. The message would quickly be fed into the computer by the duty officer, and in this case, it was soon discovered that although Akbar had actually come to England to study, in the hope of getting out of the intelligence game, he was a former "black" (or Arab) agent. His file would have shown when he was last in contact. It would also have included a large picture of him. The photos were mounted with a large one at the top and three more along the bottom, showing each profile, and the subject with or without a beard, for example.

When dealing with the PLO, no matter how remotely, extra precautions are always taken, so very strict APAM procedures would have been followed before the katsa and Akbar actually met.

Since Akbar did prove to be clean, he went on to tell them that he had been instructed by his PLO contact to go to Paris for a meeting. He suspected it was to be a large operation — that was why someone at his low level would have been called in — but at that point he had no specific information.

He wanted money. He was tense and excited. He really didn't want to get involved in all this again, but he didn't think he had much choice, since the PLO knew where he was. The katsa gave Akbar money on the spot and a phone number to call in Paris.

Because it is difficult, especially on short notice, to call in teams from Arab countries, where people are not used to European ways and can be more easily spotted in a European setting, the PLO taps its supply of students and workers who are already living in Europe and so are free to travel without arousing suspicion or requiring a cover story. For the same reason, they often use the services of European revolutionary groups in their work, even though the PLO neither trusts nor respects them.

Now it was Akbar's turn, and so he flew to Paris for a rendezvous at the Pyramides, a Metro station, with other PLO people. Mossad's Paris station was to have Akbar followed to his meeting, but somehow they got it wrong. By the time they arrived, Akbar and his hosts had gone. Had they monitored the rendezvous and taken pictures, it might have helped in sorting out the complicated web of intrigue that Black September was weaving in its zeal to murder Meir.

As an internal security precaution, PLO operatives traveled in pairs once they had received their instructions, but Akbar managed to make a quick call to the Paris number when his partner went to the washroom. He said there was another meeting scheduled. "Target?" asked the Mossad katsa. "One of yours," he replied. "I can't talk now." He hung up.

Everyone panicked. Word went out to Israeli facilities around the world that the PLO was planning to hit an Israeli target. All stations went on daylight as everyone speculated wildly as to who the target would be. At the same time, with Meir's trip still two months off and not even publicly announced, no one thought of her.

The next day, Akbar called again and said he would be leaving that afternoon for Rome. He needed money and wanted to meet, but he didn't have much time because he had to head for the airport. He was near the Roosevelt Metro station, so he was instructed to take the next train as far as Place de Concorde and walk in a certain direction, repeating in a different way the earlier security precautions.

They wanted to see him in a hotel room, but here again the seemingly simple act of renting a room is anything but simple in the spy business. To begin with, you need two adjoining rooms, with a camera monitoring the meeting room, and two armed security men sitting beside the adjoining room's door ready to burst in should the agent make a move toward the katsa. The katsa would also be given a room key in advance so that he wouldn't have to waste time at the front desk.

Because Akbar had to catch an airplane to Rome, he didn't have much time, so the hotel meeting was abandoned and he was picked up as he walked down the street. He said that, whatever the operation was, it involved something technical, some equipment that had to be smuggled into Italy. This seemingly innocuous bit of intelligence would prove to be a key element later on in putting the puzzle together. Because this operation belonged to the Paris station, it was also decided to send a katsa to Rome to act as Akbar's contact.

Two security people were then assigned to drive Akbar to the airport. Both, as it happened, were katsas because of a shortage of available security people at the time. One of them, Itsik, later became one of my teachers in the Mossad Academy. But his actions this day were no model for katsas to emulate. Quite the opposite.*

Because they were coming from a secured meeting in a secured car, Itsik and his partner felt they were clean. Still, regulations say that katsas don't hang around airports for fear of being seen and perhaps recognized later in another operation at another airport, or elsewhere. Nor do they ever break cover without cleansing the territory first.

On arrival at Orly airport, one katsa went to a cafeteria for coffee, while the other took Akbar to the ticket counter and

* See Chapter 7: HAIRPIECE

baggage check-in, staying with him long enough to make sure he was headed for his flight. They may have imagined that Akbar would be the only Palestinian headed for Rome, but he wasn't.

As the Mossad discovered years later in the documents seized during the Lebanese war, another man, a PLO member, spotted Akbar with the stranger at the airport, then alertly followed the katsa and saw him join his partner in the cafeteria. Incredibly, the two men, who should have long since left the airport building, broke into a conversation in Hebrew, at which point the PLO man headed directly to the phone to call Rome and report that Akbar was not clean.

Akbar and the Mossad would pay dearly for the sloppiness of Itsik and his partner.

* * *

Ali Hassan Salameh, better known as Abu Hassan, and called the Red Prince by the Mossad, was a dashing, adventure-seeking character whose second wife was Lebanese beauty Georgina Rizak, the 1971 Miss Universe. As brutal as he was smart, he had masterminded the Munich atrocity. Now, he decided to use Russian-made Strella missiles — called SA-7 by the Soviets and code-named "Grail" by NATO — to blow up Golda Meir's plane as it landed at Rome's Fiumicino airport.

The missiles, based on the U.S. Redeye missile system, were propelled at their targets through a 10.6 kg. launcher, hand-held and slung over the shoulder. The 9.2 kg. missile itself has a solid, three-stage rocket motor, an infra-red passive guidance system, and a maximum range of 3.5 km. As missiles go, it's not particularly sophisticated, but it can be deadly, finding its target by homing in on the exhaust pipes of hot engines. When shot at highly maneuverable, fast fighter jets, its lack of flexibility renders it useless most of the time. But when aimed at slow and large targets such as passenger jetliners, it is lethal.

Finding a supply of Strellas was no problem. The PLO had them in their training camps inside Yugoslavia, so all that was needed was a way to smuggle them across the Adriatic into Italy. At the time, the PLO also had a modest yacht, with sleeping cabins, anchored near Bari on Italy's east coast directly across the sea from Dubrovnik, Yugoslavia.

Salameh patrolled some sleazy bars in Hamburg, Germany's major port city, until he found a German who knew something about navigation and was willing to do anything for money. He then hired two women he met in another bar, who were also interested in the offer of money, sex, drugs, and a leisurely cruise on the Adriatic.

The Germans were flown to Rome, then to Bari, where they boarded the PLO vessel, which had been stocked with food, drugs, and booze. Their only orders were to go to a small island off Dubrovnik, wait while some people loaded wooden boxes into the storage area, then return to a spot on the beach north of Bari, where they'd be met by some other men and paid several thousand dollars each. They were also told to enjoy themselves, take three or four days, and indulge in whatever earthly pleasures they wanted — orders they doubtless followed religiously.

Salameh had chosen the Germans because, if they were caught, the authorities would be more likely to think they were Red Army or some other organization, rather than PLO-related. Unfortunately for them, Salameh was not in the habit of taking chances with outsiders at the end of a mission. When the Germans arrived back with the crated missiles, the PLO went out in a small boat to unload the cargo, then took the three of them away and slit their throats, punched holes in the yacht, and let it sink about a quarter mile offshore.

The Strellas were loaded into a Fiat van, and from Bari the PLO team drove to Avelino, from there to Terracina, then to Anzio, to Ostia and into Rome, staying off the main roads and driving only during daylight hours to avoid any suspicion, finally arriving at an apartment in Rome where the boxes containing the missiles would be stored until they were needed.

* * *

In Beirut, Black September leader Abu Yusuf had been immediately informed that Akbar was a mole within the organization. But rather than kill him right away and perhaps jeopardize the whole operation, Yusuf decided he'd use this knowledge to throw the Israelis off the track. While he knew they were aware that they'd been targeted, they didn't know how, because Akbar had had only limited knowledge of the operation.

"We will have to do something that will make the Israelis say, 'Ah, that's what it was,'" Yusuf told his officials.

Which is why, on December 28, 1972, less than three weeks before Meir's scheduled January 15 visit to Rome, Black September staged what at the time was seen as an inexplicable raid on the Israeli embassy in Bangkok, Thailand. It was clearly a loosely planned event. They picked the day that Prince Vajiralongkorn was being invested at Parliament House as heir to the throne, and Israeli Ambassador Rehevam Amir, along with most foreign diplomats, was attending the ceremony.

Time magazine described the takeover of the embassy on Soi Lang Suan (the lane behind the orchard): "In the hot tropical sun of high noon, two men in leather jackets climbed over the wall enclosing the compound, while two others, well-dressed in dark suits, strolled in through the front gate. Before the guard could raise any alarm, he was staring down the muzzles of submachine guns. The Black September Arab terrorist group, perpetrators of the Munich massacre, had struck again."

Indeed they had. But it was strictly a diversion. They took control of the embassy and hung the green-and-white Palestinian flag out of a window. They allowed the guard and all the Thai employees to go free, but kept six Israelis as hostages, including Shimon Avimor, the ambassador to Cambodia. Soon, 500 Thai police and troops surrounded the building, and the terrorists threw out notes demanding Israel release 36 Palestinian prisoners or they would blow up the embassy and everyone in it, themselves included, within 20 hours.

Eventually, Thailand's deputy foreign minister, Chartichai Choonhaven, and Air Marshal Dawee Chullasapya, along with Egypt's ambassador to Thailand, Moustafa el Essaway, were allowed to enter the embassy to begin negotiations. Israeli ambassador Amir stayed outside, installing a telex machine in a nearby office to keep in direct contact with Meir and her cabinet in Jerusalem.

After just an hour of talks, the terrorists agreed to an offer of safe conduct out of Thailand if they released the hostages. They then enjoyed a meal of curried chicken and Scotch whiskey, courtesy of the Thai government, and at dawn they left for Cairo on a special Thai flight, accompanied by Essaway and two ranking Thai negotiators.

The *Time* magazine account of this event also noted that because of Essaway's role, it was "a rare instance of Arab-Israeli cooperation. . . . Even rarer was the fact that the terrorists had listened to reason. The incident marked the first time that Black Septembrists had backed down."

The journalists, of course, had no way of knowing that this had been the plan all along. Neither did the Israelis, and with one significant exception — Shai Kauly, then head of the Mossad's Milan station — they believed this was the operation Akbar had tipped them off about.

Just to make sure the Mossad did fall for the diversion, Akbar was told by his PLO associates prior to the Thailand affair to stay in Rome for the moment, but that the operation was slated for a country well outside the usual terrorist battleground of Europe or the Middle East. Naturally, Akbar passed this information to the Mossad, so that when the Bangkok attack took place, headquarters in Tel Aviv was not only convinced that this had been the operation in question, but overjoyed that no Israelis had died or even been hurt. There was quite an uproar within the Mossad over the fact that there had been a warning of such an attack, but the location had not been pinpointed. There was an even larger tremor within the Shaback, which is responsible for the security of Israeli embassies and installations abroad.

Akbar was certainly convinced that Bangkok had been the target all along, so he contacted his katsa in Rome for another meeting. Since Mossad security is so meticulous, the Palestinians would not have risked following Akbar to any of his rendezvous for fear of being seen and tipping off the

Mossad that they were on to him. Their main concern was feeding him information to pass along to the Mossad.

Now, believing the operation was completed, Akbar wanted money. Since he would soon be heading back to London, he was told by the London-based katsa to bring as much documentation as he could from the PLO safe house. The meeting would be held in a small village south of Rome, but it began in the usual way — sending Akbar to a Rome trattoria — and followed standard APAM procedures from there.

What wasn't standard, however, was the result of the meeting.

When Akbar was shoved into the katsa's car and his briefcase tossed to the front seat in the usual way, the security man opened it. The car instantly blew up, killing Akbar, the katsa, and both security men. The driver survived, but was injured so badly that he remains a vegetable today.

Three more Mossad men had been following in another car, and one swore later that he had heard, over their communications system, Akbar saying in a panicky voice, "Don't open it!" as if he had known the briefcase contained an explosive device. The Mossad, however, never did determine whether or not Akbar knew his briefcase was booby-trapped.

In any event, the men in the second car called in another team, including a standby ambulance, complete with a nurse and doctor — local sayanim. The remains of their three dead colleagues, along with the severely injured driver, were quickly removed from the scene and later shipped back to Israel. Akbar's badly charred body was left in the wreckage of the car, to be found by Italian police.

As it turned out, the PLO made a mistake by killing Akbar before the Meir operation. They could easily have waited until he had returned to London. Even though the Mossad would have known who killed him, it wouldn't have particularly mattered to them at that point.

In the meantime, Meir had already arrived in France on the opening leg of the trip that would bring her to Rome. Mossad officials chuckled to themselves that Meir did not bring along Israel Galili, a minister without portfolio with whom she had been having a long-running affair. The two used to hold many of their private trysts at the Mossad Academy, making the romance an item of particular merriment around the Institute.

* * *

Mark Hessner,* head of the Rome station, had been completely taken in by the PLO's Bangkok ruse. But in Milan, Shai Kauly remained convinced there was something wrong with that scenario. Kauly was a determined, studious man with a well-earned reputation as a stickler for details. Sometimes it was a liability. He once held up an urgent message, for example, so that a grammatical error could be corrected. But more often, his meticulousness was an asset. On this occasion, Kauly's persistence would save Golda Meir's life.

He kept going over and over all the reports concerning Akbar and related PLO activities. It made no sense to him that the attack in Bangkok was the same thing that Akbar had talked about: why would it have involved smuggling technical materials into Italy? Then, when Akbar was killed, Kauly became even more suspicious. Why would they kill him unless they knew he was an Israeli agent? But if they did know, then the Bangkok attack must have been a hoax, Kauly reasoned.

Still, he didn't have anything solid to go on. The office was blaming the katsa from London for the attack, saying that when he had asked Akbar to bring documentation, he did not warn him how to handle himself so he wouldn't be caught.

As for Hessner, his personal animosity toward Kauly would be a serious complicating factor in the unfolding events. When Hessner had been a cadet in the Academy, he had been caught several times ying about his whereabouts — including once by Kauly, his instructor at the time — when he was unaware of being followed. Instead of going to

* See Chapter 4: SOPHOMORES

his assignment, Hessner had gone directly home. When he was asked by Kauly to give a report, he had given one completely different from what really happened. The fact that he was not kicked out must have meant he had a good, strong horse on the inside, but he never forgave Kauly for catching him, just as Kauly never regarded Hessner as a professional.

With Meir's visit so close at hand now, security was particularly tight. Kauly kept reading the reports over and over again, trying to piece together the missing chunks.

* * *

As often happens in such situations, Kauly's biggest break came from a most unexpected source. A multilingual and mega-talented woman in Brussels kept an apartment at the behest of PLO fighters seeking a temporary haven in the ongoing war against Israel. A high-priced hooker, she was an imaginative PLO playmate. Because the Mossad bugged both her phone and her apartment, amorous recordings of her and her friends in various states of sexual ecstasy had become a favorite diversion for Mossad officials around the world. It was said she could moan in at least six languages.

Just a few days before Meir's scheduled arrival in Rome, someone — Kauly thought it was Salameh, although he was never positive — in the Brussels apartment told the woman he had to phone Rome. He told the party who answered to "clear the apartment and take all 14 cakes." Normally, a call to Rome would not have raised suspicion, but with Meir due to arrive and Kauly already suspicious, it was just what he needed to prompt a move.

The German-born Kauly was only about five foot five, with sharp features, light brown hair, and a light complexion. He had a low-key personality and was not given to trying to impress his superiors, which is why he was in Milan, a minor station, and Hessner was in Rome.

When Kauly heard the Brussels tape, he immediately called a friend in liaison, who called his friend in Italian intelligence, Vito Michele, and said he needed an address from a phone number right away. (Because Kauly was in Tsomet [recruiting], he was registered as an attaché at the consulate, and therefore did not make himself known as a katsa to local intelligence. He would not have called Michele direct.)

Michele said he couldn't do it without permission from his boss, Amburgo Vivani, so the liaison man said he'd call Vivani, which he did. What channels Italian intelligence went through to get the information was of no concern to Kauly. He knew only that the man in the Rome apartment had been told to leave the next day, giving them very little time to track down the address and determine if it had anything to do with a PLO operation.

Vivani did get the address, but incredibly, the liaison officer in Rome, rather than give the information to Kauly in Milan, sent it to the Rome station, which knew nothing of its significance — or about the Kauly-Hessner feud — and so sat on it until the next day. Finally, Kauly tracked down the address himself and phoned the Rome station, telling them to go directly to the apartment because it could have a bearing on Meir's visit. At this point, Kauly was still guessing, but he was convinced something critical was about to happen.

By the time the Mossad found the apartment, however, it was empty. But a search did turn up an important piece of evidence: a torn piece of paper showing the back end of a Strella missile and several words in Russian explaining the mechanism.

Now Kauly was frantic. With less than two full days before the prime minister arrived, he knew there were PLO operatives all over the place, that there was an operation on, that they had missiles, and that Meir was about to land. But it was only this last he knew precisely.

As a result, Meir was notified of a security risk, but her response to the head of Mossad was, "I'm going to meet with the pope. You and your boys make sure I land safely."

At this point, Kauly went to see Hessner to debate whether or not they should involve local security. Hessner, trying a power play of his own, thanked Kauly for his help, but added, "Your station is in Milan. This is Rome." He told him to leave. As Tsomet station head in Rome, Hessner was automatically in charge. If one of his superiors in Israel wanted to take charge, he would have to come to the Rome station to do so. Then, that did not happen. Today, it probably would.

Still, Kauly was more concerned for the safety of the prime minister than worried over a jurisdictional dispute. He told Hessner to stuff it. "I'm staying," he insisted. Hessner, furious, contacted headquarters to complain that Kauly was causing confusion in command. Tel Aviv then ordered Kauly off the case and back to Milan pronto.

But Kauly didn't leave Rome. He had two of his katsas from Milan with him, leaving Milan empty, and he told Hessner they'd just snoop around and stay out of everybody's way. Hessner wasn't happy with that either, but he'd made his jurisdictional point, so he ordered all personnel out to the airport and its environs to see if they could get a break on the terrorists. The PLO, however, assuming the Mossad might know more about its plans than they did, had taken the extra precaution of moving into the beach area for the night, camping in their vehicles. Thus, a Mossad check of every hotel and rooming house in and around Lido di Ostia, plus all known PLO hang-outs the night before Meir's January 15 arrival, came up empty.

Still, since the Mossad knew the range of the missiles, they at least knew the area to search before Meir's plane landed, although it was a massive area, about five miles wide and 13 miles long, and the problem was compounded by Hessner's stupid decision not to notify the local police about the potential problem. The Strella can be activated remotely. When the target comes within range, the missile has an electric pulse that activates a beeper; once fired, it will trace a target by itself. The terrorists would have a time fix on Meir's plane, knowing from their own agents exactly when it had left Paris, and when it was due to land. And it would be an El Al jet — the only one due at that time of day.

Rome's Leonardo da Vinci Airport at Fiumicino was called by Alitalia officials at the time "the worst airport in the world." Crowded, confused, airplanes were almost always late, sometimes up to three hours, because the airport had only two runways to handle up to 500 aircraft a day in peak season.

Of course Meir's plane would receive top priority, but the constant confusion in the airport itself was no help to the Mossad officials scurrying around trying to find a group of terrorists and their missiles. They could be anywhere — in the airport itself, the nearby hangars, or in the fields surrounding the airport.

For his part as he was patrolling the airport, Kauly ran into a Rome-based katsa and asked where the Mossad liaison people were. (They were the ones who would notify the Italian police when needed, not the katsas themselves.)

"What liaison?" the man replied.

"You mean they aren't here!" Kauly was incredulous.

"No," said the Rome katsa.

Kauly immediately called the liaison man in Rome and told him to call Vivani and tell him what was going on. "Pull whatever strings are necessary. We've got to get reinforcements out here."

It seemed more likely the terrorists would be outside the perimeter of the airport within missile range of Meir's plane, since there proved to be very few good hiding spots on airport grounds. Still, they searched everywhere, soon joined by Adaglio Malti of Italian intelligence.

Malti had no idea the place was full of Mossad officers. He was there because of a tip from the Rome liaison officer that, based on reliable information received, the PLO was planning to embarrass the Italians by shooting down Meir's plane over the airport with Russian-made missiles. (That message would have been approved first by liaison command in Tel Aviv before being transferred to the Italians.)

* * *

By this time, the terrorists had split into two groups. One, with four missiles, went to the south of the airport, and the other, with eight, to the north. The fact that two of the 14 "cakes" would be unaccounted for after the operation proved to be significant later on. But at that time, the northern group set up two missiles next to their Fiat van in a field.

However, it wasn't long before a Mossad security man combing the area noticed them. He shouted. They opened fire. The scene was one of great confusion. The Italian police arrived, and the Mossad man — not expecting them, since it was Kauly who had called them, nor wanting them to see him — ran off. In the commotion, one of the terrorists tried to get away, but Mossad officers who had been observing the action soon caught up to him, tied him up, threw him into a car, and spirited him swiftly away to an airport storage shed.

Under brutal and persistent beating, the terrorist confessed that they'd planned to kill Golda Meir, and he boasted, "There is nothing you can do about it."

"What do you mean nothing we can do? We got you!" an officer replied, and the beating continued.

Kauly had, meanwhile, heard over his walkie-talkie that a prisoner had been taken. He immediately made his way to the storage shed. The officers told Kauly they had captured this terrorist, and the Italians had nabbed some more, along with either nine or 10 missiles.

But Kauly remembered the telephone call from Brussels about taking "all 14 cakes." Not only did the Mossad still have a problem, only 30 minutes remained until Meir's plane landed. There must be more missiles. But where?

By this time, the prisoner was unconscious. Kauly threw water over him.

"It's finished for you," Kauly told him. "You blew it this time. She's landing in four minutes. There's nothing you can do about it,"

"Your prime minister is dead," the terrorist taunted his captors. "You didn't get us all."

Kauly's worst fears were confirmed. Somewhere out there was a Soviet-made missile with Golda Meir's name on it.

At that, a security man smashed the terrorist unconscious. When they'd caught him, he'd been carrying an explosive device, called a "bouncing Betty," often used by terrorists. It sticks into the ground like a land mine, but is attached to a short stake with a string tied to the pin. They put the device beside him, made a longer string, walked out of the building, then pulled the string, blowing the man to bits.

The tension was incredible. Kauly got Hessner on the walkie-talkie and asked him to radio Meir's pilot to postpone the landing. It's not clear whether he ever did that or not. What is clear is that one Mossad security man, scouting a perimeter highway in his car, suddenly noticed something odd about a food-concession cart standing by the side of the road. He had already driven by it twice, but on the third time, it struck him: there were three stacks poking out of the roof, but only one was smoking. The terrorists had got rid of the cart owner, drilled two holes in the roof, and stuck Strella missiles up through the holes. The plan was that when Meir's plane got close enough and the missile began beeping, all they'd have to do was pull the trigger and approximately 15 seconds later the plane would have been totalled.

Without wasting a second, the Mossad man did a sharp U-turn on the road and drove his car directly into the cart, turning it over and pinning the two terrorists beneath it. He got out, confirmed that there were two missiles all right — and that the terrorists were trapped. Then he saw police cars heading his way, so he jumped back in his own car, turned around, and roared off toward Rome. As soon as he notified his Mossad colleagues, they all faded from the picture as if they had never been there in the first place.

The Italian police arrested five Black Septembrists, but strangely, considering the fact that they were caught red-handed with the missiles attempting to assassinate Meir, they were released within a few months and flown to Libya.

10

Carlos

ON FEBRUARY 21, 1973, the Israelis sent two Phantom jets out against an unarmed Libyan Arab Airlines Boeing 727 that had been bound for Cairo but strayed off course. They shot it down, killing 105 of the 111 people on board. That came just 12 hours after Israeli commandos had staged a daring raid in Beirut, blowing up various PLO installations, capturing a considerable amount of documentation, and killing several PLO leaders, including Black September chief Abu Yusuf and his wife.

The destruction of the civilian plane was a tragic mistake. At the time, Israel had received threats that an airplane filled with bombs would be flown to Tel Aviv. The ill-fated Boeing was headed directly over one of the largest military bases in the Sinai, and when the chief of the air force could not be found, the decision to shoot was made by a captain.

It would be another six years before the Mossad finally caught up with the Red Prince, but Golda Meir's single-minded personal vendetta against Black September drastically changed the role of the Institute. The PLO became the most important part of Mossad work — not a good situation, because less attention was paid to other enemies, such as Egypt and Syria, who were screaming war — and, in fact, preparing for war; Anwar Sadat had committees all over Egypt actually called "war committees." But the Mossad was spending nearly all its time and resources chasing down Black September terrorists.

On October 6, 1973, just a few months after the Strella incident in Rome, General Eliahu Zeira, head of Israel's military intelligence, was telling a press briefing in Tel Aviv: "There will be no war." In the midst of the briefing, an Israeli major entered the room and handed the general a telegram. Zeira read it and immediately left without saying a word.

The Egyptians and Syrians had attacked, the Yom Kippur War had begun, and the Israeli death count on the first day was 500, with more than 1,000 wounded. A few days later they managed to recover and begin pushing the invaders back, but the war forever changed Israel's image — both for others and for itself — as an invincible force.

Golda Meir was still alive, thanks to the Mossad, but one result of the war was her resignation as prime minister on April 10, 1974.

As for Shai Kauly, he knew there were still two Strella missiles unaccounted for after the attempt on Meir. However, the immediate threat was over, he was back in Milan, and concerns over the war soon overtook all other problems.

At the time of the airport incident, though, the Italian police had felt extremely embarrassed. After all, here was an attempted assassination of a major political figure right under their noses and they had done nothing, other than arrive late and pick up the pieces the Mossad had left behind. Italian intelligence had had no inkling of the plan to kill Meir. While the general public knew nothing of the episode, some of the intelligence community did. And so the Italians asked the Israelis not to make the details public.

The Mossad view was that by helping another party cover up something, it gained a certain advantage. Thus, it was always willing to help someone save face — just as long as that someone knew that, to the Mossad, he was still an idiot.

And so the LAP, or *Lohamah Psichlogit*, the Mossad's psychological warfare department, was asked to develop a cover story. At the time, the situation between Israel and Egypt was extremely tense, but because the Mossad was so busy looking for the Black September gang, the vital signs indicating war preparation had been missed. With only about 35 or 40 active katsas operating in the world at any given time, concentrating on covering the activities of the PLO — with thousands of people in its many factions — could preoccupy the whole force and create a serious gap in the monitoring of Israel's other major enemies.

In any event, LAP invented a cover story for the Italians to make public, at the same time telling the British, French, and U.S. intelligence agencies what had really happened. There is a rule in intelligence called the "third party rule": if, for example, the Mossad gives information to the CIA because the two have a good working relationship, the CIA cannot pass the information on to a third party, because it came from another intelligence agency. Of course the rule can be circumvented by simply paraphrasing some of the information and then passing it along.

At the time of the Rome airport incident and subsequent cover-up, the Mossad frequently supplied the CIA with lists of Russian military equipment being sent to Egypt and Syria, including the series numbers of weapons and individual serial numbers. The purpose was twofold: to make the Mossad look good because they could obtain this information, and to help confirm a military build-up. This would assist the CIA in convincing the U.S. government to increase its support to Israel. The CIA couldn't tell Congress where they got this information, but it did, however, confirm the same information being given to Congress by the Jewish lobby groups.

The Americans already considered Libya's Moamer al Kadhafi a dangerous lunatic, and in the mid-1970s the whole world seemed to be in turmoil, with little terrorist revolutionary groups springing up everywhere. There was Action Directe in France, the Baader-Meinhof gang in Germany, the Japanese Red Army, the Italian Red Brigade (who murdered Prime Minister Aldo Moro in 1978), the Basque ETA in Spain (which claimed to have murdered Spanish premier Carrero Blanco in 1974), and about five different Palestinian organizations. Even in the United States there were the Weathermen and the Symbionese Liberation Army — the 1974 kidnappers of heiress Patricia Hearst.

In the midst of this upheaval, many synagogues and other Jewish institutions in Europe were hit by bomb attacks, so the time was ripe for the Mossad to blame the Italian escapade on the Egyptians and Libyans, even though they'd had nothing to do with it.

The Mossad did get the list of the Strella missiles the Italians had confiscated. There were still only 12, but they'd worry about the missing two later. The serial numbers of these missiles were added to the lists they were sending the CIA of weapons sent by the Russians to Egypt, even though the Mossad knew from its interrogation of the terrorists that these particular missiles had come from Yugoslavia.

But the story devised by LAP for public consumption in Italy was that the terrorists, who got their weapons from Libya, had left Beirut by car in late December, 1972, carrying the Strellas, arriving in Italy by ferryboat and driving to Rome, supposedly on their way to attack a Jewish target in Vienna. The reason for the circular route, it was explained, was that it is easier to enter one western European country from another than it is to pass through customs coming from a Communist country. The terrorists were "officially" arrested January 26, 1973, by the Italian police for transporting explosives, having been held incommunicado since their failed airport attack while a cover story was concocted by LAP. Incredibly, the Italian police then released the terrorists, first two and, later, another three.

But in the meantime, the Americans were feeding all this Mossad-supplied information into their military computer system. When the Italians finally announced on January 26 that they'd arrested the terrorists and confiscated their weapons, they, too, passed along the serial numbers of the Strellas to the CIA, who in turn gave the data to their military intelligence. Then, when those serial numbers were cross-referenced with the ones the Mossad had included as supposedly coming through Egypt and Libya via Russia, the U.S. computer showed a match. Now the Americans truly believed that the Russians had supplied Egypt, which had, in turn, given the missiles to Kadhafi, who had armed the terrorists — further evidence that the Libyan leader was exactly what the United States believed him to be. Only the Mossad knew the truth.

It seems that the main reason the Italians freed the terrorists was that they were afraid of the case coming to trial, for the truth would have got out: Italian intelligence had allowed a cell of terrorists to come within a whisker of assassinating a world leader. Quite a scandal.

* * *

It still bothered the Mossad at the time that two of the missiles were unaccounted for. But the Italians were happy, since their embarrassment had been concealed, while the Americans thought Kadhafi was behind the whole thing.

While the terrorists were still in jail, security men from the Shaback had interrogated them and found out that Ali Hassan Salameh, the Red Prince, had indeed been involved. Now the Mossad wanted him badly.

The Italian police had allowed the Shaback to interrogate the Palestinians in Rome. In all likelihood, a team of two Shaback men would have come into a room where one prisoner was sitting on a chair, his hands cuffed behind his back; his legs, too, would have been cuffed, with a chain leading to the cuffs. The first thing the Shaback would have done was ask the Italian police to leave the room. "This is an Israeli room now. We will be responsible for the prisoner." The PLO prisoner doubtless would have been horrifed. After all, he'd probably gone to Europe to avoid ever winding up in the hands of the Israelis.

After closing the door, the Shaback officers, speaking Arabic, would have said something like, "We are your friends from the *Muchbarat.*" (Muchbarat is a catch-all name used by the Arabs to describe all intelligence. Indeed, many Arab intelligence agencies go by that name.)

They would have wanted to make sure that the prisoner knew exactly who he was dealing with and what his situation was. Next they would have removed the regular cuffs and replaced them with the much harsher type they favor. Made of plastic, they look similar to the plastic fasteners used to attach name tags to luggage, only these are much stronger and have little razor blades to hold the fasteners. Unlike regular handcuffs, which give a bit of room to move, these are pulled tight, cutting off circulation and causing considerable pain.

Then, after cuffing his arms and legs with these, all the while chatting away about his sorry situation, the Shaback officers would have probably placed a jute sack over the prisoner's head. Next, they would have opened his fly and pulled out his penis, leaving him sitting there handcuffed, blindfolded, a bag over his head, and his private parts sticking out. "Now you feel at home?" they would have mocked. "Let's start talking."

At that point, it wouldn't have taken long for the talk to come. In this case, the Shaback unfortunately had no idea the prisoners would shortly be released, and so they asked a lot of questions about Salameh. So many that once they were out, word quickly got back to the Red Prince that he was Mossad's number-one target.

* * *

At the time, Black September was pushing very hard. Letter bombs were still common, and bombings and grenade attacks were being staged quite regularly all across Europe. While the Mossad was extremely anxious to get Salameh, the Black September leaders in Beirut were equally anxious to save him. He was their favorite son. So they warned him to get out of sight for the time being.

But Black September leader Abu Yusuf — who would be killed a few weeks later by Israeli commandos in a February 20, 1973, raid on his Beirut headquarters — decided the organization must replace Salameh, at least temporarily, to handle the European operations. And so they settled on Mohammed Boudia, Algerian-born, and well known in fashionable Paris society. He started his own cell, in his own name: the "Boudia cell."

Boudia's idea was to coordinate all the terrorist groups operating in Europe into one deadly underground army. He arranged for members of various groups to train in Lebanon and, almost overnight, created a major terrorist organization, a kind of clearing house for all the factions. It was a good idea in theory, but the main problem was that the PLO organizations were extreme nationalists, while most of the other groups were radical Marxists, and Islam and Marxism simply don't mix.

Boudia had a liaison man of his own who traveled between Paris and Beirut, a Palestinian named Moukharbel. In the Israeli commando raid on Black September headquarters there, Moukharbel's file, complete with a photo, had been among the many seized and taken back to Tel Aviv.

Enter Mossad katsa Oren Riff. Everything was hot. There was no time for the normal cautious setups. Riff, who spoke Arabic, was told in June 1973 to make a frontal recruitment effort on Moukharbel, that is, simply confront him directly and offer him a deal. (There is much to be gained by this technique: it does sometimes get recruits; if it fails, it might scare a man enough to make him stop working for the other side — or, he's stopped, period, as Meshad, the Egyptian physicist, was.)*

Moukharbel was staying at a fancy London hotel. He was followed for one and a half days, and the hotel was cased. Finally, Riff was to go to his door as soon as Moukharbel returned from a walk. His room had already been checked for hidden weapons; there were none and no one else was there. On Moukharbel's way up in the elevator, a man "accidentally" bumped into him, quickly frisking him for concealed weapons as he did so. Since Moukharbel was PLO, he was considered extremely dangerous, but having taken all the precautions the circumstances allowed, Riff waited for the man to go into his room, then went to the door.

Glancing swiftly at the other man to make sure he wasn't going for a weapon, Riff quickly recited Moukharbel's Black September file: his name, address, age — everything it contained.

He then said, "I'm from Israeli intelligence and we're willing to pay you a pretty penny. We want you to work for us."

Moukharbel, a handsome, sophisticated, expensively tai-

* See PROLOGUE: OPERATION SPHINX

lored man, looked Riff straight in the eye, smiled from ear to ear, and said, "What took you so long?"

The two men had a quick, five-minute meeting and made arrangements for another that would be more formal and properly secured. It wasn't so much the money with Moukharbel, although he wanted that, too, but he particularly wanted a double cover so that if something happened to either side, he'd still be safe. It was a question of his own personal survival, and if both sides were willing to pay him, fine.

Right away, he gave Riff most of the locations where Boudia stayed. Boudia loved women and had a number of mistresses all over Paris. He knew he was a target, so he used women's apartments as safe houses, staying in a different one each night. But since Moukharbel needed to be in contact with him, he knew the various addresses. Once Riff passed them along to Metsada, the department began tailing Boudia on his rounds. They soon learned that he was busy transferring some money for an upcoming operation to a Venezuelan named Ilyich Ramirez Sanchez, who came from a rich family, had studied in London and Moscow, and was now living in Paris and doing some work for the PLO.

Metsada soon saw that Boudia was a careful man. One thing an intelligence agency looks for in such matters is a constant — something the target does regularly. This sort of work can't be done on the spur of the moment. "There he is: let's kill him!" That just doesn't happen. It must be planned to avoid any complications. The most constant thing about Boudia was that everywhere he went he drove his blue Renault 16. He also had one place, on the rue des Fosses-St-Bernard, which he visited more frequently than the others.

Even so, Boudia wouldn't get into his car without opening the hood, checking underneath the car, looking in the trunk and at the exhaust pipe for possible explosives. As a result, Metsada decided to put a pressure mine inside his car seat. But because they didn't want the French to suspect the Mossad, the bomb was deliberately made to look as if it was homemade, filled with nuts and sharp scrap iron. The bomb was fitted with a heavy metal plate at the bottom so that it would blow up, not down, when pressure was placed on it.

On June 28, 1973, Boudia left the apartment building, performed his usual check, then opened the driver's door and hopped onto the seat. As he was closing the door, the car blew up, killing him instantly. The force of the blast was so strong that many of the nuts and bolts went right through his body and peppered the roof of the car.

The French police, who knew his association with terrorist groups, believed he was blown up by accident when explosives he was carrying went off, a conclusion often reported by various police departments in lieu of other explanations.

Even though Black September had no direct evidence that the Mossad had killed Boudia, they knew it was so. They ordered the immediate revenge killing of an Israeli. A Palestinian student at UCLA, in southern California, was ordered to get a gun and go to the Israeli embassy in Washington. They reasoned that a complete unknown could do a hit and escape much more easily than someone who had been involved in a terrorist group and might be tailed by U.S. intelligence. And so, on July 1, 1973, an unidentified young man walked up to Colonel Yosef Alon, the assistant air attaché at the embassy, shot him dead on the street, and fled. The gunman was never caught. The Mossad learned of this tie-in with the Boudia operation later, from some documentation captured after the Yom Kippur War.

After Boudia's assassination, Moukharbel notified Riff that Black September had brought the Venezuelan, Sanchez, to Paris to run their European operation. The Mossad knew very little about him, but they quickly found out that his favorite alias was Carlos Ramirez — or later, simply Carlos. He would soon become one of the most famous and feared men in the world.

* * *

Ali Hassan Salameh, not a stupid man himself, was busy setting up his own personal security. He wanted to avoid the Mossad and to make Israel look bad at the same time. So he arranged with volunteers to get themselves recruited by the Mossad through two different embassies. Their job was to feed the Israelis a series of dates and locations that would map his movements. Not his real movements, of course, but the ones he wanted them to believe. This eventually led the Mossad to a little town in Norway called Lillehammer, about 95 miles north of Oslo, where a waiter in a restaurant bore an uncanny — and for him, fatal — resemblance to the Red Prince.

Metsada head Mike Harari was in charge of the operation to get Salameh. Salameh made sure that, when the unsuspecting waiter was being watched by the Mossad, some of his men walked over and talked to him, which would confirm he was who the Mossad thought he was. Though he wasn't, on July 21, 1973, the Mossad killed the innocent waiter. Three people went to jail. One of them, David Arbel,* talked a lot, and the "Lillehammer affair" became perhaps the biggest scandal and embarrassment in Mossad history.

Back in Paris, Carlos was taking over. The European intelligence community knew nothing about him. He didn't speak Arabic; in fact, he didn't even like Arabs. (Carlos said of the Palestinians, "If these guys are half as good as they say, how come the Israelis are still sitting in Palestine?") But Moukharbel, recently recruited as a Mossad agent by Oren Riff, remained as liaison man for Carlos.

In the process of consolidating the Paris operation, Carlos gained control of the stockpile of Black September weaponry throughout Europe. Among other things, he inherited the two "missing" Strella missiles that had been part of the aborted assassination attempt on Golda Meir.

Moukharbel, in addition to acting as liaison with Black September, was doing the same job for two other Palestinian groups, the Popular Front (PFLP) and the Palestinian Youth Organization. The volume of information coming from him to the Mossad was astonishing, and the Mossad, after chewing it up and keeping what it wanted for itself, began feeding Eu-

* See Chapter 7: HAIRPIECE; Chapter 15: OPERATION MOSES

ropean intelligence and the CIA so much information, they didn't know what to do with it all. It became an inside joke with other intelligence officers, who would ask, "Oh, did we get the Mossad book today?" And liaison with the CIA was so tight then, the Americans would joke about "the Mossad desk at Langley" (CIA headquarters in Virginia). This flooding the market with information perhaps didn't do anybody much good, though at least nobody could say later they weren't told. And it was a system the Mossad later used successfully.

Carlos naturally took an interest in the two leftover Strella missiles in Rome. Apparently, when the two teams had divided them, they'd simply left two behind in a safe house the Mossad didn't know about. Had they not killed the terrorist captured at the time of the assassination attempt, they might have found out. He had been one of the team using that particular house.

Although Carlos had not moved against any Jewish targets yet, the Mossad was beginning to realize he was a dangerous man. They learned of the missiles through Moukharbel, but there was no point in touching them yet. In any case, they couldn't make a move on the house without burning Moukharbel, who was phoning every two or three days with information; at one stage they actually had an operator on call 24 hours a day for him.

Carlos wanted the missiles to be used against an Israeli plane. But he would not become personally involved in an operation that required intricate planning. That was his rule — and part of the reason he was never caught. He would plan an operation, see that it was carried out, but would not participate.

The Mossad had a problem with the missiles. Clearly Moukharbel was too valuable to burn over this one operation, but if ever they let the Palestinians get to the airport with the weapons, they would be able to take out an Israeli airplane.

Oren Riff, Moukharbel's katsa, was running the show. Riff was a straightforward, no-nonsense kind of guy. At the end of 1975, he was one of the infamous 11 crack katsas who signed a letter to the head of the Mossad saying the organization was stagnant, wasteful, and had the wrong attitude toward democracy. It is known inside only as "the letter of the 11," and Riff is the only one of the 11 who survived it. Everyone else was kicked out. He was skipped over twice for advancement, however, and in 1984 when he demanded his file to see why he was not being advanced, he was told it had been misplaced — an unlikely story, since the organization had only 1,200 people altogether, including secretaries and drivers.

As a result of that letter, incidentally, the NAKA regulations were changed so that not more than one other person in the Mossad could cosign a letter.

Anyway, Riff called liaison in Rome and told them to call their friend in Italian intelligence, Amburgo Vivani, and give him the address of the safe house where the missiles were. "You tell him you'll call him at a time when all the people involved are there and he's to come into that apartment only at that particular time," Riff said. "That way he can catch them all."

A unit of neviot men were casing the place for the Mossad and on September 5, 1973, when they saw all the terrorists go in, they called Italian intelligence. The Italians were standing by — so was the Mossad, who saw the Italians but weren't seen by them — and they entered the apartment, arresting five men — from Lebanon, Libya, Algeria, Iraq, and Syria — and confiscating the two missiles.

The story given out was that the five had planned to shoot down civilian airliners from the roof of their apartment as they were taking off from Rome's Fiumicino airport. This was a ridiculous story, because the airplanes didn't fly over that apartment. But it didn't matter. People believed it.

At that time, the head of Italian intelligence was very close to the Mossad. In fact, the Italian, carrying a concealed camera, used to travel to Arab countries and photograph Arab military installations for the Mossad.

Even though they caught the terrorists red-handed with two heat-seeking missiles, the Italians released two of the five on bail immediately. Naturally, they left Rome. The other three were released to Libya, but on March 1, 1974, after they had been flown there, the Dakota plane that had carried them blew up on its way back to Rome, killing pilot and crew. There is an ongoing police investigation into that bombing.

The Italians claim the Mossad did it, but they didn't. It was most likely the PLO. They probably thought the crew had seen something when they let them off in Libya, or might recognize them in some other operation. If the Mossad had blown it up, they would have done it when the terrorists were on board.

On December 20, 1973, Carlos was in Paris. He had a place on the outskirts of the city, a storage place for PLO ammunition. The Mossad was looking for a reason to give the address to the French without burning their valuable agent, Moukharbel.

That morning, Carlos performed his own style of terrorist act — his infamous "bang, bang" and get out. He left his apartment carrying a grenade, hopped in his car, and drove down a street, lobbing the grenade at a Jewish bookstore, killing one woman, and wounding six other people. That was reason enough for the Mossad to pass on the address of the ammunition depot, but when it was raided by French police, they found weapons, guns, grenades, TNT sticks, propaganda leaflets, about a dozen people, but no Carlos. He had left France the same day.

The next day he called Moukharbel from London, wanting to meet him there. Moukharbel said he couldn't go because the British police wanted him. The Mossad tried to persuade him to go but he wouldn't, so for a time they lost contact with Carlos.

Then on January 22, 1974, Carlos called Moukharbel again. "It's Ilyich," he said. "I'm coming back to Paris. I just have to sign a deal tomorrow or the next day."

All Israeli installations in Britain immediately went on alert. But it couldn't be a visible alert in case the call was simply a test by Carlos of Moukharbel's loyalty. They knew that Carlos was always one step ahead of everybody else.

Two days later, on January 24, a car went by an Israeli bank in London, and the lone man inside the car threw a hand grenade at the bank, injuring one woman.

The next day, Carlos called a meeting with Moukharbel in Paris. He told him that he had to lay off Israeli targets for the time being because things were too hot, but he had some debts to pay to the Japanese and German gangs, which had to be done before he could do anything for the PLO.

That more or less put the Mossad at ease, and it tied in with other information they had. But with Carlos, you could never be at ease for long. On August 3 that year, three car bombs were set in Paris, two outside newspaper offices and one (detected before it exploded) outside a radio station. The French police thought it was the work of Action Directe. It was, but Carlos had helped them rig and plant the bombs. Then he had driven to another part of Paris so as to be far from the actual operation.

The Mossad subsequently learned that Carlos had received a batch of Russian-made RPG-7 rocket anti-tank grenade launchers. The RPG-7 is a compact, easy-to-carry weapon that weighs only 19 pounds and has a maximum effective range of 555 yards on a static target, and 330 yards on a moving target. It will penetrate armor up to 12 inches thick.

On January 13, 1975, Carlos and a colleague, Wilfred Bose, headed for Orly airport looking for trouble. (Bose, a member of the Baader-Meinhof gang, was killed on June 27, 1976, in the famous hostage-saving raid on Entebbe, Uganda.) In any event, the two men spotted the tail of an Israeli airplane on the tarmac.

Carlos drove by again to take another look, stopped the car, and tossed a small bottle of milk onto the road, spilling the liquid as his signal for the spot where he could best see the Israeli plane. With Carlos's feet planted under the roof racks of his Citroën Deux Chevaux, Bose backed down the road, then drove ahead slowly, at about 10 miles an hour. As he approached the milk spot, Carlos rose from his squatting position and fired, missing the Israeli plane, but damaging a Yugoslavian plane and one of the airport buildings. They drove down the road a few yards and stopped the car. Carlos jumped down, got in the passenger seat, and off they went.

When he returned to the apartment, he told Moukharbel

what he had done, but Moukharbel told him he'd heard about it on the radio and that he'd missed the Israeli plane.

Carlos replied, "Yes, we missed this time, but we're going back on the nineteenth to do it again."

Naturally, Moukharbel fed this tidbit to Oren Riff. Again, they did not want to burn such a valuable agent, so Riff ordered double security and had all Israeli planes moved to the north side of the airport so that there was just one approach to them, should Carlos fulfill his threat.

Sure enough, on January 19, after the French had been warned there might be a terrorist attack, Carlos arrived with three men in the car. They made three passes and then stopped, but the French police, their sirens roaring, closed in. The men didn't fire. Instead, appearing to throw down their weapons, they ran off, leaving their car behind. Carlos grabbed a passer-by and put a gun to her head. One of his colleagues followed suit. For the next 30 minutes, there was a standoff while they negotiated.

Although no guns were fired, somehow they got away. Their equipment was left behind, and Carlos disappeared. Even Moukharbel didn't know where he was.

* * *

For the next five months, things were quiet. Moukharbel was still supplying valuable information, but he had heard nothing about Carlos. At this point he was becoming nervous, too: friends had told Moukharbel that some people in Beirut were getting suspicious of his activities and wanted to talk to him. By this time, the Mossad had decided to hit Carlos, but all Moukharbel wanted was a new identity and to get out of the game as quickly as he could. He had begun to fear that Carlos was on to him.

Headquarters didn't want Riff to tackle Carlos himself, nor did they want the Metsada to eliminate him, so it was decided that they should leave the whole thing to the French, although they were prepared to help out with some information.

On June 10, 1975, Carlos phoned Moukharbel, who was

panicky, telling Carlos he had to leave Paris. But Carlos invited him over to an apartment he had in a house on the rue Toullier in the Fifth District. It was one of those houses that actually sits behind another and can be approached either by going through the house closest to the fronting street and through a garden, or by walking up some stairs and crossing a walkway. With only one entrance, and therefore, only one real exit, it was an odd place for Carlos to be.

Through an apartment sayan, Riff had managed to rent the apartment in the front building that overlooked the courtyard and the Carlos apartment. It was a small place of the sort tourists rent by the day or week, and Riff was in the top-floor apartment looking down on the action.

The French police were notified that there was one man in the apartment who was in league with a known arms dealer, and another (Moukharbel) who wanted to get out of a tricky situation and was willing to talk. The police were not told it was Carlos, nor were they told that Moukharbel was an agent.

The story Riff told Moukharbel was that he would get the French police to go to him. "You tell them you want to get out and go to Tunis. We'll make sure they have nothing on you. You know you're not safe as long as Carlos is roaming around. They'll show you a picture of Carlos and yourself, and ask you who the other man is.

"Try to wiggle out of it, say he's a nobody. They'll still want to see him, so you'll take them to Carlos. They'll arrest him for interrogation, and then we'll make sure they get the information about him and he'll be locked up forever, while you'll be free and living in Tunis."

The plan had some giant holes, but if it brought in Carlos, the Mossad didn't care.

Riff asked permission from Tel Aviv to transfer most of Carlos's file to the French so that they would know who they were dealing with. His argument was that the Mossad was handing them an agent, and if they didn't know who Carlos was, their agent, Moukharbel, would be in great danger. What's more, he was afraid the French would also be in danger if they weren't properly prepared for Carlos. After all, they still knew very little about him.

The answer Riff got was that liaison would handle the transfer of information when needed, after Carlos was in custody, and depending upon items that were negotiable with the French. In other words, if the French wanted information, they were going to have to pay something for it.

The reason the French were not tipped off about Carlos was a simple matter of rivalries and jealousies between two Mossad departments: Tsomet, or later Melucha, which handled the Mossad's 35 active katsas and was the main recruiter of enemy agents; and Tevel, or Kaisarut, the liaison department.

Tevel was always struggling with Tsomet to give out more information. Their view was the more they could give other agencies, the friendlier they became and the more they would get back in return. But Tsomet always resisted, arguing that information shouldn't be given out easily, that something should be received back directly for everything given out.

On this occasion, however, when the department heads were meeting to discuss the request from Oren Riff (then with Tsomet) to give the French most of the Carlos file, the normal situation was reversed. Tsomet wanted to release details, but Tevel didn't. So the head of Tevel, seizing the opportunity to make an internal point, said, "What is this? They want to give the French information? When we want to give out information, you won't let us. So now, we won't let you." They could get away with it because there was nobody who could look at it later. Nobody they had to answer to. They were a law unto themselves.

On the appointed day, Riff watched Carlos enter his apartment. The liaison officers had spoken to the French and told them where to pick up Moukharbel, which they did. There was a group of other South Americans in Carlos's apartment. They were having a party.

Moukharbel arrived in an unmarked police car along with three French policemen. Two of them stayed with him near the stairs, while the third knocked on the door. Carlos opened the door, the plainclothes policeman introduced himself, and Carlos invited him in. They talked for about 20 minutes. Carlos no doubt seemed like a nice guy, no problems. They'd never seen him or heard of him. As far as they were concerned, they were just acting on a tip. No big deal.

Riff would say later that he was becoming so nervous watching that he wanted to throw the book away, rush over, and warn the police. But he didn't.

Finally, the cop must have told Carlos he had someone with him that he might know. "I'd like you to talk to him. Do you mind coming with me?"

At this point, the cop signaled to his two colleagues on the walkway to bring Moukharbel. When Carlos saw him, he assumed he'd been burned. But Moukharbel's plan was just to tell Carlos not to worry, that the cops had nothing on them. Carlos said to the cop, "Sure, I'll come with you."

All this time, Carlos was holding the guitar he'd been playing when the cop had knocked on the door. The others in the room had no idea what was happening, so the party continued. Carlos asked if he could put the guitar away and get a jacket, and the cop saw no reason why not. In the meantime, the other three men were approaching the door.

Carlos went into the next room, threw the guitar down, picked up his jacket, opened the guitar case and took out a .38 caliber submachine gun. He approached the door and immediately opened fire, wounding the first cop seriously with a bullet through the neck. He then killed the other two cops on the spot, then hit Moukharbel, downing him with three bullets in the chest and one in his head — this last from point-blank range as insurance that Moukharbel was indeed dead.

Riff was hysterical as he saw all this from his apartment. He had no weapons. He watched helplessly as Carlos finished off Moukharbel, then calmly left the scene.

But Riff knew one thing: the French police knew who *he* was. They knew he had brought their men there, and as far as they were concerned, it would look like a trap. Two and a half hours later, Riff, in the uniform of a flight attendant, boarded an El Al flight for Israel. *

The wounded policeman was helped by the people at the party, who called an ambulance. They had no idea who Carlos was. The policeman survived, revealing later that, as Carlos fired, he kept shouting, "I am Carlos! I am Carlos!" over and over again.

Carlos became famous that day.

* * *

On December 21, 1975, Carlos was thought to have been involved in an operation at OPEC headquarters in Vienna where six pro-Palestinian guerrillas burst into an OPEC conference, shot three people to death, wounded seven others, and seized 81 hostages. During the next few years, dozens of bombings and other terrorist acts were attributed to him. In 1979-80 alone — the last time the Mossad heard of him — about 16 explosions that were attributed to Action Directe had all been done in the Carlos style.

One of the problems with intelligence agencies is that they do things behind closed doors that affect people on an international scale. But because they do it behind closed doors, they don't necessarily take responsibility for it. An intelligence agency with no supervisory body is like a loose cannon, only with a difference. It's a loose cannon with malice aforethought. It can be blinded by internal rivalries.

There was no reason for the deaths of those French policemen, or the deaths of any of the other people killed by Carlos. There was no reason, in fact, for Carlos to be out on the street. What the Mossad is doing, then, because it is not accountable to anyone, is not just hurting the Institute, but hurting Israel.

Cooperation cannot be sustained on the basis of a quid pro quo. Over time, the liaisons of other countries' agencies will stop trusting the Mossad. Then it starts losing credibility

---

* See Chapter 2: SCHOOL DAYS

within the intelligence community. This is what it is doing. Israel could be the greatest country in the world, but the Mossad is destroying it by manipulating power, not in the best interests of Israel, but in its own best interests.

11

Exocet

O<small>N A RAINY MORNING</small>, September 21, 1976, Orlando Letelier, 44, left his home on Washington's elegant Embassy Row and, as he usually did, got behind the wheel of his blue Chevelle. Letelier, a former senior cabinet minister under Chile's ill-fated Marxist president, Salvador Allende Gossens, was accompanied by his American research colleague, Ronni Moffit, 25.

Moments later, a bomb, detonated by remote control, ripped the car to pieces, killing both men instantly.

As often happens in these affairs, many people blamed the CIA. After all, the CIA had been credited with a larger role than it actually played in Allende's 1973 downfall, and it had long been a favorite international whipping boy to explain all kinds of violent acts. Others pointed, correctly, to the Chilean secret police, DINA, which was, in fact, disbanded a year later, under considerable U.S. pressure (although it would be reborn under a different hierarchy), by the country's new head, General Augusto Pinochet Ugarte.

Nobody pointed the finger at the Mossad.

And while the Mossad had no direct involvement in the hit ordered by Chilean DINA Chief Manuel Contreras Sepulveda, it had played a significant indirect role in the execution through a secret deal with Contreras to buy a French-made Exocet surface-to-surface naval missile from Chile.

The death squad didn't use Mossad personnel in killing

Letelier, but they certainly used Mossad know-how, taught to them as part of the deal Contreras made to supply the missile.

In August 1978, a U.S. federal grand jury indicted Contreras, along with DINA operations director, Pedro Espinoza Bravo; DINA agent, Armando Fernandez Larios; and four Cuban exiles who were members of a fanatical anti-Castro organization in the United States. All seven were charged with murder.

The key evidence for the 15-page indictment came from U.S.-born Michael Vernon Townley, who had moved to Chile with his parents at age 15, stayed on as an auto mechanic, and been recruited by DINA. He was named an unindicted co-conspirator and cooperated with the prosecution in return for a light sentence of three years and four months. The Pinochet regime turned over the Chileans to U.S. prosecutors — the Cuban exiles escaped, although one was arrested April 11, 1990, while living in St. Petersburg, Florida — but Chile steadfastly refused to give them Contreras, the man who had orchestrated the assassination of Letelier. Contreras was never tried for the crime, although in October 1977, he was forced by Pinochet to resign his post, in an effort to improve the military junta's battered international image.

* * *

Once a year, all the military intelligence organizations in Israel get together to plan upcoming events, one of which is the annual meeting of all intelligence agencies in the country, both military and civilian, called *Tsorech Yediot Hasuvot*, or *Tsiach* for short, meaning simply "necessary information." At the meeting, the information customers — for example AMAN, the prime minister's office, and military intelligence units — go over the quality of information received during the past year and what is required for the next year, in order of importance. The document that flows from this meeting is also called Tsiach, and amounts to a purchase order to the Mossad and the other suppliers — for example, the military intelligence corps — for intelligence over the next year.

There are essentially three kinds of intelligence suppliers: *Humant*, or intelligence-gathering from people, such as Mossad katsas working with their various agents; *Elint*, or signals, a task done by Unit 8200 from the Israeli army intelligence corps; and *Signt*, or intelligence-gathering from regular media, a job that keeps hundreds of people busy in another special military unit.

At the Tsiach, the customers not only decide what they need by way of intelligence, but they grade agents based on their performance over the past year. Every agent has two code names, an operational name and an information name. The operational reports, filed by Mossad katsas, are not seen by the intelligence customers. They don't even know they exist. The information report, broken down into various categories, is sent separately.

Based on these reports, the intelligence customers rate agents from A to E. Actually, no agent rates A, though combatants can. But a B is a very reliable source; a C is so-so; a D, take his word with caution; and an E, don't work with him. Each katsa knows his agents' gradings and will try to improve them. The grade sticks for an entire year and agents are paid according to their grades. If one had been a C for a year, then went up to a B, for example, he'd get a bonus.

When katsas make these reports, they fill in a little two-square box at the top. On the left is the agent's grade, while beside it is a number, beginning with 1, which means the agent heard or saw the item reported himself; to 2, meaning he heard about it from someone reliable but didn't actually see it himself; to 3, meaning he heard it third-hand as rumor. Hence, a report with B-1 at the top would mean it contained information from a good agent who had seen or heard the event in person.

While the head of army intelligence is the senior man in military intelligence, each branch of the Israeli armed forces has its own unit. Thus, there is infantry intelligence, tank-battalion intelligence, air-force intelligence, and navy intelligence. (The first two are now grouped as ground forces intelligence.) The head of the army, formally called the Israeli Defense Force or IDF, is a lieutenant general, whose shoulder-pad symbol is a sword crossing an olive branch, plus two fig leaves, or falafels.

Unlike the United States, with its separate forces, the IDF is basically one army with various branches, such as navy and air force. The heads of those branches, major generals, wear the sword and olive symbol but just one falafel. One rank below them are the brigadier generals, the heads of the various military intelligence branches. One below that is colonel — my rank when I joined the Mossad and was promoted one rank.

Underlining the importance of intelligence to the Israelis is the fact that the head of the army intelligence corps holds the same rank — major general — as the heads of the navy, air force, field forces, tank battalions, and the military judicial system. The head of naval intelligence is one rank lower.

The head of AMAN, or military intelligence, holds the same rank as the other service heads, but in practice outranks all other military intelligence officers because he is answerable directly to the prime minister in the chain of command. The difference between AMAN and the intelligence corps is that AMAN is the recipient of intelligence, while the corps is charged with gathering tactical information in the field.

In late 1975, naval intelligence went to the annual military intelligence meeting and announced its need for an Exocet missile. The missile, manufactured by France's Aerospatiale, is called a sea skimmer; it is fired from a ship, rises to find its target through a homing device, then drops to level out just above the water line, making it difficult to detect with radar and also to defend against. The only way to determine a defense against such a missile is by testing it.

Israel's main concern was that some Arab countries, Egypt in particular, would be buying Exocets. In the event they did, the navy wanted to be prepared. In fact, they did not need a whole missile to test — only the head, where all the electronic systems are located.

The man selling a missile won't give the buyer the full information about it. He won't test it on the defense side, either, only on the attack side. And even if you did get the specs from a firm like Aerospatiale, they would show the missile's maximum performance. They're trying to sell it, after all!

That was why Israel wanted to have their own to test, but they couldn't openly buy it from the French. France had an embargo on selling weapons to Israel. A lot of countries still do, because they know that the moment Israel has certain weapons, it will copy them.

The task of acquiring an Exocet head was passed on to the Mossad chief, who in turn ordered the Tevel to take care of the navy's request.

The Mossad already had considerable information about the Exocet, thanks in part to a sayan who worked at Aerospatiale and had passed along details. They had also conducted a small operation, sending a team to break into the plant accompanied by a missile expert flown in from Israel for the occasion. He was taken into the plant "with handles," and materials brought to him for his expert opinion. His task was to determine what they should photograph. The team spent four and a half hours inside the plant before leaving without a trace.

But despite photographs they had taken of the missile and its complete plans, an actual working model was essential. The British had the missile but they weren't about to give one to Israel.

Europe was a dead end for the project, but the Mossad knew that several South American countries had Exocets. Normally, Argentina would have been a good source, but at the time, they had a deal with Israel, purchasing made-in-Israel jet engines, and the Mossad was wary of any operation that might jeopardize that lucrative contract.

The best bet, then, was Chile. As it happened, that country had just placed a request with Israel for training a domestic security service — something in which Israel's special expertise is well known. Israel may not brag openly about it, but it has trained such diverse units as Iran's dreaded Savak, security forces in Colombia, Argentina, West Germany, South Africa, and in several other African countries, including former Ugandan dictator Idi Amin's secret police. Israel also trained the secret police of recently deposed Panamanian strongman Manuel Noriega.* In fact, Noriega, who trained personally in Israel, always wore the Israeli paratrooper wings on the right side of his military uniform (they are normally worn on the left). And just to show how nondiscriminatory the Mossad is, it trained both sides in the bloody ongoing civil unrest in Sri Lanka: the Tamils and the Sinhalese, as well as the Indians who were sent in to restore order.

Because of the bad international reputation of Chile's DINA, Pinochet was looking to revamp the service, and he assigned its chief, General Manuel Contreras, to look after the details.

Because Contreras had already approached Israel with this request, the then liaison chief, Nahum Admony, asked his MALAT branch in the liaison department to follow up on the navy request. MALAT, which covered Latin America, was a small branch, with just three officers and their chief. Two of the officers spent time traveling around South America, mainly trying to initiate business ties with Israel. One of them, a man named Amir, was in Bolivia at the time, looking at a factory built by Israeli industrialist Saul Eisenberg,** a man so powerful the Israeli government had passed a special law making him exempt from many high taxes so that he would bring his headquarters to Israel. Eisenberg specialized in what are called turnkey operations — building factories, then handing the keys of a completely finished project to its owners.

In 1976, Eisenberg was the central figure in a political scandal and police investigation in Canada after the federal auditor-general's report questioned the payment of at least $20 million to him and his various companies for their role as agent for Atomic Energy of Canada Limited (AECL) in trying to sell the CANDU nuclear reactor to Argentina and

---

* See Chapter 5: ROOKIES
** See Chapter 6: THE BELGIAN TABLE

South Korea. AECL President L. Lorne Grey admitted at the time that "no one in Canada knows where the money went."

Before Amir left Bolivia, all the relevant background information was forwarded to him at the embassy there. It would give him as much information as possible on whom he was meeting, their strengths and weaknesses — anything headquarters believed would help him. His flights, hotel room, and all the necessary details were arranged from Tel Aviv — even to a bottle of Contreras's favorite French wine, a label listed in his Mossad computer file.

Amir was told to attend a meeting in Santiago, but not to make any commitments.

Headquarters in Tel Aviv had already replied to the Chilean request for secret-police training, saying they would send Amir, an administrative officer, to discuss the project, but taking care not to suggest any commitments one way or the other. The purpose of the meeting, they said, was simply an initial evaluation.

At the airport in Santiago, Amir was met by an official from the Israeli embassy and taken to his hotel. The next day, he met with Contreras and some of his senior personnel. Contreras disclosed that they had some CIA help at the time, but they didn't think the CIA would assist with certain things they needed to do. Basically they wanted to train an internal security unit to handle local terrorism — kidnappings and bombings — and also to protect visiting dignitaries.

Following the meeting, Amir flew to New York to see the MALAT department head in a house the Mossad had secured there. (It was actually being lent to MALAT by another department, "Al," which works exclusively in the United States and has safe houses there, making it more secure to meet there than to fly another man into Chile for a meeting.)

After listening to Amir's detailed description of the meeting, his boss said, "We want something from these guys. Let's suck them in first. Let's start something and then turn around and make our request. We'll give them the end of the rope, and then we'll pull it in."

It was decided that Amir would meet again with Contreras to work out a deal for training the police unit. At the time, such training courses were offered only in Israel. Subsequently, there have been occasions where Israeli instructors were sent abroad, to South Africa and Sri Lanka, for example. But in 1975-76, the policy was to make trainees come to them.

* * *

Training still takes place at a former British air-force base just east of Tel Aviv called Kfar Sirkin. Israel had used it at one time as an officers' training base, then it became a special-services base, used mainly for training foreign services.

The courses usually last between six weeks and three months, depending on the extent of training required. And they are expensive. Israel at the time was charging fees between $50 and $75 a night per trainee, plus $100 a day to pay for the instructors. (The instructors saw no part of that money, of course. They still had to make do on their regular army pay.) There were also charges of $30 to $40 a day per trainee for food, plus about $50 a day for weapons, ammunition, and other incidentals. A unit of 60 trainees, for example, would cost about $300 each a day, for a total of $18,000. For a three-month course, that would be about $1.6 million.

On top of that, they would be charged $5,000 to $6,000 an hour for helicopter rental, and as many as 15 helicopters could be used in a training exercise. Add to that the cost of special ammunition used in training: a bazooka shell, for example, cost about $220 a unit, while heavy mortars were about $1,000 each; anti-aircraft guns, some with as many as eight barrels, can fire thousands of rounds in a few seconds — at between $30 and $40 a shell.

It's pure profit. They make a lot of money on these training operations, even before selling any weapons. Then, since these people are trained using Israeli weapons, when they go back home, they naturally want to buy those weapons and that ammunition to take with them.

Amir told Contreras to choose 60 of his best men for the training program. The command would be set up in three levels: soldiers, sergeants, and commanders, with specific training methods for each level. Three groups of 20 would arrive for basic training. Out of that, the best 20 would go on to command training. From that group would come the sergeants and the higher ranks.

When Amir had laid the entire proposal out for Contreras, without hesitation, the Chilean said, "We'll take it." He also wanted to buy all the equipment his men were going to be trained on, and asked for either a small manufacturing plant to be set up, or a shelf stock of up to six years' supply of ammunition and replacement parts.

Having decided to buy the package, Contreras then began to haggle a bit over the price, at one point offering Amir several thousand dollars as a bribe to lower it. But Amir refused, and Contreras finally accepted the price.

Just before the end of the program's basic-training phase, Amir flew back to Santiago to meet with Contreras.

"The training went very well," Amir told him. "We're just about to pick the men for sergeant training. They were very good. We only had to turn away two of them."

Contreras, who had handpicked the men for training, was pleased.

After chatting about the program for a while, Amir finally said, "Look, there's something we need from you."

"What is it?" asked Contreras.

"The head of an Exocet missile."

"That should be no problem," said Contreras. "You hang around your hotel for a day or two while I make some inquiries. I'll be in touch."

Two days later, Contreras called Amir to a meeting.

"They won't give you one," he said. "I asked, but they won't approve it."

"But this is something we need," said Amir. "We've done you a favor with the training. We were hoping you'd be able to help us out now that we need something."

"Listen," Contreras replied. "I'll get it for you personally. Never mind the official channels. You pay $1 million, in U.S. cash, and you've got it."

"I'll have to get approval for that," said Amir.

"You do that. You know where I am," said Contreras.

Amir called his boss in New York and told him about Contreras's deal. They knew the general could deliver, but the branch head couldn't give the go-ahead on his own, either, so he called Admony in Tel Aviv, and the Mossad, in turn, asked naval intelligence whether the navy was willing to pay $1 million for the missile. They were.

"We've got a deal," Amir told Contreras.

"Fine. You bring a man who knows what we need and we'll go to a naval base here. He can show me exactly what it is you want. Then we'll take it."

An Israeli missile expert from Bamtam, Israel's missile manufacturer in Atlit, a town south of Haifa where the Gabriel missile was developed, was flown in. Because they wanted an actual working missile, he insisted on taking one right off a ship — an active head. This way they could be sure they weren't being duped with a phony head or one that needed repairs, and so was not operational.

On orders from Contreras, the missile was unloaded from the ship and placed on a trailer. The Israelis had already paid the $1 million in advance.

"Is this what you want?" Contreras asked.

After the Israeli naval officer had inspected the missile, Amir said, "Yes, it is."

"Good," Contreras replied. "What we're going to do now is put the head in a crate, secure it with wires and clamps, and take it to a room in Santiago. You can guard it if you want, I don't care. But before you take it, there's something I want."

"What?" said Amir, concerned. "We had a deal. We lived up to our part of the bargain."

"And so will I," said Contreras. "But first, you call your man and you tell him I want to talk to him."

"I don't have to do that. I can talk," said Amir.

"No, you tell your man I want him here. I want to talk to him face-to-face."

Amir had little choice. Clearly, Contreras realized that Amir was relatively junior, and he was pressing to take all the advantage he could. From his hotel room, Amir called his boss in New York, who in turn called Admony in Tel Aviv to explain the situation. That very day, Admony caught a flight to Santiago to meet the Chilean general.

* * *

"I want you to help me build a personal security force," Contreras told him.

"We're already doing that," said Admony. "And your men are doing extremely well."

"No, no. You don't understand. I want a force that can help me eliminate our enemies, wherever they are. Like you do with the PLO. Not all our enemies are in Chile. We want to be able to hit people who are a direct threat to us. There are terrorist groups out there threatening us, just as groups are threatening you. We want to be able to eliminate them.

"Now, we know you have two ways of doing this. You can agree that when a problem arises, your people will do the job. We know, for example, that you were asked by Taiwan to perform this service and that you refused.

"We prefer to use our own men — that you train a group of our men in how to deal with terrorist threats from abroad. You do that, and the missile is yours."

This new wrinkle came as a shocker to both Admony and Amir, and given the nature of the request, Admony told Contreras he'd have to get permission from his own superiors before committing himself.

To do that, Admony returned to Tel Aviv for a top-level meeting in Mossad headquarters. The Mossad was angry that Contreras had added an unexpected rider to the deal. They decided a political decision, not a security decision, was required: that the government would have to rule on whether to give Contreras what he wanted or drop the whole project.

Now, the government was hardly anxious to become involved in this sort of deal, either, so that its decision was the kind that means: "We don't want to know of such things."

A private person would have to be hired to complete the deal. Chosen for the job was the head of a major Israeli insurance company, Mike Harari, the recently retired Mossad department head who had been in charge of the botched Lillehammer hit. As one of dictator Manuel Noriega's most influential advisers, Harari also helped train the Panamanian elite special anti-terror unit, K-7.

In addition to his other attributes for hammering out a deal with the Chilean general, Harari was then in direct business partnership with a large shipping firm, a perfect vehicle for safely, and quietly, transporting the missile head to Israel.

As a Mossad officer, Harari had been head of Metsada, the department in charge of combatants, and its sub-unit, the kidon. He was instructed to tell Contreras he'd teach his special anti-terrorist unit everything he knew. While he may not have taught them everything — he needed Mossad approval for what he did teach, and they prefer to keep some techniques to themselves — he certainly taught them enough to organize a hit against their enemies, real or perceived, abroad. Payment for this training was sent directly to Harari from a slush fund administered by DINA.

This special group were Contreras's people. They weren't an official group at all. He picked them. He paid them. They did his work. Maybe their ways of interrogation even went beyond what was taught, but there is no doubt he got his special unit trained and Israel got its Exocet. Harari taught such torture techniques as electric wire shock, pain points, pressure points, and time endurance. The major goal of interrogation is to get information. But the Chileans gave it a special twist. They seemed to like interrogation just for the sake of it. They often weren't even after information. They just loved inflicting pain.

* * *

On that damp Washington day in September 1976, however, when Letelier took his final drive, no one had the slightest idea that the killer had been trained through the Mossad. The connection was never made. And nobody knew Israel had the Exocet, either.

The Israelis tested the missile head by attaching it to the underbelly of a Phantom jet, hooking up all the outlets to a series of sensors that could be read under various conditions, conducting fly-bys and simulating missile flights. They tested how it was picked up by radar, how it could be tracked by the ships, and how its telemetry worked. The testing process took four months and was conducted by jets flying out of the Hatsrim air base near Beersheba.

12

Checkmate

As a young boy growing up in Syria, Magid had dreamed of one day playing chess on the world circuit. He lived and breathed chess, studied its history, and memorized the moves of the masters.

Magid, a Sunni Muslim, had lived in Egypt since the heady days of the late 1950s, a time when Gamal Abdel Nasser, whose goal was a broadly based, Egyptian-led union of Arabs, headed 1958's formal union of Egypt and Syria into the United Arab Republic.

Now it was the summer of 1985, and Magid had just arrived in Copenhagen, hoping to set up in business as a private investment banker. On his first day there, he noticed a well-dressed man sitting in his hotel lobby studying a chess book and a board. Magid had been late for an appointment and didn't have time to stop. The next day, however, the man was there again. The board was like a magnet for Magid and he walked over to the man, tapped him on the shoulder, and in remarkably good English said, "Excuse me."

"Not now, not now," the man snapped.

Startled, Magid stood back momentarily, watched quietly for a brief period, then suggested a logical defensive move.

Now the stranger was interested. "Do you know chess well?" he asked.

The two men struck up a conversation. Magid was always thrilled to talk chess, and for the next two and a half hours he and his new-found friend, who had introduced himself as Mark, a Canadian entrepreneur — a Christian of Lebanese background — talked about the game they loved.

Mark, in reality, was Yehuda Gil, one of a pool of katsas stationed in Brussels and assigned to make initial contact with Magid. Not that it was Magid they wanted. It was his brother Jadid, a ministerial-level official with the Syrian military whom they hoped to recruit. They had tried once before in France, but time had been too short and it hadn't worked. As with most of these operations, however, Jadid hadn't even known the attempt was made — and certainly didn't know that the Mossad had given him the code name "Corkscrew."

* * *

This story actually began on June 13, 1985, when a katsa named Ami, on duty at the Danish desk on the seventh floor of Mossad headquarters in Tel Aviv (then at the Hadar Dafna Building on King Saul Street) received a routine message from the Mossad liaison officer in Denmark. He was forwarding a request from "Purple A," the code name for the Danish Civil Security Service (DCSS), for a check to be run on a list of about 40 people with Arabic names and/or backgrounds applying for visas either to visit Denmark or to move there.

What the Danish public does not know — and only a few Danish government officials do know — is that the Mossad routinely checks all these applications on Denmark's behalf, putting a checkmark next to the name on a copy of the Danish visa application if there is no problem with the applicant. When there is a problem, they either tell the Danes or, if it's to Israel's advantage, hold back the application for further study.

The relationship between the Mossad and Danish intelligence is so intimate as to be indecent. But it's not the Mossad's virtue that is compromised by the arrangement; it's Denmark's. And that's because the Danish are under the mistaken impression that because they saved a lot of Jews in World War II, the Israelis are grateful and they can trust the Mossad.

For example, a Mossad man, a marats, sits right in DCSS

headquarters monitoring all Arabic and Palestinian-related messages coming into their listening department — an extraordinary arrangement for a foreign intelligence service. As the only Arabic-speaking man there, he understands the messages, but sends the tapes to Israel for translation (everything goes through a liaison code-named "Hombre" in the Mossad's open station in Copenhagen). This information is not always shared with Denmark when the transcripts, often heavily edited, are returned. The original tapes are not returned by the Mossad.

Clearly the Mossad does not hold the Danes in high esteem. They call them *fertsalach*, the Hebrew term for a small burst of gas, a fart. They tell the Mossad everything they do. But the Mossad doesn't let anybody in on its secrets.

Normally, checking 40 names through the Mossad computer would take about an hour. But it happened to be Ami's first time dealing with the Danes, so he began by calling up the DCSS information on his computer terminal. Up popped a letter numbered 4647, marked "secret," a detailed description of the Danish security service's functions, personnel, and even some operations.

Once every three years, Danish intelligence officials go to Israel for a seminar conducted by the Mossad to discuss the latest developments in terrorist activities and anti-terrorism techniques. Through this relationship, Israel receives a complete picture of the 500-strong Palestinian community in Denmark and receives "total cooperation on subject of dance (following people) coordinated when needed with Purple."*

The letter listed Henning Fode, then 38, as head of DCSS, appointed in November 1984 and scheduled to visit Israel in the fall of 1985. Michael Lyngbo was second-in-command, and although he lacked intelligence experience, he handled the Soviet bloc for the organization. Paul Moza Hanson was legal adviser to Fode, the Mossad's contact man, who was scheduled to finish his term shortly. Halburt Winter Hinagay was head of the department of anti-terrorism and subver-

* See APPENDIX II

sion. He, too, had taken part in the last seminar on terrorism held in Israel.

(In fact, the Mossad holds a series of such seminars, inviting one intelligence service at a time, and consequently generating valuable contacts while perpetuating the notion that no organization deals with terrorism better than they do.)

Another document on Ami's computer screen showed the full name of Denmark's overall intelligence service: *Politiets Efterretingsjtneste Politistatonen* (PEP). It listed a series of departments.

Telephone tapping comes under Department S: in an August 25, 1982, document, the Danes had told Hombre they were planning a new computer system and could afford to give the Mossad 60 "listenings" (60 locations where they actually installed listening devices for the Mossad). They had also installed a number of listening devices in public telephones "at our (Mossad) suggestion in areas known to be sensitive to subversive activities."

The head of service had to hold the rank of what was called detective inspector — a district-attorney level in Israel. The Mossad report went on to complain that their following unit was of poor quality: "Their people are easy to detect. They do not blend in well, probably due to high rotation of personnel in that unit . . . about two years and they go to different jobs."

The police were responsible for recruiting people for the service, but that was difficult to do since there was little room for promotion. On July 25, 1982, Hombre asked about a North Korean secret operation in Denmark, but was told it was being done for the Americans, so "don't ask again."

Still searching his computer for more information, Ami pulled up a sheet called "Purple B," which detailed the Danish Defense Intelligence Service (DDIS), the intelligence arm of the Danish military under direct orders from the head of the army and the defense minister. The service is structured into four units: management, listening, research, and gathering.

For NATO, its job is covering Poland and East Germany and the movement of Soviet ships in the Baltic, with the help of sophisticated electronic equipment supplied by the Americans.

Internally, it is responsible for military and political research, "positive" gathering within Danish borders (information from Danish citizens about what they have seen), as opposed to "negative," which would be getting information from outside the borders. It also handles international liaison and gives national assessments to the government. At that time, it was planning to set up a unit to handle Middle East concerns (beginning with one man working on it one day each week).

The service is renowned for its sharp photographs of Soviet air, ground, and sea activities. It was the first intelligence service to supply Israel with pictures of the Soviet SSC-3 system (or surface-to-surface missiles). Purple B had been headed by Mogens Telling since 1976. He had visited Israel in 1980. Ib Bangsbore was head of the human section, slated to retire in 1986. The Mossad had good sources within the DDIS and also within the Danish Defense Research Establishment (DDRE). Danish intelligence also worked more closely with Sweden (code-named "Burgundy") than it did with its NATO partner, Norway. On occasion, Purple B met with "carousel," the code name for British intelligence, working with them on a case-by-case basis and cooperating in several operations against Russian intelligence.

Ami would retrieve all this information and read it before calling up a reference form, which entails feeding available information into the computer: a name, a number, whatever he had, for a search of the computer's memory bank. If the person in question was Palestinian, and no information appeared on the screen, Ami would transfer the form to the Mossad's Palestinian desk. They might want to check further or simply store the name in the Mossad computer. All Mossad departments are connected to one giant computer in Tel Aviv headquarters. Each night, a hard disk copy of the entire day's information is taken out and put in a safe place.

Ami was just four names from the end of the file he was checking when Magid's name popped up. The family name rang a bell. Ami had been chatting with a friend in the research department earlier and had seen a photo of a man with that name standing next to Syrian President Hafez al-Assad. Many Arab names are similar, but it's always worth checking. There was nothing on the computer regarding Magid, so Ami called research and asked his friend on the Syrian desk to bring a copy of the photo to lunch in the ninth-floor dining room so that he could compare it with Magid's on the Danish visa form.

After lunch, with the photo of Jadid on hand, Ami searched the computer for more details, checking whether Jadid had any relatives, which is how he discovered that he did have a brother whose description and history matched Magid's.

This opened the possibility of a "lead": recruiting one person to get at another, so Ami wrote his report and placed it in the daily internal mail. In the meantime, the Danish form would be attached to the file with no reply on it, meaning the Danes would assume there was no problem with the visa application, or the Mossad would have let them know.

In Tsiach, the Mossad's annual book of "need to know information," Syrian military data has remained a top priority for many years. As a result, the Mossad had AMAN, Israeli military intelligence, prepare a list of what they needed to know about Syrian military preparedness, graded from the most important on down. The AMAN's resulting 11-page questionnaire* included: the number of available Syrian battalions; the status of Armored Brigades 60 and 67 and of Mechanized Brigade 87; the number of brigades in Special Forces Division 14; and a whole series of related questions, such as details of the then-rumored replacement of Ahmad Diab, head of office for national security, by Fefat Assad, President Assad's brother.

The Mossad already had a number of sources in place in Syria — what they called their early-warning system — in hospitals and in construction work, for example, wherever people could obtain and pass on snippets of information that cumulatively could tip Israel off about war preparations.

* See: APPENDIX III for full questionnaire

For their part, the Syrians have been in an attack formation for years along the Golan Heights, so that current and reliable military intelligence has always been considered crucial — and recruiting a high-level Syrian source would be viewed as a major event.

The Mossad considers Syria a "whim" country. Simply put, this means that since it is run by one man, Assad, he can wake up one morning and say, "I want to go to war." The only way to find out quickly if that happens is to have a source as close to the top as possible. At the time, the Mossad knew he wanted to take back the Golan Heights. Assad knew he could gain ground with a quick strike, but couldn't hold off the Israelis for long; so, for several years in the 1980s, he sought a guarantee from the Russians that they would intervene, through the United Nations or otherwise, to stop any such war quickly. They would not agree, however, so Assad never did send in his tanks.

* * *

This was the delicate situation that made recruiting Magid's brother a top priority, and within hours, Yehuda Gil (Mark to Magid) was heading to Copenhagen to await his man's arrival. Another team was assigned to Magid's hotel room to install the necessary listening and viewing devices — anything to assist in recruiting him and through him, his important brother.

The idea to use a chess game for making initial contact with Magid was Gil's, although it had evolved from a lengthy tension-filled meeting in a Copenhagen safe house.

During Magid's long first conversation with Mark, he must have felt he'd found a friend he could trust. He told Mark most of his life story and suggested they meet for dinner that night. Mark agreed, and returned to the safe house to discuss the upcoming dinner with his colleagues.

Over dinner he would explore what Magid had to offer, how much he knew. In the meantime, Mark would present himself as a wealthy entrepreneur (always a favorite cover story), with access to various buying and selling transactions.

Magid explained that his family was in Egypt and he wanted to bring them to Denmark, although not immediately; he wanted to have a good time first. He was looking for an apartment to rent for the moment; later on, when his wife joined him and they were more established, they'd buy. Mark offered to help, promising to send a real-estate agent over to Magid's hotel the next day. Within a week, Magid had his apartment. And the Mossad bugged it thoroughly, even installing pin-hole cameras in the ceiling.

During the subsequent safe-house session, it was decided that Mark should tell Magid he had to return to Canada on business for a month, which give the Mossad time to use the surveillance equipment to good advantage. They learned that Magid didn't do drugs, but he certainly loved normal sex, and lots of it. His lavish apartment was also cluttered with the latest electronic gadgets: videos, tape players, and such.

Luckily for the Mossad, Magid telephoned his brother twice each week. It soon became clear that Jadid was no angel himself, but was working on some shady money-making deals with Magid. Jadid had been buying considerable quantities of pornographic material in Denmark, for example, and selling it for huge profits in Syria. In one conversation, he told Magid he would be visiting him in Copenhagen in about six weeks.

Armed with that information, Mark set up another meeting with Magid and, playing the role of a senior executive of the Canadian company (never the top boss since that would eliminate buying time to take the proposal to the "boss" — in reality, the safe-house group), he began pushing him harder to try to set up a business deal.

"What we normally do is to give investment assessments to our clients," Mark said. "We advise them whether or not to invest in a country, so we must gather information on that country. We are almost like a private CIA."

Mention of the CIA had no discernible effect on Magid, something that worried the Israelis at first. Since mentioning the CIA to Arabs usually prompts a violently negative response, the Mossad began to fear Magid might have already been recruited by someone else. He hadn't been. He was just a cool customer.

"Naturally," Mark went on, "we're willing to pay for information that will allow us to analyze whether investments are safe — if they can be guaranteed in various parts of the world. We're dealing with big players, you understand, so we've got to have detailed and reliable information, not just something anyone can pick up on the street corner."

As an example, Mark used Iraq, which is known worldwide for its dates. "But would you order dates with the [Iran-Iraq] war on? Only if you knew a shipment could be guaranteed. Then you'd do it. But to know that, you must bring political and military knowledge to the regular market. That's what we do."

Magid was clearly interested. "Look, this is not really my business," he said. "But I know somebody who might interest you. I can introduce you to him. But what's in it for me?"

"Well, we usually offer a finder's fee plus a percentage on whatever we get. It depends on the value of the information, the countries involved. We could be talking a few thousand dollars, or hundreds of thousands. It all depends."

"What countries are you interested in?" asked Magid.

"Right now, we need to know about Jordan, Israel, Cyprus and Thailand."

"How about Syria?"

"Possibly. I'll have to check on that. I'll let you know. Again, much depends on our client's needs and what level the information comes from."

"Okay, you check," said Magid, "but my guy is very high up in Syria."

So the two men agreed to meet again in two days. Mark, still playing a cool hand, told Magid that Syria was of some interest. "It's not our top priority," he told the Arab, "but it could be profitable if the information is really good."

A day earlier, however, Magid had already called his brother to tell him he'd got something important for him and that he should come to Copenhagen even sooner. Jadid readily agreed.

The day after Jadid arrived, Mark met with the two brothers in Magid's apartment. He did not let on that he knew Jadid's position, but asked a series of questions about the sort of information he could expect from him so that he could assess what his company's offer would be. Mark spoke about military matters, but mixed in considerable nonmilitary information to disguise his focus. After a few negotiating sessions — each followed by reports to the safe house — Mark offered a $30,000 finder's fee to Magid, $20,000 a month for Jadid, plus 10 percent, or $2,000 a month for Magid. The first six months would be paid in advance, deposited in a Copenhagen bank account Mark would set up for Jadid. If Jadid came out of Syria after that time with more information, then he'd be paid for the next six months, and so on.

The next step was to teach Jadid how to write secret letters using a special chemically treated pencil. He would send them information by this means on the back of his regular letters to his brother.

They offered to give Jadid the working materials to take back to Syria with him, but he refused, so they agreed to have it all sent to Damascus. "You people really do work like an intelligence agency," he said at one point.

"Definitely," replied Mark. "We even employ ex-intelligence people. The difference is, we're in the game to make money. We only share our information with people who are willing to pay for it and use it for investment purposes."

Mark then had to go over the questions with Jadid. Many oddball questions were thrown in: real-estate values and changes in government departments, for example, always to camouflage the questionnaire so that military questions would not dominate. After several trial runs with the special pencil, and assurances he'd be contacted and told where to pick up the list of questions in Damascus, Jadid seemed satisfied that everything was in order.

Throughout the exercise, the Mossad suspected that both brothers knew they were working for Israel, but the game was kept up in any event. However, because of their suspicions, security for the katsa was upgraded.

While the promise to deliver the goods to Jadid sounds simple enough, in fact, it involved an intricate series of maneuvers to avoid any chance of discovery.

The Mossad made use of a white, or non-Arabic, agent: in this case, one of their favorite carriers, a Canadian UN officer stationed in Naharia, a beach city in northern Israel near the neutral zone separating it from Syria. These officers are free to cross borders at will. The Canadian was paid the standard $500 fee to leave a hollowed-out rock containing the papers at a specific spot at the side of the road to Damascus: exactly five steps from a post with a particular kilometer marking on it.

Once the Canadian had come safely back across the border, a Mossad combatant picked up the rock, took it to his hotel room, unfastened the false side, and removed questionnaire, pencil, and some of Jadid's money. He checked the whole package at a parcel station, pocketed the claim check, and flew to Italy. From there, he sent the claim check special delivery to Mossad headquarters in Tel Aviv. They, in turn, put it in an envelope and sent the claim check to Magid who, finally, mailed it to his brother.

So it arrived in Jadid's mail as a normal letter from his brother, with no suspicions aroused. Soon, the letters started coming back, as Jadid went studiously through the detailed questionnaire, telling the Israelis everything they wanted to know about Syrian military preparedness.

This scheme worked well for about five months, with the Mossad convinced they had an unwitting accomplice in high places for a long time to come. Then, as happens all too often in the intelligence business, things changed.

While the Syrians had no idea Jadid was spying for the Israelis, they had been growing increasingly suspicious that he was involved in pornography and drugs. To make sure, they would set him up: Jadid would be arrested by Syrian police carrying a shipment of heroin from Lebanon as he was leaving the country on a trip to several European capitals. He was to be part of a team that would audit the books that recorded the military operations of several Syrian embassies.

Ironically, Jadid was saved from being caught by the greed

of another Syrian, a man named Haled, who was assistant military attaché at the country's London embassy. Haled had been recruited by the Mossad in an earlier operation and was selling them the embassy code, which changed every month. So it was they could read all messages to and from Syrian embassies worldwide.

One of those messages tipped them off that Jadid was scheduled to be part of the audit team. But another message, sent from Damascus to Beirut, said Jadid would be arrested for smuggling heroin out of the country. The message had serious ramifications for both Jadid and Haled.

The Mossad had to get a message to Jadid. With only three days left before the bust was planned, they sent a combatant in, posing as an English tourist. From his hotel room, the man phoned Jadid, telling him simply that there had been a hitch and he was not to go to the planned meeting with the dealers or pick up the shipment. It would be delivered to him after he arrived at his destination in Holland.

When the dealers did arrive for the meeting, the police were not far behind, and made several arrests. Now Jadid was wanted by the dope dealers, too: they naturally assumed he had set them up.

At the time, Jadid knew nothing about all this. So when he arrived in Holland and was still not contacted about the deal, he called Syria to find out what had happened. It was then he learned that he was suspected by both the government and the dope dealers and had best not return home. So it was that after pumping him for any more information he had — it was considerable — the Mossad set him up with a new identity and relocated him in Denmark, where he still lives.

* * *

In London, Haled was a different story. When auditors arrive, they put a black-out order on an embassy, meaning no communication is allowed with other embassies until it is lifted. As with that of most countries, the Syrians' military side was an operation separate from the diplomatic side of the embassy. As assistant military attaché, Haled had free access to the military safe, access he'd used to "borrow" $15,000 to buy a new car. Though he had planned to repay the "loan" from his regular monthly Mossad check, he hadn't counted on a surprise audit.

Fortunately for Haled, the Mossad knew about the audit. But just to be safe, his katsa called Haled on his private number at the embassy, using his regular code name and message to set up a meeting. Haled would know that the signal meant meeting at a certain restaurant — changed regularly to avoid detection — at a prearranged time. He would know that he must wait there 15 minutes; if his katsa didn't show, that was the signal to phone a certain number. If there was no answer, it meant he was to go to another prearranged meeting spot — almost always a restaurant. But if Haled was being tailed, or there was any reason to avoid either meeting place, the katsa would answer the phone call and give him separate instructions.

In this case, there was no problem with the first restaurant: the katsa met Haled, told him a team of auditors was coming the next day, and left when Haled assured him there was nothing to worry about. Or so he thought . . .

An hour later, with the katsa back in the safe house writing his report, Haled phoned the special number he'd been given. Though he didn't know it, he was calling a number inside the Israeli embassy (each embassy has several "unlisted" lines). His message in code would have been something like: "Michael is calling Albert." When the man taking the call punched the code into his computer, it showed the request for an emergency meeting. Haled, a colonel by rank, had never used the emergency code in his three years on the Mossad payroll; according to Israel's psychological reports on him, he was extremely stable. Something was obviously wrong.

Since they knew Haled's katsa was still in the safe house, a bodel was sent to him. After making sure he wasn't being followed, the bodel phoned the safe house with a coded message, such as: "I'll meet you at Jack's place in 15 minutes." Jack's place might be a particular pay phone arranged in advance.

The katsa immediately left the safe house and, after completing a route to make sure he wasn't being followed, went to the designated pay phone to call the bodel who, in turn, told him in code that Haled wanted to meet him at a particular restaurant.

At the same time, the other two katsas on duty at the embassy left, did their route, then went to the restaurant to make sure it was clean. One went inside and the other to a prearranged spot so that Haled's katsa could meet him and find out just what was going on. Because Haled was a Syrian and the Mossad did not yet know what was wrong, this meeting was considered dangerous. After all, at the meeting with his katsa only an hour earlier, everything seemed fine.

After speaking with the man stationed outside, Haled's katsa phoned the restaurant and asked to speak with him — by his code name — telling him to go to yet another restaurant for the meeting. The katsa inside the restaurant made sure Haled didn't phone anyone before he left for the new location.

Normally, an operation like this would not have been handled by the on-duty katsas, but because this was an emergency, they used a "station work-out" to arrange the meeting: meaning simply that katsas from the station did the work.

When the two men finally met, Haled was pale and trembling. He was so frightened that he defecated in his pants, making a dreadful smell.

"What's wrong?" the katsa demanded. "We just met and everything was fine."

"I don't know what to do. I don't know what to do!" Haled kept repeating.

"Why? Calm down. What's the problem?"

"They're going to kill me," he said. "I'm a dead man."

"Who is? Why?"

"I put my life on the line for you. You've got to help me."

"We'll help you. But what's the problem?"

"It's my car. It's the money for the car."

"Are you crazy? You've called me in the middle of the night because you want to buy a car?"

"No, no, I've got the car."

"Well, what's wrong with the car?"

"Nothing. But I took the money for the car from the safe in the embassy. You told me they were going to check. Tomorrow morning I'll go to work and they're going to kill me."

Haled hadn't been worried initially because he had a wealthy friend who'd bailed him out of temporary jams before. He'd anticipated borrowing the money only for a couple of days while the auditors were there; after they left, he could take it out again, repay his friend, then gradually replace the "loan" from his Mossad retainer. But Haled discovered that his friend was out of town. Now he had no way to raise that kind of money overnight and replace it in the embassy safe. He told his katsa he wanted an advance. "I'll pay it back over six months. That's all I want."

"Listen, we're going to solve it. Don't worry. But I need to talk to somebody first."

Before the katsa left with Haled, he called his colleague at the pay phone, giving him a coded message that meant he must go quickly to a nearby hotel and reserve a room under a prearranged name. Once in the hotel room, the katsa sent Haled to the bathroom to clean up.

In the meantime, because of the emergency, the station went on "daylight," and Haled's katsa called the station head at the safe house, outlining the problem in general terms and requesting $15,000 in cash. Technically, anything over $10,000 had to be cleared through Tel Aviv, but in this emergency the station head approved it, telling the katsa he'd meet him in 90 minutes and adding, "It's your ass if it doesn't work."

The station head knew a sayan who operated a casino and always had large amounts of cash on hand (they'd used him before and usually repaid him the next day), so he borrowed the money. The sayan even gave him $3,000 extra, saying, "Maybe you'll need it."

In the meantime, the station's second-in-command happened to be meeting with an attack katsa named Barda, who was in London on another assignment. Barda, posing as an officer from Scotland Yard, had recruited the two night guards at the Syrian embassy when preparing for another operation that had involved breaking into the embassy.

Now that they had the money, the problem was putting it back in the safe before morning. Haled, who knew the combination and could make up some excuse for being in the embassy at night if he was seen, was assigned that task.

Barda, for his part, arranged meetings with first one guard, then the other, at different restaurants (each thought the other was still on duty), leaving the way clear for Haled to return the money.

Afterward, back in the hotel room, Haled's katsa told him the money was not an advance (they reasoned that if they paid him an advance he would have no motive to cooperate), but that $1,000 a month would be deducted from his retainer for the next 15 months.

"If you bring something special, we'll double the bonus so that you can pay it off more quickly," the katsa told him. "But if you do anything illegal at the embassy again, I'll kill you."

Obviously Haled believed him, as he should have. It seems he hasn't "borrowed" a penny since.

13

Helping Arafat

IT WAS A BUSTLING YEAR, 1981. The same day that Ronald Reagan was sworn in as U.S. president, Iran released 52 hostages after 444 days in captivity. On March 30, John Hinckley shot Reagan. In Poland, Solidarity hero Lech Walesa was pursuing freedom, a pursuit that would help to open the door for the massive political changes in Eastern Europe at the end of the decade. In London, on a bright July 29 morning, Prince Charles and Lady Diana Spencer captured the hearts of romantics and royalty buffs everywhere with a wedding broadcast around the world. In Spain, Basque terrorists fought pitched battles with government authorities. And in Washington, CIA director William Casey was under pressure to resign for supporting failed clandestine efforts to assassinate Libyan strongman Moamer al Kadhafi and for appointing his political crony, Max Hugel, as head of the CIA's clandestine operations, even though Hugel had no apparent qualifications for the job. Hugel himself resigned under pressure on July 14 when two former business associates accused him of illegal stock manipulation.

Inside Israel, it was a tumultuous year even by that country's standards. In 1980, inflation had hit 200 percent and was still spiralling so fast, there was one joke that you could buy some cottage cheese with six price increases pasted on the package and the cheese would still be fresh. Now that's inflation!

Prime Minister Menachem Begin, 67, and his ruling Likud Party were facing a severe political challenge from Shimon Peres, 57, and his Labor Party, further complicated by the fact that one of Begin's ministers, Abu Hatsrea, had been caught in an election payoff scandal and sent to jail. The June 29 election, in fact, ended in a 48-48 tie, but Begin was able to enlist the help of some splinter parties to build a bare majority of 61 in the 120-member Knesset.

Shortly before that, on June 7, Israel had provoked the ire of the United States by attacking and destroying an Iraqi nuclear plant,* and the Americans had clamped a temporary embargo on the shipment of F-16s to Israel, even supporting a UN resolution condemning the attack. Israel also stepped up its attacks in Lebanon and, for a time in late July, appeared headed for all-out war against Syria. U.S. special envoy Philip Habib, a retired career diplomat of Lebanese descent, was hopping around the Middle East trying to negotiate agreement on a peace plan. U.S. State Department counsellor Robert McFarlane was sent to see Begin in July to attempt to get him to rein in his war machine.

For the Mossad, this wasn't all bad. The one thing they didn't want to happen was to see peace breaking out all over. So, there was a lot of activity designed to prevent serious negotiations — yet another example of how dangerous it is to have such an organization with no one to answer to.

For Yassar Arafat and his PLO, it wasn't a quiet year, either. In 1974, Arafat had denounced terrorist acts by his organization outside the borders of Israel, chiefly in Europe. And while Palestinian terrorism did continue in Europe, it was conducted by a variety of factions opposed to Arafat. Indeed, outside the occupied territories, Arafat is not that powerful in the Palestinian movement. His strength derives from the West Bank and Gaza Strip where, except with Muslim fundamentalists, he enjoys overwhelming personal popularity.

* See PROLOGUE: OPERATION SPHINX

One of Arafat's biggest problems was the Black June Organization (BJO) headed by Sabri Al Banna, better known as Abu Nidal. The BJO, who are Palestinian Muslims, have a religious fervor that makes them more dangerous than many of the other factions. This organization had nearly been wiped out by a combined force of Syrians and Lebanese Christians in the late 1970s, but Nidal had survived, under a death sentence from Arafat. Any Palestinian deaths that couldn't be pinned on Israel were blamed on Abu Nidal, considered the bad boy of the terrorist world.

It was the BJO's attempted assassination of Shlomo Argové, Israel's ambassador to London, in 1982, that Israel used as an excuse to launch a full-scale war against Lebanon. Begin called it the "War of Choice," meaning that Israel had entered this war not because it had to — as with all its previous wars — but because it chose to. It may have been a poor choice, but Begin's own demagoguery got in the way. In any event, the attempt on Argové left him alive but essentially in a vegetable state. And it was blamed on Arafat, even though he had nothing to do with it.

Before the Argové affair, Israel had negotiated an under-the-table unofficial ceasefire with Arafat's PLO to get them to stop firing their Russian-made Katyusha rockets from southern Lebanon into Israel, a deal that was made to appear as if it was a unilateral one on behalf of the PLO. Arafat was charging around to various East Bloc countries at the time shoring up his support. The Mossad knew he was going to attempt to purchase a large supply of light weapons in Europe and have them shipped to Lebanon. The question was why? After all, he could just go to Czechoslavakia, for example, and say he wanted weapons. They'd say, "Sign here," and send everything he needed. It was like living by a fountain but walking five miles down the road to get water. If you don't explain that the fountain is salt water, it makes no sense.

Arafat's salt water was a 20,000-strong force of well-trained fighting men called the Palestinian Liberation Army, or PLA, headed by Brigadier General Tariq Khadra, who in 1983 would denounce Arafat as PLO leader and formally withdraw his support. This army was attached to the Syrian army, prompting a saying within the Mossad that the "Syrians will fight Israel to the last Palestinian."

The East Bloc countries, always willing to supply the Palestinians with weapons, nonetheless dealt through formal channels. That meant for them that, in 1981, if Arafat wanted weapons they would be sent to the PLA.

That was fine as far as it went. But after the Munich massacre in 1972, Arafat had formed a special personal security force. At PLO headquarters in Beirut, Arafat could reach his special force on telephone extension 17. Hence, the name of this unit became Force 17, at the time headed by Abu Tayeb, and varying in number between 200 and 600 crack fighters. Arafat also relied heavily on Abu Zaim, his head of security and intelligence.

* * *

For the Mossad, the most important player in all of this was a man named Durak Kasim, Arafat's driver and personal bodyguard and member of Force 17. Kasim had been recruited as a Mossad agent in 1977 when he was studying philosophy in England. A greedy man, he was reporting to them almost daily, sending messages through a burst radio communications system, receiving $2,000 a report. He also telephoned information and mailed it periodically, and once even showed up at the "submarine" — the Mossad's underground station in Beirut — a reckless thing to do, and a rude shock to his operator that Kasim would know the address. During the siege of Beirut, Kasim was actually with Arafat, reporting to the Mossad from inside PLO headquarters.

Kasim was Arafat's closest personal aide. He was the one who helped find boys for Arafat. Certainly homosexuality is against Islamic beliefs, but given the way of life, it's not that uncommon. It's not as badly regarded as it is in the West. The Mossad didn't actually have any proof to support the claim that Arafat liked teenage boys. They had no photos, nothing. It could have been just another way to discredit Arafat; they did that with many other Arab leaders, saying how they lived the good life by skimming off the system. But they couldn't say that about Arafat. He actually lives a humble life, with his people. During the siege of Beirut he had many opportunities to escape but he didn't leave until he got his people out, so the Mossad can't claim that he operates out of self-interest, either. Perhaps they used the story about him liking teenage boys as a substitute.

At the time, however, the right-wingers in the Mossad were pushing to have Arafat killed. Their argument was that if they assassinated Arafat, the Palestinians would replace him with someone more militant who would not be acceptable to the West, or to the left in Israel, and therefore there would be no peaceful solution to the problem. Violent clashes and ultimately unconditional surrender were the only way the Mossad could conceive of achieving peace.

The argument against killing Arafat is that he is the best of a bad lot, an educated man, a uniting force among the Palestinians, so that if talks do get somewhere, there will be someone to talk with who legitimately represents the Palestinians. Through intelligence in Israel, both the Mossad and the Shaback know that Arafat is widely respected and yes, revered, in the territories, although they do not transfer that picture to their political superiors.

By mid-1986, this debate was just about over. The right was winning. But Arafat had become too much of a public figure. The Mossad didn't have an excuse to get him. But it's still not off the agenda. The moment it's feasible, they'll do it.

Another major player at this time was Mostafa Did Khalil, known as Abu Taan, head of the Palestinian Armed Struggle Command (PASC), Arafat's coordination group. It used to be called the Palestinian Coordination Council, but after Arafat denounced the use of force outside Israel in 1974, many of the PLO organizations adopted more militant, bombastic names for internal use, to avoid any suggestion they were going soft.

Another group to be kept in mind was the Arab Liberation Front (ALF) headed by Abdel Wahab Kayyale. He was assassinated in Beirut in December 1981 and replaced by Abdel Rahim Ahmad, his second-in-command.

In any event, Arafat wanted small arms to expand Force 17. The inevitable power struggles were going on within the organization, and Arafat felt he needed more personal fire-power. But when he asked General Khadra, the army chief of staff, he was turned down. Khadra told Arafat not to worry, he'd protect him. Arafat worried.

It was because Khadra controlled the weaponry coming in from the East Bloc to the PLO that all the factional organizations went through other Arab countries, such as Libya and Iraq, to obtain their weapons from the East.

On January 17, 1981, Arafat flew to East Berlin to meet East German President Erich Honecker, who gave him 50 German "advisers" to help train PLO people in Lebanon. On January 26, Arafat again met East German representatives, this time in Beirut, and again asked for weapons, trying to arrange a quiet deal without going through Khadra. Thanks to constant reports from Kasim, the Mossad knew Arafat was deeply worried about problems from within and a possible Israeli attack.

On February 12, Arafat met Vietnamese representatives in Damascus, trying to arrange a deal. They offered missiles, but he wanted small arms. Three days later, he went to Tyre, Lebanon, for a meeting with the heads of various PLO factions, trying to persuade them to stop fighting each other and concentrate on the real enemy, Israel. By March 11, Arafat was becoming increasingly nervous, hoping to get a commitment before the April 15 general PLO meeting in Damascus. On that single day in Beirut he held three separate meetings with the ambassadors from Hungary, Cuba, and Bulgaria, but still failed to obtain any specific commitments.

The Mossad was by now very nervous itself, assuming that eventually Arafat would get his weapons. What really spooked them was that the PLO leader was beginning to say he wanted to have someone meet with Israeli diplomats on his behalf to begin negotiations toward stopping an attack on Lebanon. The Mossad knew the big secret long before the Israeli government did, which was usually the case.

On March 12, Arafat met in Beirut with Naim Khader, the

PLO's representative in Belgium, asking him to use his connections there with the Israeli foreign office to get negotiations under way and avoid more bloodshed. The Mossad was very anxious about this. The idea was that if they could get Israel involved in Lebanon to help the Christians, then they could wipe out the Palestinians there. But if the Mossad started talking, they wouldn't get that chance. There was a real undercurrent between them and the foreign office. The foreign office didn't know this, but the Institute was trying to get the war started, at the same time that they were busy trying to avoid it. The Palestinians were trying to find a lead to the Israeli diplomats, and the Mossad was trying to cut it off.

At the same time, the Mossad had learned that Arafat would try to make use of François Ganud, then a 65-year-old Geneva banker and financial supporter of Carlos's. Arafat's idea, passed along to the Mossad by Kasim, was to get the money from Ganud to buy weapons in Germany with the help of a group called the Black Bloc, an offshoot of the Red Army Faction (RAF), who in February had received training in Lebanon from the German advisers sent by Honecker.

The Mossad was not happy with U.S. envoy Philip Habib's apparent progress in his peace mission, so their idea was to involve the CIA, telling them the PLO was preparing for war while they were talking about peace, in the hopes that this would kill the initiative, or at the very least stall it. At the time, Begin was running for re-election and had no knowledge of the Mossad plans. The military operation already had a name, "Cedars of Lebanon," and they had begun feeding information to CIA liaison. But on March 30, with John Hinckley's attempted assassination of President Reagan, the CIA became distracted, and that part of the operation was put on hold.

On April 10, Arafat was again meeting Honecker in East Berlin. The next day he was in Damascus at the fifteenth session of the Palestinian Council.

On May 15, the Mossad contacted the German anti-terrorist unit, GSG-9 (*Grenzschutzgruppe*), which they wanted to bring into the operation for future use.

On June 1, nearly three months after his meeting with Arafat, Naim Khader made an early morning telephone call from his home to an official in the Israeli foreign office in Brussels arranging a meeting for June 3 to explore the possibility of getting peace talks started. On his way to work, a dark-complexioned man wearing a tan jacket and sporting a pencil mustache walked up to Khader, shot him five times in the heart and once in the head, walked off the curb, climbed into a passing "taxi," and disappeared. Although Arafat didn't know it then, the Mossad had struck.

Nevertheless, Kasim was reporting that Arafat was extremely agitated at this time. He couldn't sleep at night. He was run ragged. He wanted protection and really wanted to get the arms deal for Force 17 under way.

At the beginning of July, there was a series of demonstrations in Germany against U.S. missiles stationed there. On July 9, Arafat was in Belgrade, Yugoslavia, still pursuing his goal of getting weapons. About the same time, an Argentine plane coming from Israel and loaded with armaments for Iran, crashed into a Russian plane over Soviet airspace. The Americans, angered by the Israelis' selling of arms to Iran, sent Robert McFarlane over to meet with Begin, an event that signaled the beginning of the Iran-Contra affair, which would blow up publicly several years later.*

At the same time, the Syrians had brought missiles into Lebanon, precipitating another crisis, and Lebanese strongman Bashir Gemayel was warning Syria that this could lead to all-out war.

The Syrians, incidentally, are always switching their military support in Lebanon from one group to another based on what they call the "balance of weakness." They believe that if one of the fighting factions gets strong, they should back another group to fight it. That way, they keep everyone down and exercise overall control of the situation.

The Mossad was still trying to con the Americans, and Mossad head Yitzhak Hofi ordered the LAP department to

---

* See Chapter 17: BEIRUT

concoct a scenario to convince them that the PLO was planning war, not peace. The idea was to justify to the United States an Israeli takeover of southern Lebanon.

LAP produced photographs of all the armament depots of General Khadra's PLA. Since they were a unit of the Syrian army, it was hardly surprising that they had armaments depots for their supplies, but it served to provide convenient "evidence" that the PLA was preparing to attack Israel, even though the Mossad knew about Arafat's frantic efforts to avoid a war.

LAP also showed the CIA documents that had been captured from the PLO, showing actual attack plans of northern Israel. Again, this is neither unusual nor necessarily indicative of an impending attack. In any military base, you could find such detailed plans. Whether the PLO intended to implement them, or whether they had even been approved, was a different matter. But the Mossad had no intention of allowing such considerations to get in the way of their own mischievous plans.

Even before hostilities began, news releases and photographs were being prepared. And afterward it would be easy to come up with documentation to authenticate the "threat" to Israel from the Palestinians.

On instructions from Arafat, Abu Taan, head of his PASC coordination unit, sent two men to Frankfurt to organize the small-arms deal. The man is charge was Major Juad Ahmed Hamid Aloony, a 1969 graduate of the military academy in Algiers, who'd had political training in China during 1978 and 1979, and graduated from a military school in Hungary in 1980. He was joined by Sergeant Abd Alrahaman Ahmed Hassim Alsharif, a 1979 graduate of Cuba's military academy, and of the same school Aloony attended in Hungary.

The Mossad and the federal German police were not on friendly terms. But the GSG-9, who were Israeli-trained, were very cooperative, as were the Hamburg special anti-terrorist police unit, which the Mossad code-named *Tuganim*, or "French Fries."

The Tuganim would provide Mossad people with identification, just as if they were working for them. The Mossad had trained them, after all. They had even helped them interrogate Arabs.

Because the Tuganim were so cooperative, the Mossad wanted to set up the entire operation in Hamburg. As with the federal police, the Mossad's relationship with the central German federal intelligence was poor. But every German district has its own police and intelligence force, so the Mossad connections are directly with those.

The Mossad also knew that Arafat planned to involve Isam Salem, a doctor, who was the PLO representative in East Berlin, in the deal to arrange a loan with the Swiss banker, Ganud, for the small arms needed for Force 17. Ganud had already been placed on standby in the event the PLO needed an interim loan. Since weapons are considered "hot" items, no one wants them around for long, so large interim loans are often necessary to swing deals quickly.

At the same time, Arafat had decided to bring a large shipment of hashish from Lebanon. A group of Black Bloc members, in return for their just-completed training in Lebanon, would transport the hashish and unload it through the European underworld for cash, then give the cash to Isam Salem. He, in turn, would either pay for the weapons or pay back Ganud if interim financing had been required. Arafat also planned to use these Black Bloc members to transfer the arms back to Lebanon.

All this information came to Mossad headquarters through *Yahalomim* ("Diamonds"), the department that handles communication from agents. Once an agent goes to a target country, he is not handled any more by his katsa. Rather, communication between the agent and the Mossad is done through Tel Aviv headquarters.

Armed with this information, the head of Mossad sat down with the heads of Tsomet, Tevel, and security operations to map out their strategy. They had four major objectives: to stop Arafat from getting the weapons; to stop the attempted negotiations between the PLO and Israel's foreign office; to obtain the full load of hashish and dispose of it for cash; and to extract the loan from Ganud, leaving the PLO holding the bag. In addition to the obvious political and strategic benefits of this operation, the Mossad at the time had a serious cash-flow problem, as did the state of Israel, and they were always searching for new sources of revenue.

* * *

To prepare for this giant sting operation, a neviot team was sent to Hamburg in May 1981 to begin setting up a secure dock and warehouse. A katsa from the London station was sent in to start setting up the sting.

About the same time, a team from Metsada was assigned to Naim Khader in Brussels to make sure he did not get serious peace negotiations under way. He was to be taken out. How they planned the hit can only be speculated upon, but it was done in a fashion that was the signature of the Mossad: simple, quick, and total; on the street in broad daylight; the more witnesses the better; all that's left as a calling card are some unmarked shell casings and the body.

The assassin would have used a pistol containing nine bullets, with only six for the hit. From the time the hit was dead to the time the killer got in the car, anybody who tried to stop him would have joined the man on the ground.

It was set up so that Abu Nidal of the BJO would be blamed for the hit, not only by outsiders but by Arafat and the Israeli foreign office, as well. Sure enough, not long after Khader's assassination, stories naming Nidal as the world's most dangerous, and wanted, terrorist appeared in the media.

In Hamburg, the five-man neviot team was headed by Mousa M., a relatively new Mossad man who had come from the Shaback and had a history in Unit 504. They stayed in the exclusive Atlantic Hotel Kempinksi, on Lake Alster in this, West Germany's second-largest city.

The Mossad love Hamburg, first for the good working relationship with the local anti-terrorist police and intelligence, and then for the infamous live sex shows and red-light districts where hookers display their charms in the windows or even by walking naked on the streets. Of course, that was for the evenings. During the day, the team was busy in Hamburg's dockland on the south shore of the Elbe River searching for some suitably obscure warehouses that would give relatively easy access and also allow them to observe and take photographs without being seen.

It was quite a leisurely assignment, because at this time, Arafat still hadn't made his weapon arrangements, so Mousa, who eschewed the sex shows and hookers himself, decided to have a little fun with one of his men. Since it was not yet an actual operation, the men were not doing APAM, their normal operational security. Mousa easily followed one of them to a hotel where the man met a high-class hooker. When his man went to the washroom, Mousa photographed the hooker standing by herself at the bar, then left. The next night, the man met the same hooker and again spent most of the night with her.

The following morning, when he arrived for a meeting at Mousa's hotel room, the other members of the team were already there. Everyone was just sitting around smoking and looking concerned. He could feel the tension in the air.

"What's up?" he asked Mousa.

"We've got an emergency situation here," Mousa replied. "We've got to scour the city. We got a notice from headquarters that a Soviet black agent is masquerading as a hooker and has made contact with a Mossad person. We need to get her and interrogate her, and get him and ship him back to Israel where they'll charge the bastard with treason."

The man was still tired and hung over, but he had no reason to worry. At least not until Mousa gave them all an 8-by-10-inch photograph of the "Soviet agent," at which point his complexion turned positively waxen.

"Can I speak to you a moment, Mousa?" he mumbled.

"Sure, what is it?"

"Ah, privately."

"Yeah, sure."

"Are you certain this is the agent?"

"Yeah, why?"

"When was she seen with the guy?"

"This week, as far as I know," said Mousa. "More than once."

It took several minutes before the man finally confessed

he'd been the one with the hooker, but he insisted he hadn't told her anything and that she hadn't asked him anything. He pleaded with Mousa to believe him and help him. In the end, Mousa just looked straight at him and started to laugh.

That was Mousa. Always waiting with something up his sleeve. Others just hope it wasn't their balls.

Eventually, the team did find a suitable warehouse and Mousa notified the London katsa, saying, "You'd better get this done quickly, so I can get my guys out of here before they catch some kind of disease!"

* * *

Through its relationship with Saudi Arabian billionaire Adnan Khashoggi, who had been recruited as an agent,* the Mossad knew another Saudi who was a legitimate European arms dealer. He had the rights to supply Uzis and other weapons to the private market in Europe. The plan was to get Khashoggi's friend to provide the necessary U.S.-made arms to fill Arafat's order. They would, of course, be presented as having been stolen from various stockpiles at European military bases.

At this time, Mossad katsa Daniel Aitan, using the cover name Harry Stoler, contacted Isam Salem, Arafat's man in East Berlin. Arafat had not even asked him to get the weapons yet, but thanks to Kasim's ongoing communications, the Mossad knew he would soon do so and decided to get in one step ahead.

The German-speaking Aitan, a straightforward individual, presented himself to Salem as "Harry Stoler," a businessman who dealt in what he referred to as "various equipment and materials." Most important of all, he told Salem, he could guarantee good prices and secure delivery. Stoler also told Salem that while he avoided getting into politics, he thought the Palestinian cause was just, and he hoped to see them succeed.

They made another appointment to meet. Even though Salem was PLO and so considered dangerous, they knew he

* See Chapter 17: BEIRUT

was not involved in terrorist activities in Europe. The katsa's safety was therefore not in question, and, indeed, Salem fell for the pitch completely.

At the next discreet meeting — called "a meeting in four eyes," or just the two of them — Stoler mentioned that from time to time he learned of "stray equipment" from U.S. military bases in Germany — items with a short-term life on the outside. He said he could also take orders for such "back door" deliveries if Salem was interested.

In the meantime, the Mossad was assuring GSG-9 that they had tabs on the Black Bloc and would notify them when and where they could be picked up with enough evidence to put them away.

As they knew he would, Arafat finally passed on a request to Salem in East Berlin, carried personally by Major Aloony and Sergeant Alsharif, PASC chief Abu Taan's men. They gave Salem the list of equipment necessary for Force 17, with orders that the deal be done in extreme secrecy, that the equipment come from the West, and that Arafat's two messengers deal directly with Abu Taan. Salem was ordered to contact their friends in the RAF (Black Bloc), or any other known source available to complete the arms deal for Arafat.

"We will be sending first-grade 'tobacco' to be used as currency," the order said. "If needed, we can receive interim financing through Abu Taan.

"The carriers of this letter are fresh in the field and so can be used as go-betweens, and therefore put under your command."

When Salem got the message, he naturally called Daniel Aitan, a.k.a. Harry Stoler. Salem said the deal had to be coordinated quickly and quietly and that he would send a representative (Aloony) with a shopping list of the necessary equipment. He wanted to know how long it would take to fill the order and ship it.

Up to now, the Mossad plan had been to appropriate all the PLO money and their hashish by way of clever dealing, but a new piece of information from Kasim alerted them that Arafat had a backup plan.

He had planned a similar arms order with Ghazi Hussein,

the PLO representative in Vienna, just in case Salem didn't come through. Another unit was immediately sent to Vienna to keep tabs on Hussein. Vienna was a sensitive area for the Mossad because it was the terminal for Russian Jews on their way to Israel. The ties between Israel and Austria at the time were very cordial. For the Mossad, there was nobody there to talk to. The Austrians took their neutrality seriously. They had hardly any security services at all.

The hashish to be brought in by the Black Bloc terrorists was packed in the usual fashion, a series of bales called "soles" because they look like the soles of shoes. The idea was to ship it by sea from Lebanon to Greece, where the Black Bloc would use its customs contacts to load it into cars, with each of the 25 or 30 European terrorists putting some of it in their cars and driving back through Europe to a warehouse in Frankfurt.

One of them was to handle the sale of the hash and deal with Salem. But the GSG-9, tipped off by the Mossad, arrested him on a trumped-up charge of subversive activities aimed at U.S. bases. The Germans were not told about the hash, but once they had the man in custody, the Mossad was allowed to interrogate him. A German-speaking Mossad man, posing as German security, managed to extract the name of his second-in-command by offering to cut a deal. Then they arranged with the Germans that the man would be held incommunicado until the "deal" was wrapped up.

"I know about the dope," the Mossad man told the prisoner. "If you don't tell me who to deal with, you'll spend the rest of your life here, not because of subversive activities, but for dealing in hash."

And so, with Arafat's shopping list in hand, the Mossad went to Khashoggi's Saudi dealer friend to fill the order. Aloony, a military man, was told he would be responsible for checking the equipment and making sure it was sealed for delivery to Lebanon.

The weapons were brought by truck to Hamburg. The Mossad didn't tell the Germans. But if we had happened to meet them, we would have explained.

In the meantime, Stoler was talking to Salem about a Bei-

rut address to ship the arms to. The idea was just a shot in
the dark; at that stage the Mossad did not expect the sting to
reach the stage of an actual shipment. But Stoler told Salem
the shipment would need a cover of some sort because it
had to go through Lebanese customs. In these affairs, such
arrangements are wise, simply to make a deal look "legitimate." As for Salem, he said he had a relative in Beirut in the
raisin business who might give them a shipping address.

"Raisins from Germany?" said Stoler. "Isn't that like bringing strudel from Senegal?"

Not exactly. It seems there is some exporting of packaged
raisins and other dried fruits that come into Germany in
large quantities and are then shipped out again at a better
price than Greece and Turkey can offer.

So Stoler asked Salem to get him a "legitimate" raisin
order. "That way, I can get things rolling," he added.

The idea of this exchange was to get Salem to do as much
of the planning as possible so he would not realize he was
being led. Next, Stoler said he had no ship available, but
Salem told him that would be no problem because it would
be a container shipment, meaning simply one extra container joining a shipment to Lebanon.

In the meantime, a Mossad liaison man passed on information from Tsomet to another katsa planning to make contact
with the second-in-command from the Black Bloc. He met the
man, telling him his jailed colleague got a message delivered
to him through mutual contacts in jail. He said the plans had
changed. Instead of selling the hashish, it would be exchanged for arms.

The deadline was approaching. The Mossad had already
ordered the weapons and they knew Salem would have to
get his money through Abu Taan, since now he couldn't get
it from the hashish. The Mossad was gaining control of that.
Salem wouldn't have been worried. He knew he could get the
interim loan, and *thought* he could pay it back once the hash
was sold. In addition, the Mossad promised the Black Bloc
some missiles, and planned to deliver some dummies — the
plastic, display-style that look exactly like real missiles but
won't fire because there's nothing inside them.

The pieces were falling together nicely in Hamburg and Frankfurt, but Ghazi Hussein in Vienna was still a problem. Fortunately, however, he had called Salem when he got the arms order from Arafat. While he'd never admit it to Arafat, he told Salem he had no contacts in this area of activity. Salem said he knew someone who might be able to help. They both knew they shouldn't be liaising on this, but what could they do?

* * *

Mossad security was pulling its collective hair out. Here they were, in the midst of a big operation with the ever-treacherous PLO — and with no security at all. But apart from holding meetings in open courtyards or cafés, and avoiding any closed-door meetings with the PLO men, there wasn't much they could do under the circumstances except complain a lot and send messages that condemned such unsecured activities, saying they would accept no responsibility should anything go wrong.

By the beginning of June, the plan had pretty well taken shape. It takes time to gather weapons, but while they were waiting, everyone was getting nervous. In late June, both Hussein in Vienna and Salem in East Berlin notified Arafat that his request had been met and would be ready within two or three weeks.

In the meantime, Major Aloony was becoming rather nervous about the money he'd been expecting from the hash deal. He hadn't heard from the contacts. Nor did he know who, or where, they were. The only contact Aloony had was the address and phone number of one of the Black Bloc men. But the leader was in jail and his second-in-command had been told by the Mossad man posing as a friend to call everybody in the unit and tell them that, in case anybody made inquiries, they were trading hash for arms. If they had any problems at all, or if anybody called about them, they were to call him immediately.

When Aloony finally called his contact, he was told the Black Bloc leader was in jail, but another man was handling the deal. As instructed, Aloony's contact then telephoned the second-in-command. The Mossad katsa working with the Saudi arms dealer was putting pressure on the dealer to obtain the weapons quickly, because someone was rushing them.

Because of Aloony's call, the Mossad knew he was asking questions, but it was no great problem, because he'd got the answer they wanted. The man the Mossad was dealing through assured Aloony it was no problem. Everything was being handled. He had been instructed just to say that, and nothing more, other than that he would let Aloony know as soon as the deal was complete. Aloony understood these deals take time, so he didn't seem unduly concerned. He also knew that in their training camp, the PLO had instilled the fear in the Germans that if they double-crossed the PLO they would be dead, the old saying that you can run, but you can't hide.

It also helped matters that even the PLO players didn't know as much as the Mossad about what was happening. Salem in East Berlin, for example, didn't know the request to Hussein in Vienna was a backup request. It had not been made through Abu Taan, who was dealing with Salem, but by Arafat's personal security chief, Abu Zaim. While Salem knew the weapons were for Arafat's Force 17, Hussein had no idea what they were for.

In any event, the Mossad man in Vienna and Hussein made their own arrangements for payment and delivery of the weapons. Hussein had a way of transporting goods on Libyan aircraft without their being checked; he did not explain how, only that he wanted the arms in containers, which he would then take to Beirut. The plan was to supply him with *some* real weapons; however, as in Hamburg and Frankfurt, all the shoulder-carrying missiles would be dummies.

The key was to ensure that everything was synchronized in Vienna, Hamburg, and Frankfurt. If the plan failed in any of the three locations, it could not only ruin the whole scheme, but create considerable danger.

In Hamburg, where the weapons were stored in one of a series of look-alike warehouses, the plan was to show Aloony and Sergeant Alsharif the weapons, stored in a container with the raisins on the top and the bottom. They would then seal the container, lock the warehouse doors, give Aloony the key, and set up an appointment to bring him there the next morning. The container would then be loaded on a truck and taken to the ship for passage to Beirut.

After taking Aloony back to his apartment, the Mossad would go to the warehouse, take the lock and the number off the door, and put them next door on the look-alike warehouse. There they would completely fill another container with low-grade raisins. That was what Aloony would ship off to Arafat.

Stoler (Aitan) told Aloony to bring the money with him because he wanted several hours to get away. "No problem," said Aloony. "I'll bring the money. But I sleep with the raisins in the warehouse."

"Okay," said Stoler, his heart stopping for a moment. "I'll pick you up tomorrow at 6 p.m."

"But you said in the morning," said Aloony.

"I know, but it's not a good idea to go in there in the daytime with weapons. Too many people around."

With Aitan and the others all back at the safe house, they knew they had a problem. How would they switch the containers in the warehouse if Aloony was sleeping with them?

Meanwhile, a small, single-family house outside Vienna was now loaded with the weapons Hussein had ordered. The katsa notified Hussein that his assistant would make the transaction, asking him to bring $3.7 million to the meeting place, after which he would be given the key to the house and the address. The plan was that they would pick up one of Hussein's men, then take him blindfolded to the house so he could check the equipment. He would be allowed one phone call to Hussein (then they would cut the line), telling him everything was in place. Next he would be locked in, the money would be transferred, and Hussein would be given the address and the key. Hussein bought it.

It was now July 27, 1981, and back in Hamburg they were still wrestling with the Aloony problem. The weapons to be loaded into a container were inside the warehouse. A duplicate container was hoisted high above it, right up to the ceiling, on one of those double-track hoists used to cart heavy equipment and crates. In Geneva, Ganud had already provided about $5 million in interim financing for the Hamburg deal and $3.7 million in Vienna.

At 6 p.m. on July 28, Aloony was picked up and driven to the warehouse. He asked to do a spot check of several cartons. Once he was satisfied, they loaded the goods into the containers, with raisins covering them, and sealed the container. Aloony was ready to hand over the money, but Stoler said, "Not here, there are too many people around. Let's go to the car. It's more private."

While they were in the car, Stoler completed a spot check of his own, using an electronic device on some of the bundles to make sure the U.S. dollars were not counterfeit. As that was going on, the duplicate container hooked onto the chain at the top of the warehouse was quickly lowered, and the container with the weapons was hoisted to the ceiling, hauled along to the back of the warehouse, and dropped behind some other containers.

The whole switch took only about 10 or 15 minutes, but when Aloony came back, he saw what appeared to be the identical container with the identical seal. What he didn't see was its new contents. The next day, his raisins safely stowed, Aloony set sail for Beirut.

After Aloony had left, the Mossad men went into the warehouse, loaded the weapons from the first container onto a truck, and took them back to the dealer. As for the surplus raisins, they were sent off to Israel.

The same night, the deal to trade the hashish for the missiles was completed in Frankfurt, and the Black Bloc man was told to bring his team next day to remove the weapons. The hashish was handed over to a man from Panama's F-7 (the special security unit Harari had trained). The hash was taken to Panama in exchange for a credit of about $7 million. The idea was to sell it on the U.S. market where it commands a much higher price than in Europe. Once the Panamanians sold it, they would give the Mossad the $7 million and keep for themselves whatever profit they made.

The next day, when the Black Bloc members came to pick

up their phony missiles, the police were there waiting for them. About 20 men were arrested that day.

Also on July 29, three men at the Vienna airport, with a partial load of the weapons from the suburban house, were arrested by local police who had been told by the Mossad that Hussein and his helpers had just arrived on a flight from Lebanon and were smuggling weapons into Vienna to hit a Jewish target. Hussein was later deported. His two helpers were jailed. The bulk of the weapons, still at the house, were recovered by the Mossad. They left some behind for the police to discover when they checked out the story that Hussein had been stockpiling them.

In total, the Mossad pocketed between $15 and $20 million and burned a lot of valuable ground. They had Khader killed, Hussein expelled, his two helpers and about 20 Black Bloc terrorists jailed, and the PLO name blackened in a few countries.

The success was wonderful for Mossad morale. Not only did the PLO lose everything, they still owed everything to their banker. For a time, the sting kept Force 17 short of weapons, and it made the PLO feel really stupid. What happened to the raisins that were shipped to Israel remains a mystery.

* * *

A further postscript to this story is the fate of Arafat's driver/bodyguard, Mossad agent Durak Kasim. He lost a leg in an Israeli air attack on a Tunis Palestinian base. He had been reporting from the camp, but wasn't told about the imminent attack. Furious, Kasim quit both jobs and moved to South America.

14

Only in America

WHEN JONATHAN J. Pollard,
31, and his wife, Anne Henderson-Pollard, 25, were arrested
in late November 1985, after a failed attempt to gain asylum
at the Israeli embassy in Washington, the predictable political fall-out focused attention for a time on an embarrassing
and explosive question: does the Mossad actively operate in
the United States?

Officially, the Mossad says no, no, a thousand times no.
Absolutely not. Indeed, Mossad katsas are forbidden even to
carry phony U.S. passports or use U.S. covers in their work,
so delicate is the situation between the state of Israel and its
largest and most influential supporter.

How to explain Pollard, then? Easy. He wasn't Mossad.
Rather, he had been receiving $2,500 a month since early
1984 from an organization called *Lishka le Kishrei Mada* or
LAKAM, the Hebrew acronym for the Israeli defense
ministry's Scientific Affairs Liaison Bureau, and was spiriting
secret documents to the home of Irit Erb, a secretary at the
Israeli embassy. LAKAM was then headed by Rafael Eitan,
who publicly denied any connection, but was a former
Mossad katsa who had taken part in the 1960 abduction of
Adolf Eichmann from Argentina.

Pollard, a Jew, worked in research at the U.S. Intelligence
Support Center in Suitland, Maryland, near Washington, part
of the Naval Investigative Service. In 1984 he was switched to

the Anti-Terrorism Alert Center in NISC's Threat Analysis Division, an odd transfer given the fact that he had previously been warned by security officials about leaking information to the South African military attaché — and his new job gave him access to considerable classified material.

It didn't take long to determine that Pollard was sharing this information with the Israelis, and when confronted by the FBI, he actually agreed to cooperate with them in getting to his Israeli contacts. He was placed under 24-hour surveillance by the FBI, but panicked and sought asylum. He and his wife, arrested as an accomplice, were stopped as they left the embassy.

Naturally, the Americans demanded an explanation. After a telephone call from U.S. Secretary of State George Schultz in California to Israeli Prime Minister Shimon Peres, at 3:30 a.m. Jerusalem time on December 1, Peres, who had set up LAKAM himself when he was deputy defense minister in the 1960s, formally apologized: "Spying on the United States stands in total contradiction to our policy. Such activity, to the extent that it did take place, was wrong, and the government of Israel apologizes."

Peres went on to say that if government officials were involved, "those responsible will be brought to account, the unit involved . . . will be completely and permanently disbanded, and necessary organizational steps will be taken to ensure that such activities are not repeated." (All they did was change the mailing address and attach LAKAM to the foreign affairs department.)

But even if Peres didn't really mean it, his statement seemed to satisfy the U.S. administration. Former CIA director Richard Helms said it wasn't uncommon for friendly nations to spy on each other. "You do what you can. Getting caught is the sin," he said.

And while the Pollards were carted off to jail for spying — the Mossad considers LAKAM raw amateurs in the craft — Shultz later told reporters, "We are satisfied with the Israeli apology and explanation." After a brief flurry of unhappy publicity for Israel, the controversy died.

Suspicions lingered, of course, about Pollard's exact status, but it seems that even the CIA believes that apart from the odd questionable exercise, the Mossad, except for liaison, simply does not operative actively in the United States itself.

Well, they're wrong.

Pollard was not Mossad, but many others actively spying, recruiting, organizing, and carrying out covert activities — mainly in New York and Washington, which they refer to as their "playground" — do belong to a special, super-secret division of the Mossad called simply *Al*, Hebrew for "above" or "on top."

The unit is so secretive, and so separate from the main organization, that the majority of Mossad employees don't even know what it does and do not have access to its files on the computer.

But it exists, and employs between 24 and 27 veteran field personnel, three as active katsas. Most, though not all, of their activity is within U.S. borders. Their primary task is to gather information on the Arab world and the PLO, as opposed to gathering intelligence about U.S. activities. But as we shall see, the dividing line is often blurred, and when in doubt, Al doesn't hesitate to cross over it.

To say it doesn't gather information on the Americans is like saying mustard is not the main course, but you do like a little on your hotdog. Say, for example, there's a senator on the arms committee who interests Mossad. Al rarely uses sayanim, but that senator's paperwork, anything happening in his office, would be important information, so an aide would become a target. If an aide was Jewish, he or she would be approached as a sayan. Otherwise, the person would be recruited as an agent, or even just as a friend, with whom to mingle and listen.

The Washington cocktail circuit is very important for that. Certain attachés keep track of it. There is no problem adding someone to that circuit and giving it a legitimate ring.

Suppose, for instance, McDonnell Douglas wants to sell U.S.-made airplanes to Saudi Arabia. Is that a U.S. issue or an Israeli issue? Well, as far as the Institute is concerned, it's Israel's business. When you have something like that in place, it's very difficult not to use it. So they do.

One of the more famous of Al's activities involved the theft of research material from some major U.S. aircraft-manufacturing firms to help Israel secure a five-year, $25.8 million contract in January 1986 to supply the U.S. navy (shipboard) and marine corps with 21 16-foot-long drones, or unmanned Mazlat Pioneer 1 aircraft, plus the accompanying ground control, launch, and recovery equipment. The drones, which have a television monitor mounted underneath, are used in military reconnaissance work. Mazlat, a subsidiary of the state-run Israeli Aeronautical Industries and Tadiran, "won" the contract after outbidding U.S. firms in a 1985 tender.

In reality, Al stole the research. Israel had been working on a drone, but was not nearly far enough advanced to enter this competition. When you don't have to include research recovery costs in your bid, it makes a substantial difference.

After winning the contract, Mazlat went into partnership with AAI Corp. of Baltimore, Maryland, to complete it.

Al is similar to Tsomet, but it does not come under the jurisdiction of the head of Tsomet. Rather, it reports directly to the head of Mossad. Unlike normal Mossad stations, it does not operate inside the Israeli embassy. Its stations are located in safe houses or apartments.

The three Al teams are set up as a station, or unit. Let's say that for some reason relations between Israel and Great Britain collapsed tomorrow and the Mossad had to leave the United Kingdom. They could dispatch an Al team to London and have a complete clandestine setup the next day. The Al katsas are among the most experienced in the Institute.

The United States is one place where the consequences for messing up are immense. But not working through the embassy creates difficulties, especially with communications. If Al people are caught in the United States, they're jailed as spies. They have no diplomatic immunity. The worst that can happen to a katsa in a normal station, because he has diplomatic immunity, is deportation. Officially, the Mossad has a liaison station in Washington, but nothing else.

Another problem that precludes working out of the Israeli embassy in Washington is that it is located behind a shopping center part way up a hill on International Drive. There is little else around there except the Jordanian embassy farther up the hill, overlooking the Israeli embassy — hardly a good setting for carrying out clandestine activities.

Incidentally, despite rumors to the contrary, the Mossad does not have a station in the Soviet Union. About 99.99 percent of information it gathers on the Eastern Bloc comes through "positive interrogation," which means simply interviewing Jews emigrating from the Soviet Bloc and analyzing and processing that information. Quite a good picture of what's going on in the USSR can be created and put on the face of an intelligence agency actively gathering data there. But it has been too dangerous to work there. The only activity was to help get people out — creating escape routes, that sort of thing. A separate organization under the auspices of the Mossad does that; it's called *nativ*, which means "pathway" or "passage" in Hebrew. The Eastern Bloc information has a good exchange value. That, coupled with data gathered in other countries — for example, the radar information from the Danes — helps in presenting a picture of knowledge.

The Americans don't realize how much information is given to us through NATO, information that can be manipulated to present a much more vivid picture. In the pre-Gorbachev era, of course, the Soviet news media sources weren't that great, but you could always get data by rumor and word of mouth. Even military movements. Somebody might complain that his cousin was moved somewhere and hadn't been heard from. Even if only 10 people a day were arriving in Israel from the Soviet Bloc, you could still get an extraordinary amount of information from that.

Al's stations, while outside the embassy, still operate like stations for the most part. They communicate directly to Tel Aviv headquarters either by telephone, telex, or computer modem. They do not use burst communications systems, because even if the Americans couldn't break down the messages, they would know there was clandestine activity in the neighborhood, something the Mossad wants to avoid. Distance is also a factor.

Al katsas are the only ones in the entire organization who use American passports. And they are breaking two fundamental rules: they're operating in a target country; and they're using the cover of the country they are in. The rule is that you never play an Englishman in England, or a Frenchman in France. It makes it just too easy for the locals to investigate your documentation. If you hand a Paris cop your local driver's license, for example, he can check it immediately to see if it's valid.

Al gets away with it because the quality of their documentation is top grade. It has to be. In *enemy* territory, you don't want to get caught because they're going to shoot you. In *the United States*, the friendliest country, you don't want to get caught because they're going to shoot your whole country. The FBI probably suspects something from time to time, but they don't really know.

* * *

The following story was told to me by Ury Dinure, at one point my NAKA instructor, who was then in charge of Al's New York station. Dinure had been actively involved with an operation that affected U.S. international policy, created a serious domestic problem for then president Jimmy Carter, and stirred up some ugly racial conflict between U.S. Jews and leaders of the U.S. black community. Had the Americans known about the extent and the nature of the Mossad's involvement, it could have jeopardized — perhaps even severed — the historic good relations between the two countries.

First, a look at 1979.

The most momentous event that year was the final outcome of the September 1978 Camp David agreement on a "framework for peace," signed by Carter, Egyptian President Anwar Sadat, and Israeli Prime Minister Menachem Begin. Most of the Arab world had reacted with shock and anger at Sadat. As for Begin, he began to regret the whole thing almost immediately after leaving Camp David.

U.S. Secretary of State Cyrus Vance had tried an eleventh-hour shuttle diplomacy approach to reach an agreement before the December 17 treaty-signing deadline set at Camp David, but that fell apart at the last minute when Begin refused to negotiate seriously, creating considerable distrust between Washington and Jerusalem. Early in 1979, Begin sent his legendary foreign minister, Moshe Dayan, to Brussels to meet with Vance and Egypt's Premier Moustafa Khalil to explore ways of resuming the deadlocked talks. But Begin bluntly announced that Dayan would discuss only "how, when, and where" negotiations might be resumed, rather than discussing the actual content of the Camp David agreement.

In late December 1978, Israel's usually divided Knesset had voted 66 to six in support of Begin's tough position toward Washington and Cairo. As an illustration of their mood, Israel halted a military equipment pullback that had been planned to help speed the Sinai withdrawal following a peace treaty. Israel also stepped up its attacks on Palestinian camps in Lebanon, prompting Florida Democrat Richard Stone, head of the Senate Subcommittee on Near Eastern and South Asian Affairs, to say that the Israelis appeared to have "drawn the wagons into a circle."

Following the Knesset vote, Begin telephoned U.S. Jewish leaders, urging that pro-Israeli groups launch a write-in and telegram campaign to the White House and Congress. A group of 33 Jewish intellectuals, including authors Saul Bellow and Irving Howe, who had criticized Begin's past inflexibility, sent Carter a letter calling Washington's support of Cairo's position "unacceptable."

In February 1979, hoping to get the talks moving again, the United States asked both Israel and Egypt to meet with Cyrus Vance at Camp David. Both sides agreed, although Israel was angry about a report to Congress on human rights prepared by Vance's department that referred to reports of "systematic" mistreatment of Arabs in the occupied West Bank and Gaza.

Two weeks before the *Washington Post* published this report, Israeli army tanks had moved into West Bank villages at dawn and crushed four Arab homes. The government also established a new outpost, the forerunner to a civilian settlement, at Nueima, northeast of Jericho — making it the fifty-first on the West Bank — where about 5,000 Jews were living among 692,000 Palestinians.

In the midst of this chaos, Carter, in March, launched his own six-day mission to Cairo and Jerusalem. Despite the odds against it, he managed to persuade the two sides to agree to a U.S.-written compromise, bringing the two hostile nations closer to peace than they'd been in more than 30 years. The price Carter paid for this was more than $5 billion in extra aid over the next three years to Egypt and Israel. Two of the major stumbling blocks had been oil-starved Israel's concerns about giving Egypt back its captured oil fields in the Sinai and, of course, the still-unsettled question of Palestinian autonomy.

In May, Carter appointed Texan Robert S. Strauss, 60, former chairman of the Democratic National Committee, as a super-ambassador for the second stage of the peace negotiations. While Israel formally approved, it continued to launch assaults on PLO bases in Lebanon. Begin's cabinet voted eight to five to establish yet another new Jewish settlement, at Elon Moreh on the occupied West Bank, prompting 59 prominent U.S. Jews to send Begin an open letter criticizing Israel's policy of setting up new Jewish settlements in the densely populated Arab areas.

To further complicate matters, Begin had a mild heart attack, and Dayan discovered he had cancer. Inflation inside Israel was pushing 100 percent. The country's balance-of-payment deficit was approaching $4 billion, and total foreign debt had doubled in five years to $13 billion, prompting a domestic political crisis. This was exacerbated by Jewish outrage at Carter's comparison of the plight of the Palestinians with the U.S. civil rights movement.

Both Sadat and Carter began to pressure Israel to agree to a plan for Palestinian autonomy. The Arab countries favored an independent sovereign state in the West Bank and Gaza, home for the Palestinians already there, and the millions in the diaspora. The Israelis were totally opposed to the notion of a hostile state — particularly one run by PLO chieftain

Yasser Arafat — sitting on its own border. Israel was suspicious that U.S. reliance on Arab oil was tilting its priorities more toward Arab interests.

In the absence of Begin, who was still recuperating, Dayan was attempting to run the government. In August, he warned the United States against recognizing the PLO or strengthening the chance of a wholly independent Palestinian state's emergence in the West Bank and Gaza. At the end of a stormy, five-hour cabinet session, the Israelis voted to warn the United States to keep its previous commitments, particularly its promise to veto any attempt by Arab states to alter the 1967 United Nations Resolution 242, acknowledging Israel's right to exist. Israel threatened to withdraw from the stalled negotiations over "autonomy" if the Americans pressed too hard to establish relations with the PLO.

What had infuriated the Israelis was an orchestrated power play launched earlier in the summer by Saudi Arabia, Kuwait, and the PLO in an attempt to get things going their way. It began with the Saudis raising their oil production by one million barrels a day in July on a three-month basis, easing the shortage that had sparked long gas lines in the United States during May and June. In addition, the PLO had adopted a conciliatory stance, in public at least, hoping to enhance its rather unwholesome image in the West; Kuwaiti diplomats at the UN were proposing a draft resolution that would tie in Israel's right to exist (Resolution 242) with international recognition of the Palestinians' right to self-determination.

The plan had grown from a June meeting, when Saudi Arabia's Crown Prince Fahd had invited Arafat to Riyadh and persuaded him to build a better relationship with the United States, beginning by curtailing terrorist activities, at least for a time. Kuwait was enlisted because of the widely respected diplomatic abilities of its ambassador, Abdalla Yaccoub Bishara, then on the UN Security Council.

To placate Israel, the Americans flatly rejected voting for any draft endorsing an independent Palestinian state, but they did not rule out a possible milder resolution aimed at simply affirming the Palestinians' legitimate political rights, bringing the language of Resolution 242 in line with the Camp David accords.

When Egyptian Premier Moustafa Khalil announced at the autonomy negotiations, held at a Mount Carmel hotel over-looking Haifa harbor, that his country would support a UN resolution on Palestinian rights, Israeli's justice minister, Shmuel Tamir, accused Egypt of "endangering the whole cur-rent peace process."

Inevitably, the Mossad was also worried about how events were unfolding, particularly over the growing domestic role of Israeli Defense Minister Eizer Weizman. The Mossad did not trust Weizman, a former pilot who was second-in-com-mand of the armed forces during the Six Day War, a heroic commander and father of the legendary Israeli air force. They regarded him as an Arab-lover to the point of believing he was a traitor. Their animosity toward him was ridiculous. Even though he was the minister of defense, no top-secret in-formation was shared with him. Weizman was a free spirit, the kind of man who would agree with you on one thing but disagree completely on something else. He never toed the party line. He did what he believed was right. Men like that are dangerous because they're unpredictable.

But Weizman had certainly proven himself. In a country where just about everybody serves in the army, military ser-vice is important. That's why you end up with a government that is 70 percent generals. People don't seem to understand what's wrong with that — with people whose nostrils flare at the smell of gunpowder.

Even Begin and Dayan were having their disagreements. Dayan, historically a Labor man, had left that party to join the charismatic, right-wing Begin. But the way they looked at the Palestinians was completely different. Dayan, as did most Labor people from his generation, looked at them as an adversary, but as people. Begin and his party, when looking at the Palestinians, didn't see people; they saw a problem. Dayan would say, "I'd rather be at peace with these people and I remember times when we were." Begin would say, "I wish they weren't here, but there's not much I can do about that." That's such a different outlook, it's not surprising there was growing friction between them.

In the midst of all this, the Mossad had made its first contact with the opium growers in Thailand. The Americans were trying to force farmers to stop producing opium and grow coffee instead. The Mossad's idea was to get in there, help them grow coffee, but at the same time help them export opium as a means of raising money for Mossad operations.

One of those operations was the continuing efforts of Al in New York and Washington to undermine Arab determination to enlist U.S. assistance in helping the PLO — or Palestinians generally — achieve a higher status through the UN.

The Israelis were understandably not very happy about that. There had been constant attacks on Israeli villages, massacres, a state of ever-present danger. Even if the shelling stopped for a while, they still felt the same way. Bags were being checked in department stores and movie theaters. If someone saw a bag left on a bus with no one attending it, they told the driver, he'd stop the bus, and everyone would get off. If someone left their attaché case somewhere by accident, they could expect it to be confiscated and blown up.

There was a big influx of Palestinians from the West Bank working in Israel. Many Israelis had served on patrol in the West Bank, and they knew the Palestinians hated them. Even if you were a left-winger and you thought they had a right to hate you, you still didn't want to end up in pieces.

It was common for people from the right to express their distrust of Palestinians; they felt that dealing with them was only a vicious circle. A left-winger might say, "Let them have elections," and the right would say, "Forget it. They'll elect somebody I don't want to talk to." So the left would say, "But they've announced a ceasefire." The right would respond, "What ceasefire? We don't recognize the Palestinians as a group that can give a ceasefire." Then the next day something would blow up and the right would say, "See, I told you they wouldn't keep the ceasefire!"

* * *

Al had been operating in New York since about 1978, trying to get a line on Arab activities around the peace talks being pushed by Carter. In September 1975, Secretary of State Henry Kissinger had officially pledged that the United States would not recognize or negotiate with the PLO until it affirmed Israel's right to exist. First, former president Gerald Ford and then Carter announced they would uphold that pledge. Still, the Israelis didn't completely believe it.

In November 1978, after the Camp David talks, Illinois Republican Congressman Paul Findley, a member of the House Foreign Affairs Committee, had carried a message from Carter to a meeting with Arafat in Damascus, at which Arafat said the PLO would be nonviolent if an independent Palestinian state was created in the West Bank and Gaza with a connecting corridor.

Carter had already called for a Palestinian "homeland" as early as 1977, and in spring 1979, U.S. ambassador to Austria Milton Wolf, a prominent Jewish leader, met with the PLO's representative there, Issam Sartawi, first at an Austrian government reception, then at an Arab embassy cocktail party. Wolf was acting under instructions from Washington to meet with Sartawi, but not to discuss anything of substance. In mid-July, when Arafat went to Vienna to see Austria's chancellor, Bruno Kreisky, and former West German chancellor, Willy Brandt, Wolf and Sartawi held a serious meeting to discuss the negotiations. When news of that leaked out, the State Department said Wolf had been officially "reminded" about the U.S. policy against negotiating with the PLO, but the Mossad knew Wolf had been acting on direct instructions from Washington.

There was a growing momentum in the United States to achieve a certain peace alignment. Even the Arabs had begun to see the advantages of this, and the Mossad, through their network of electronic bugs at the homes and offices of various Arab ambassadors and leaders in New York and Washington, learned that the PLO was leaning toward agreeing to the 1975 Kissinger position and recognizing Israel's right to exist.

At this time, the U.S. ambassador to the UN was Andrew Young, a Southern black liberal and close friend of Carter's, who had been one of the president's earliest supporters and was considered the administration's main conduit between the White House and the black community.

Young, an outspoken and often controversial ambassador, was a product of the U.S. civil rights movement and had a weak spot for the underdog, a view that Israel saw as more anti-Israeli than pro-Palestinian. Young believed that Carter wanted a solution, a settlement that would relieve the Palestinians from the situation they were locked into, while creating a peaceful situation in the region.

Young opposed new settlements in the West Bank, but he wanted to postpone the planned presentation by the Arabs of a resolution seeking PLO recognition before the UN. Young's argument was that it would lead nowhere, so it was better to forge a milder resolution that could ultimately achieve the goal but would have a better chance of approval.

Kuwaiti Ambassador Bishara was the driving force behind the Arab resolution and was, of course, in constant contact with the UN's unofficial PLO representative, Zehdi Labib Terzi. Because Al had rented apartments all over New York and Washington and installed numerous listening devices, they overheard a July 15 conversation between Bishara and Young, to the effect that the Arabs could not postpone the Security Council debate on the resolution, but suggesting that Young should discuss it with someone from the PLO.

Young informed Bishara that he "could not meet with representatives of the PLO," but he added, "neither could I refuse an invitation from a member of the Security Council to come to his home to talk business." Bishara, of course, was on the Security Council, and Young added that, in addition to being unable to refuse an invitation, "I can't tell you who you can have in your home."

On July 25, 1979, a cable arrived from New York at Mossad headquarters in Tel Aviv. It read: "U.S. Ambassador to UN to meet with PLO representative to UN." The cable was marked, "Urgent. Tiger. Black," which meant it was only for the eyes of the prime minister and a few of his top officials — probably no more than five people altogether.

It was handed in code to the office of the head of the Mossad, Yitzhak Hofi. Hofi personally took the decoded message to Begin. The senior Israelis were horrified to read that Young was going to meet Terzi. The message also gave the information source as recordings from Bishara's private line in his UN office, revealing that Young had been invited to his house and had accepted.

The question then was whether to prevent the meeting or let it happen. The decision to let it happen would prove that Israeli fears were well founded, that there was a shift in the U.S. attitude toward Israel. This would help prove to the country's American friends in high places that such a danger existed from this particular administration, thereby creating a pro-Israel change. It would show the whole process was jeopardizing Israeli security.

In addition, it would help get rid of Young who was seen as too much of a threat because of his open-minded approach and positive attitude toward the PLO. He didn't fit Israel's needs.

On July 26, Young, along with his six-year-old son, Andrew, walked into Bishara's Beekman Place town house. With the AI microphones picking up every word, Young was greeted by Bishara and the Syrian ambassador. Five minutes later, Terzi arrived, and while the boy played alone for 15 minutes or so, the three diplomats talked and seemed to agree that the Security Council meeting should be postponed from July 27 to August 23. (It *was* postponed.)

Right after that, Young and his son left. Within an hour, a complete transcript of the meeting was taken by AI katsa and station head, Ury Dinure, aboard an El Al flight from New York to Tel Aviv. He was met at the airport by Yitzhak Hofi, in response to the cable that had preceded him: "The spider swallowed the fly." The two men then took the transcript directly to Begin. Hofi read it on the way there.

Dinure was in Israel for just six hours before returning

with a copy of the transcript to deliver to Israel's ambassador to the UN, Yehuda Blum, a Czechoslovakian-born expert on international law.

Hofi did not want news of the meeting to leak to the media. He particularly didn't want to burn the setup in New York. He argued that Begin could achieve more by going to the administration and talking to them — the same approach they had taken after Milton Wolf's meeting with the PLO in Vienna. Hofi said it wouldn't be good politics in the United States to hurt Young, who was popular among the blacks, and anyway, they could get more concessions from the Americans by working it out behind the scenes.

But Begin wasn't interested in diplomacy. He wanted blood. "I want it out," he said. They agreed there was no point in letting out all the information, thereby running the risk of burning the source, and so *Newsweek* magazine was told simply that Young and Terzi had met. That, of course, sparked a query to the State Department, and Young was asked for an explanation. His first version was that he had been out for a walk with his son and decided to stop in to see Bishara where, to his surprise, he had met Terzi. He said the two men were involved in "15 or 20 minutes of social amenities," but nothing more.

Secretary Vance, flying back from Ecuador, was cabled Young's explanation. Relieved that it was simply a chance encounter, Vance authorized State Department spokesman, Tom Reston, to release Young's version at noon, Monday, August 13.

Once the whole thing seemed to be blowing over, the Mossad arranged for rumors to be leaked to Young that if he thought Israel was going to be quiet about this, he was gravely mistaken.

Concerned, Young requested, and got, a meeting with Yehuda Blum that lasted two hours. He did not know that Blum had the transcript of his meeting with Bishara and Terzi. Because of that, Blum was able to get Young to admit far more than he had told the State Department.

Blum was not that crazy about Young in the first place. In most of his reports, Young did not get high praise. But Blum was an experienced diplomat. Because he had the transcripts and knew exactly what had happened, he was able to extract the story. That meant they could use Young as the source, so they would not have to expose the fact that they already knew everything.

Young, who still thought Israel's main intention was to get the negotiations going, didn't know he was being set up. After the meeting with Blum, and Young's admissions, the U.S. ambassador to Israel was called by Begin and given a formal complaint. That complaint went to the ambassador and to the media at about the same time to make sure it didn't get lost in the shuffle.

By 7 a.m. on August 14, an urgent cable from the U.S. embassy in Israel to Washington was on Vance's desk, outlining what the Israelis claimed Young had told Blum, which was considerably at odds with what Young had told the State Department, and what they in turn had told the media the day before. Vance went to the White House and told Carter that Young had to resign. Carter tentatively agreed, but said he wanted to "sleep on it."

Young arrived at the White House family quarters at 10 a.m. the next morning, August 15, 1979, carrying his letter of resignation with him. After a 90-minute session, he left for a while, then rejoined Carter. They went into Hamilton Jordan's office, where senior White House staffers had gathered. With Carter's arm around his shoulder, Young told his friends he had resigned. Two hours later, Press Secretary Jody Powell, barely able to keep his composure, announced that, sadly, Young was resigning.

U.S. peace envoy Strauss, on the plane to the Middle East, said, "The Young affair . . . reinforces the unfounded suspicions that the United States is dealing in the dark with the PLO."

Young later tried to defend his actions, saying, "I did not lie, I didn't tell all of the truth. I prefaced my remark [to the State Department] with: 'I'm going to give you an official version,' and I *gave* an official version, which did not in any way lie."

But the damage had been done. Young had been stopped, and it would be a while before any Americans attempted to deal with the PLO again. And so, Al, through its extensive network of clandestine activity, had managed to end the career of one of Carter's closest friends — but a man seen as no friend to Israel.

* * *

Within a few days of the story's making headlines, Ury Dinure reported that it was too hot to stay around and requested a transfer. All the Mossad safe houses were closed, with the entire New York operation shifted to other apartments. The Mossad was sure there would be a crackdown on them, but it didn't come. It was like listening to the whistle of a bomb when it's falling. You sit there waiting for it to fall, to go boom, but then nothing happens.

The political fallout from this escapade, however, quickly turned into one of the ugliest chapters in Jewish-black relations in the United States.

American black leaders were appalled at Young's departure. Mayor Richard Hatcher of Gary, Indiana, told *Time* magazine it was a "forced resignation" and "an insult to black people." Benjamin Hooks, executive director of the National Association for the Advancement of Colored People (NAACP), said Young had been made "a sacrificial lamb for circumstances beyond his control." He said Young "should have received a presidential medal" for his "brilliant diplomatic coup," rather than losing his job over it.

The Reverend Jesse Jackson, who would later be a U.S. presidential candidate, said, "There's a tremendous tension in the air around the nation over the forced resignation." He described relations between Jews and blacks as "more tense than they've been in 25 years."

Young himself said there would not be a polarization between black and Jewish leaders, but predicted there would be "something of a confrontation as friends." He said the black community's evolving attitude toward the Middle East should "in no way be seen as being anti-Jewish. It may be pro-Palestinian in a way that it was not before, in which case the Jewish community will have the responsibility of finding a way to relate to that without being anti-black."

Other black leaders wanted to know why Young got dumped for meeting with the PLO, while U.S. Ambassador Wolf, a prominent Jewish leader, was not fired, in spite of having several meetings with the PLO. The main difference, of course, was that Wolf wasn't caught lying about them.

Indeed, the main winner in this game of intrigue seemed to be the PLO, not Israel, as more and more U.S. black organizations came out in support of Young, and the PLO cause, widely ignored before by the media, suddenly began enjoying more favorable attention. In late August, the Reverend Joseph Lowery, president of the Southern Christian Leadership Conference, headed a delegation to New York, conveying to Terzi their unconditional support for the "human rights of all Palestinians, including the right of self-determination in regard to their homeland." The next day, meeting with Ambassador Blum, the group said they had "no apologies for our support of Palestinian human rights, just as we make no apologies to the PLO for our continued support of the state of Israel." Blum was quoted as replying, "It's ridiculous to equate us with the PLO. It's like equating criminals [with] a police force."

A week later, a group of 200 American black leaders met at NAACP headquarters in New York and declared, "Some Jewish organizations and intellectuals who were previously identified with the aspirations of black Americans . . . became apologists for the racial status quo . . . Jews must show more sensitivity and be prepared for more consultation before taking positions contrary to the best interests of the black community."

A group of eleven Jewish organizations responded that it was "with sorrow and anger that we note these statements. We cannot work with those who resort to half-truths, lies, and bigotry in any guise or from any sources . . . We cannot work with those who would succumb to Arab blackmail."

Jesse Jackson was pictured in the October 8 *Time* magazine embracing Yasser Arafat, part of a self-appointed Middle

East mission initiated when Begin refused to meet him because of his sympathy with the PLO. Jackson called the refusal "a rejection of blacks in America, their support, and their money." During that same trip with Jackson, Lowery joined Arafat in a chorus of "We Shall Overcome."

Later that month, National Urban League head Vernon E. Jordan, Jr., attempted to calm the stormy waters in a Kansas City speech, saying, "Black-Jewish relations should not be endangered by ill-considered flirtations with terrorist groups devoted to the extermination of Israel. The black civil rights movement has nothing in common with groups whose claim to legitimacy is compromised by cold-blooded murder of innocent civilians and schoolchildren."

Jackson, calling the PLO "a government in exile," met Jordan in Chicago and afterward Jordan explained, "We agreed to disagree without being disagreeable."

Not so Moshe Dayan. In October 1979, tired of Begin's hard-line policies in dealing with the Palestinians, Dayan resigned — right in the middle of a Sunday morning cabinet meeting — leaving Begin to take over the foreign ministry himself. In a subsequent interview with *Time*'s Jerusalem bureau chief, Dean Fischer, and correspondent, David Halevy, Dayan said, "The Palestinians want peace and they're ripe for some kind of settlement. I'm convinced it can be done."

Perhaps. But he didn't live to see it.

* * *

The whole thing gave way to quite a few other operations gathering information from senators and congressmen, because it seemed almost to have got the nod. They must have known something about the Mossad's involvement, yet nothing happened. Nobody said anything. In the intelligence game, if you see someone operating and you look the other way, he will be encouraged to try something more daring until you hit him on the hand or hit him over the head, whichever comes first.

Al would have been gathering the recordings from the various homes, getting data from the Senate and Congress, making approaches, mingling, recruiting, getting copies of documentation, opening the odd diplomatic pouch, all the general operations of a station. Katsas were going to parties in Washington and New York. They were all running their businesses. One of them ran an escort service that still exists.

The Mossad still doesn't admit to the existence of Al. Inside the Institute, it's said that the Mossad does not work in the United States. But most Mossad people know that Al exists, even if they don't know exactly what it does. The biggest joke in all this is that, when the LAKAM broke out with the Pollard case, Mossad people always said, "There's one thing for sure. We don't work in the United States."

Which only goes to show, you can't always take a spy at his word.

15

Operation Moses

THEY WERE ALL there: foreign diplomats escaping the oppressive heat of Khartoum; tourists from right across Europe anxious to learn diving techniques in the Red Sea, or enjoy escorted tours of the Nubian Desert; and senior Sudanese officials, all relaxing in the newly constructed tourist resort 75 miles north of Port Sudan across the sea from Mecca.

How were they to know it was a Mossad front? Indeed, on the morning in early January 1985, when the 50 or so customers woke up to find the staff had vanished — except for a few locals left behind to serve breakfast — they still didn't know what had happened. Few people know even today. As far as legitimate tourists were concerned, the resort's European owners had gone bankrupt, as the notes left behind claimed, though they were assured of a full refund (and actually got it). The staff, either Mossad or Israeli navy workers, had disappeared quietly during the night, some by boat, others by air. They had left plenty of food behind, along with four trucks to carry the tourists back to Port Sudan.

But what happened at this camp is one of the great mass-escape stories of history, a story only partially known to the world as Operation Moses: the rescue of thousands of black Ethiopian Jews, or Falashas, from drought-ravaged, war-torn Ethiopia, to Israel.

Many stories, even books, have documented Israel's daring and covert airlift of the Falashas out of refugee camps in Sudan and Ethiopia. A Belgian-chartered Trans-European Airways Boeing 707 was used to fly them on a circuitous route from either Khartoum or Addis Ababa, through either Athens, Brussels, Rome, or Basel, then to Tel Aviv.

The stories — all fed by Mossad disinformation specialists — claim that 12,000 black Ethiopian Jews were rescued in this short, spectacular operation. In fact, about 18,000 were rescued, and only about 5,000 of those by way of the publicly celebrated Belgian charter. The rest came through the Red Sea "tourist resort."

* * *

At the turn of this century, there were several hundred thousand Falashas in Ethiopia, but by the 1980s their numbers had dwindled to at most 25,000, scattered mainly throughout the country's remote northwestern Gondar province. For two centuries, the Falashas had longed for the promised land, but it wasn't until 1972 that they were officially recognized as Jews by Israel. Sephardic Chief Rabbi Ovadia Yosef decreed that the Falashas were "undoubtedly of the tribe of Dan," which made them the inhabitants of the biblical land of Havileh, today's southern Arabian peninsula. The Falashas believe in the Torah, the basic Jewish scriptures; they're circumcised and observe the Sabbath and the dietary laws. Ironically, one of the keys to the rabbinate's conclusions that the Falashas are indeed Jews was the fact that they do not observe Hanukkah. This festival celebrates the victory of Judah the Maccabee over Antiochus IV in 167 B.C., after which the Temple was cleansed and Jewish worship restored. But this was not part of the Falashas' history, because they had left Israel with the Queen of Sheba long before, during Solomon's reign.

As a result of the Chief Rabbinical Council's findings, a government committee then decided that these Ethiopians were covered by Israel's Law of Return, which allows all Jews automatically to become citizens the moment they arrive in Israel to live.

In 1977, when Menachem Begin became prime minister, he vowed to help the Falashas come to the promised land. Ethiopian leader Mengitsu Haile Mariam, struggling with a bitter civil war in the early 1970s, had ordered harsh punishment for any Ethiopian attempting to escape, so Begin drew up a plan for secret arms deals with that country in exchange for covert missions from both Ethiopia and Sudan to rescue the Falashas. Only 122 black Jews had been flown out of Addis Ababa when Israeli foreign minister Moshe Dayan told a radio reporter in Zurich on February 6, 1978, that Israel was selling weapons to Ethiopia. Mariam, who had demanded the deal be kept secret, immediately called it off.

In 1979, when Begin and Anwar Sadat of Egypt signed the Camp David agreement, Begin persuaded Sadat to talk Sudan's President Jaafar al-Nemery into allowing the Falashas to flow out of refugee camps in Sudan into Israel. Over the next few years, a trickle of Falashas, perhaps as many as 4,000, did make their way to Israel, although that plan died, too, when Sadat was assassinated in 1981, and al-Nemery converted to Islamic fundamentalism.

By 1984, however, the situation had become critical. The Falashas, along with legions of other Ethiopians, were suffering horrible drought and famine. Now they began to pour into Sudan in search of food. In September 1984, when Israel's then deputy prime minister, Yitzhak Shamir, met U.S. Secretary of State George Shultz in Washington, Shamir asked the Americans to use their clout with both the Egyptians and the Saudi Arabians to persuade al-Nemery to allow a rescue operation under cover of the International Food Aid operation. Sudan, which had its own problems with drought, and with civil war in the south, was not unhappy at the prospect of having a few thousand less mouths to feed. But again, both the Sudanese and the Ethiopian officials demanded absolute secrecy.

Indeed, between November 1984 and January 1985, the operation was secret. During the first week of January 1985, George Bush, then U.S. vice-president, having received al-Nemery's approval, ordered a U.S. Hercules aircraft into

Khartoum, where it picked up 500 Falashas and flew them directly to Israel.

This part of the operation was widely reported later in books and newspaper stories. Many people knew about it, including the Americans, British, Egyptians, Sudanese, the Ethiopians themselves, as well as numerous airline officials in Europe. But they all kept it secret until Yehuda Dominitz, a senior official with the United Jewish Agency, told a reporter for *Nekuda*, a small West Bank Jewish settlers' newspaper, that the rescue operation was on. And that ended not only the operation he was speaking of, but also the secret one organized by the Mossad on the shores of the Red Sea.

As usual in these affairs, the journalism fraternity in Israel knew about the operation all along — or at least, they knew what the Mossad and the prime minister's office wanted them to know — but they agreed to withhold the story until they were given leave to print it. There is a committee of editors, called the *Vaadat Orchim*, of all the major media outlets in Israel that meets regularly with government officials for background briefing on current events. Israeli television is government controlled, as is all but one rogue radio station, so that broadcasting is never a problem to control.

Journalists are fed these government-vetted stories and made to feel they are part of them. They may even be taken on missions, always with the understanding that when it's in Israel's best interest to release the story, they'll have all the information they need. Some feel this is better than censorship (although Israel does that, too).

Once news did break of the covert operation, Arab reaction was swift and predictable. Libya requested a special session of the Arab League, and newspapers in many Arab countries condemned Sudan for cooperating with Israel. For its part, the Sudanese government denied any role in the airlift, and foreign minister Hashem Osman called in Arab, African, and Asian diplomats to accuse Ethiopia of "closing its eyes" to the Falasha exodus in return for money and weapons from Israel. Ethiopian foreign minister Goshu Wolde replied that Sudan had been bribing "a large number of Ethiopian Jews to flee Ethiopia." Kuwait's *Al rai al A'am*, in a strongly worded editorial, said: "The smuggling of Ethiopian Jews across Sudan can be regarded not as a passing event but as a new defeat inflicted on the Arab nation."

Think how upset they would have been had they known the whole story.

* * *

At the time of the operation, Prime Minister Shimon Peres declared publicly, "We shall not rest until all our brothers and sisters from Ethiopia come safely back home." In the spring of 1984, with the situation for the starving Falashas worsening, Peres set out to make his dream come true. While talks were proceeding with other governments for an airlift through the Brussels connection, Peres called in Nahum Admony, then head of the Mossad, code-named "ROM," to see if he could come up with a scheme to rescue even more Falashas.

Admony, recognizing the urgency of the situation, got permission from Peres to use resources outside the Mossad if he had to, either civilian or military.

After this meeting, Admony called in David Arbel, then head of *Tsafririm*, which means "morning breeze," the department whose sole purpose is to save Jews wherever they are threatened. Arbel, as we've seen, had made a name for himself, of sorts, in the Lillehammer debacle.

Arbel's department was responsible for setting up Jewish defense groups, called "frames," or *misgerot*, all over the world, now including some parts of the United States, where anti-Semitism is regarded as a threat. Often people with particular skills, such as doctors, are on reserve and called in for short periods to help with these frames. Normally, heads of the stations for the frames in the various countries are retired Mossad workers. The job is widely regarded as a sort of bonus for faithful service, a *tshupar*, the idea being that they've got all this expertise, why not use it?

The main job is to help the leaders of Jewish communities outside Israel plan for their own security. Part of this is done through the *hets va-keshet*, or "bow and arrow," Israel's paramilitary youth brigades. While all Israeli youths, boys and girls, belong to this *eduday noar ivry,* or "battalion of Hebrew youth," often youths from other countries are brought over to spend the summer learning about security, picking up such skills as completing obstacle courses, pitching tents, and learning how to use a sniper rifle and Uzi assault rifle. Still others learn upgraded security skills, such as how to build a slick, for hiding weapons or documents, when and how to do security checks, as well as the fundamentals of investigation and intelligence gathering.

Any use of the frames other than for self-protection has never been approved by any government official, although Mossad officials all know of such use. Thus, Yitzhak Shamir knew, but Peres, never a Mossad man, would not have known, even though he was prime minister. Israel does not sell the weapons directly to these foreign frames, but it does provide arms indirectly in a round-about arrangement with known arms dealers.

The Mossad does not see these frames as information gatherers, although the station heads know from experience that the shortest route to getting praise is by supplying useful information. Many of the youths trained at the summer camps in Israel later become sayanim, and it certainly provides a strong group of willing helpers, well trained, undaunted by the lingo, who have already shown the ability to take chances. With the exception of Canada and most of the United States, Jewish communities outside Israel have frames, trained and armed, ready to defend themselves if needed.

For this particular operation, however, the Mossad would have to recruit helpers. After his meeting with Admony, Arbel summoned all his senior officials in the Tsafririm department.

"I want an Entebbe for me," he said. "I want my name to go down in history."

Arbel told his officials he wanted as many Falashas out of Sudan as possible: "All of them." Then he told them to figure out how to do it.

Arbel's department usually operated on a shoestring budget, but this time it was clear that whatever they needed they could get. Hayem Eliaze, who headed the division that specialized in clandestine operations to rescue Jews from behind enemy lines, was put directly in charge of this undercover Moses project, with orders to produce an operational plan as quickly as possible

Within three days, Eliaze gathered his team for a lengthy brainstorming session in their offices outside the main Mossad headquarters building, on Ibn Gevirol Avenue, just one floor above the South African embassy in Tel Aviv.

With detailed relief maps on the walls, and the information they'd gathered about Sudan in front of them, each man took turns delivering what he saw as the situation and how best to approach it. For the most part, the Falashas were located in camps in the Kassala and Alatarch areas west of Khartoum, toward the Ethiopian borders. The Sudanese rebels in the south, who'd been fighting the central government for years, could not be counted on for assistance of any kind.

During one session, one of the men studying the map of the area said it reminded him of an incident near Magna, on the northwest tip of the Red Sea, when an Israeli missile boat on its way back through the Suez Canal had developed technical problems with its radar when the gyrocompass got stuck, sending the boat accidentally off course. It had plowed into a Saudi Arabian beach in the dead of night, nearly setting off an international incident.

Miraculously, the missile boat, cruising along at a healthy 30 knots, had somehow found a hole in the coral reefs before ending up on the beach. Within hours, responding to radio reports from the boat, Israeli navy commandos were sent in to take over. All documents were removed, the ship's crew was taken aboard another missile boat, the commandos set up a beachhead to defend their position if necessary, and as the sun rose, there was the bizarre spectacle of an Israeli missile boat, guarded by commandos, sitting smack on Saudi Arabian sand.

Since the two countries weren't actually speaking, Israeli officials requested that the Americans tell the Saudis that it wasn't an invasion but only a mishap, also warning them that if anyone came close to the ship, they were dead. Normally, there would have been no one within hundreds of miles of this remote desert spot, but it happened that a Bedouin tribe was having a celebration about a mile away. Fortunately, they didn't come any closer. The Saudis sent in some observers, and a deal was struck that if the commandos left their fortifications on the beach, the Saudis would leave the Israelis to get the ship back out to sea.

The first plan was to blow up the ship, but the navy nixed that (several of these missile boats, incidentally, were later sold to the South African navy, which uses them to this day). Instead, they brought in a helicopter with a supply of liquid Styrofoam which they sprayed over the entire hull of the ship, hooked a cable harness over the nose to two other missile boats, yanked it off the beach, and towed it all the way back to Eilat harbor.

As often happens in these brainstorming sessions, the retelling of such a story sparks other ideas. During the course of the telling, one man said, "Wait a minute, we actually have passage right next to the shores of Sudan. We can get quite close to shore with our missile boats. Why don't we take the Falashas out by ship?"

The idea was kicked around for a time, but ultimately rejected for a host of reasons. It would simply take too much time to load people onto ships and could never be accomplished without someone noticing. "Well, we could at least have some sort of station there," he said.

"What are you going to do? Post a sign saying 'Mossad Base of Operations. Please Don't Enter?'" one of the men quipped.

"No," he replied. "Let's have a diving club. The Red Sea is a haven for divers."

At first, the group dismissed the idea, but as time passed, and other ideas came and went, the notion of a diving school and club began to take hold. They already knew a man along that beach who operated a so-called club. Although he spent more time diving and lounging on the beach than he did teaching or renting out his equipment, he did at least have an established presence there. With proper planning, and the appropriate approvals from Khartoum, it could be turned into a full-fledged resort.

Arabic-speaking Yehuda Gil, one of their most experienced katsas, was sent to Khartoum to pose as the representative of a Belgian tourist company that wanted to promote Red Sea diving and desert sight-seeing tours in Sudan. Normally, katsas are not sent into Arab countries because of the amount of knowledge they have and the danger that they could be forced to share it with the enemy if they were captured. But because of the urgency of the situation, it was decided to take the risk this time.

Gil's job was to obtain the necessary permits, which entailed bribing several officials, to expedite his company's tourism plans. He rented a house in the upscale northern section of Khartoum, and set about his labors.

At the same time, another Tsafririm man flew to Khartoum, then to Port Sudan, and from there drove up the beach to find the man operating the tiny diving club. As luck would have it, the man was getting tired of the place. After considerable haggling, it was agreed to send him to Panama (where he still leads the life of the classic beach bum); his club would immediately come under new ownership.

* * *

The Mossad was beginning to see this operation as another "Magic Carpet" (a famous rescue in the early 1950s of Jews from Yemen who were flown into Israel by Hercules aircraft). They had already decided to use the reliable Hercules to airlift the Falashas out, but the tourist camp would have to be drastically enlarged as a cover for the operation. In the meantime, Gil had arranged for the registration of the new company and was already organizing legitimate tours from Europe to bring visitors to the site. Next, they discovered a sunken ship about 100 yards out from shore in some 65 feet of water: it was perfect for shallow diving, and a good tourist draw.

At the site, they began a recruiting drive for workers among local villagers. At the same time, Tsafririm officials in Tel Aviv were quietly recruiting the cooks, diving instructors, and others needed to operate the resort. They wanted people who spoke French or English. Knowing Arabic was an advantage, however, because it would enable comprehension of conversations among Arab diplomats and officials who might be there as guests.

Recruits were drawn from people who had been involved in past operations through Tsafririm, and they went through navy intelligence for the necessary divers to act as instructors for the tourists.

A team of about 35 Israelis was put together to whip the resort into shape. Each had the necessary papers, but because time was critical, they organized the whole operation into teams. For the local construction workers, they had four teams, each working every fourth day. In the meantime, a team of Israelis would come in during the night to expedite construction. Because of the alternating day shifts, however, no one was suspicious when they returned later in the week to find some part of the building completed.

As for the Israeli workers, they were changed regularly, too; rather than going through the process of getting credentials for everyone, they simply had documents made up in a certain name for each; a new team would show up with credentials showing them to be the people with those names.

They could obtain permission to bring in only three vehicles — a Land Rover and two pickup trucks — but they actually had nine trucks. They simply made duplicate license plates and registrations and hid the extra vehicles.

The entire operation almost collapsed because of a silly mistake. Someone decided to ship in a load of turf on a landing craft overnight, so that when a team of local workers showed up the next morning, there was suddenly a large, green lawn where there had been nothing but sand for centuries. How do you grow grass overnight? And even if you explained that it was turf, where could you find that in Sudan? Fortunately, apart from some quizzical looks, the locals just carried on with their work.

In Khartoum, Gil produced brochures showing the club, and had already begun distributing them in travel agencies throughout Europe, offering special individual rates. The resort did not cater to groups at all, the logic being that groups often know each other already and so are more curious about what's going on around them.

The resort was constructed in about a month. Besides the main buildings for the tourists, the kitchen, the bedrooms, and so on, there were several sheds to house communications equipment and weapons. (The Mossad wouldn't go into a place like that unarmed.) They also sneaked in all the gear needed for lighting up impromptu airfields in the desert: beacons, lights, sidelights, controls, wind-direction finders, and laser distance finders.

Food and other necessary supplies were brought in on Israeli missile boats that came within a few yards of shore about half a mile down the beach. Because a half-dozen locals were working in the place, their whereabouts had to be known before a shipment came in so that they wouldn't accidentally chance upon an Israeli ship being unloaded.

While all this was going on, the other Mossad operation, involving the Belgian charter, was also working, with Mossad officials paying enormous sums to bribe Sudanese officials. One of those, General Omer Mohammed Al-Tayeb, a former vice-president who became chief of security for Sudan under President al-Nemery, would receive two life sentences and a fine of 24 million Sudanese pounds in April 1986, for his part in helping the Falashas escape.

During this period, word filtered back to Mossad headquarters that one of the senior Sudanese officials wanted a 10-speed bike to help expedite moving documents for the Falashas. Because things are usually not what they seem in this business, Mossad officials were perplexed by the request and sent a message back to their contact asking for clarification. Again, the message came that the official wanted a 10-speed bike. Mossad officials tried to figure out what this meant. Did he want the weight of a bike in gold? Was this a code they didn't understand? Still confused, they sent another request for clarification and were told again that he wanted a 10-speed bike, period.

They finally realized that he actually wanted a bike, so they sent him a Raleigh, which was the least they could do.

At the resort, the Israelis were studying intelligence on the Sudanese radar system. Eventually, they found a small hole in that system, only partially covered by Egyptian and Saudi Arabian radar, in the area of Rosal-Hadaribah, a mountainous region near the border between Egypt and Sudan, where a low-level flight could get through without being detected.

So, it was decided that the Hercules aircraft would leave the military base at Eilat, called Uvda, fly over the Gulf of Aqaba and the Red Sea, down all the way to this gap in enemy coverage, before flying back up to landing strips that were being constructed in the desert. To locate suitable landing sites, they brought four Israeli pilots to the resort posing as desert tour guides. That way, they could be driving around the desert legitimately, while marking landing locations on a map. They also explained to other personnel at the resort how to set up the landing strips, and instructed them on dimensions, lighting, and communications.

Even spies have a sense of humor from time to time. At one point, a Tsafririm man took one of the Israeli pilots to Khartoum on business, and they ended up at a villa owned by a local businessman. Gil was also there, and while he and the Tsafririm man both knew what business they were in, the pilot thought Gil was a legitimate businessman. At one point, when the host had excused himself, the Tsafririm official asked Gil about his business, and then Gil said to him, "What do you do?"

"Oh, I'm an Israeli spy," came the reply.

The pilot turned white, but the other men laughed and the pilot said nothing until they were on their way back. Several miles out of Khartoum, he suddenly shouted at his companion, "You idiot! You don't do that sort of thing, even as a joke!" It took the Tsafririm official about 15 minutes to calm the pilot enough to let him in on it.

Getting the Falashas out of the camps remained a challenge for the organizers of this operation. At the time, there were hundreds of thousands of Ethiopian blacks who had fled the war and famine in their own country and spilled over into the Sudanese refugee camps, so the problem was also how to tell the Jews from the rest.

To do that, some courageous Falashas who were already safe in Israel — and would be killed if caught — agreed to go back to the camps to organize their people into groups. Very quickly, word spread about this project among the Falashas, but knowledge of it stayed completely within the Falasha community, and it wasn't long before that phase of the operation was ready.

Around March 1984, the first batch of European tourists had arrived, and word was getting around diplomatic and government circles in Khartoum about this wonderful resort. From the time they opened until the night they left in a hurry, the resort was booked to capacity, a resounding commercial success. At one point, they even toyed with the notion of enticing the senior PLO leaders to hold a convention there. The PLO would have felt perfectly safe in Sudan, across the sea from Mecca, and the proposed plan was to send in the commandos one night, herd the PLO leadership onto Israeli missile boats, and cart them back as prisoners to Israel. It might have worked.

* * *

Now they were ready for the final phase. A landing strip was set up and a desert meeting place determined, where the refugees would be met by the trucks and taken on a grueling six-hour drive to meet the Hercules aircraft. There were only supposed to be about 100 people each time, but often twice as many would crowd onto the trucks, weak, emaciated people jammed under a tarpaulin for a long, rough ride. Hundreds of Falashas, their bodies just too racked by hunger and disease, would die on this part of the trip, and hundreds more en route to Israel aboard the crowded Hercules aircraft, but because they had been identified as Jews they were taken, whenever possible, for proper burial in Israel.

Before each trip, Israeli high-altitude reconnaissance aircraft located Sudanese roadblocks (usually set up in mid-afternoon) and notified the communications center at the resort of their location by digital burst radio communications.

On the first night, everything seemed to be going without a hitch. They'd met at the right spot in the desert. They'd avoided all the roadblocks. And they arrived at the runway well before the Hercules landed, using two strips of light strung out in the desert sand. As the Hercules came through the night, the Falashas, who had never seen such a thing at close range, watched as this giant bird landed against the wind, then turned and came back toward them, its engines roaring, kicking up sand and dust.

Overcome with fright, the 200 Falashas ran off into the pitch darkness, hiding wherever they could find a spot to escape this horrid machine. The Israelis managed to round up only about 20 of them on the spot. After searching for a while longer, it was decided to let the Hercules go. They would have to take the rest of the Falashas the next night.

By morning, they had managed to find all but one of the Falashas — an old woman who miraculously survived a three-day walk back to her camp and went to Israel later with another group. The Israelis decided that from then on, they'd leave the Falashas in the trucks until the Hercules had stopped and opened its rear doors. Then they'd drive the truck right up and load the people directly onto the aircraft.

Until news of the other Moses operation became public, this secret desert airlift proceeded with little problem. They flew most nights, and often would have two or three airplanes working at one time, in order to get as many Falashas out as they could in the shortest time possible.

There was the odd hitch, however. One time an empty truck on its way back ran into a roadblock, and since the driver and passenger didn't have proper identification, they were arrested by the two Sudanese soldiers on duty, tied up, and put in a nearby tent. These roadblocks, meant mainly to track activities of the southern rebels, consisted of only two soldiers with no communications equipment. They were left there for a few days at a time.

When the two men failed to return to the resort, a search party was sent out to find them. Once their truck was spotted, a rescue plan was quickly worked out. The rescuers' truck proceeded swiftly up to the blockade, and the driver shouted at the two prisoners in the tent to lie down. The Sudanese soldiers were just approaching the truck when the back opened and submachine-gun fire cut them down on the spot. The Israelis then set the tent on fire, stuck a rock onto the gas pedal of the other truck, and sent it out into the desert — all to make it appear as if there had been a guerrilla attack. In any event, the incident passed into oblivion.

The only Israeli casualty in the operation was a passenger in a truck headed toward Khartoum. Again, they ran into a roadblock, but when the truck didn't stop, the enemy soldiers opened fire, killing the passenger, while the driver kept on going. The two Sudanese soldiers, with no communications or transportation equipment, could do nothing more than fire until the truck was well out of range.

But then, on that night in early January 1985, the message came from Israel with orders to "fold" immediately. In Khartoum, Yehuda Gil quickly packed a few personal things, plus all his documents, and caught the next flight to Europe, and from there back to Israel. While the tourists slept at the Red Sea resort, the Israelis loaded all their equipment onto ships, loaded a Land Rover and two trucks onto a Hercules, and quietly slipped out of the country unnoticed. Hayem Eliaze, the man who had been in charge of the resort, fell off a truck as it was being loaded onto the aircraft and broke his leg.

Still, two and a half hours later, Eliaze was back home in Israel, enjoying the adulation of his peers, but regretting the fact that a talkative official and a newspaper reporter had put a sudden end to what was perhaps the most successful undercover rescue mission ever.

Unfortunately, several thousand Falashas remained behind, out of reach now of Operation Moses. Falasha activist Baruch Tanga was quoted as saying: "All the years it was hard to leave. . . . Now, with half of our families still there, they publish everything. How could they do a thing like that?"

It wasn't his sentiment alone.

16

Harbor Insurance

BY THE SUMMER of 1985, Libya's President Moamer al Kadhafi had become the devil incarnate for most of the western world. Reagan was the only one who authorized warplanes to attack him, but the Israelis held Kadhafi responsible for facilitating much of the arms supply to the Palestinians and their other Arab enemies.

It is difficult to recruit Libyans. They're not liked anywhere, which is a problem in itself. They need to be recruited in Europe, but they're not big travelers.

Libya has two main harbors: at Tripoli, the capital; and at Benghazi, on the Gulf of Sidra in the northwest. The Israeli navy had been monitoring Libyan activities, largely through regular patrols around the entire length of the Mediterranean. Israel regards the corridor from Israel to Gibraltar as its "oxygen pipe." It's the tie to America and most of Europe for both imports and exports.

In 1985, Israel had relatively sound relations with the other countries bordering the southern Mediterranean: Egypt, Morocco, Tunisia, and Algeria, but not Libya.

They had a fairly big navy, but they had a serious problem with manpower and maintaining the navy. Their ships were falling apart. They had large Russian submarines they'd purchased, but they either didn't know how to submerge them, or they were afraid to try. At least twice, Israeli patrol boats came upon Libyan submarines. Normally, a sub would go "ding, ding, ding, ding," and go down. But these subs would steam back to port making their escape.

The Israelis have a listening substation on Sicily, which they enjoy through liaison with the Italians, who also have a listening station there. But it's not enough, because the Libyans, with their support of the PLO and other subversive activities, endanger the Israeli shoreline. Israel regards its shoreline as its "soft belly," the most vulnerable border to attack, home to most of its population and industry.

A considerable amount of the arms and ammunition supplied to the PLO comes via ship from Libya, much of it passing through Cyprus on the way — or going by what is called the TNT route: from Tripoli, Libya, to Tripoli, Lebanon. The Israelis were gathering *some* information about Libyan activities at the time through the Central African Republic and Chad, which was engaged in serious border clashes with Kadhafi's forces.

The Mossad had some "naval observers," usually civilians recruited through their stations in Europe simply to take photographs while ships were entering the harbor. There was no real danger involved, and it gave some visual indication of what was going on inside the harbors. But while they did catch arms shipments — more by luck than anything else — there was a clear need to have access to specific information about traffic coming in and out of Tripoli and Benghazi.

At a meeting involving Mossad's PLO research department and the head of the Tsomet branch dealing with France, the United Kingdom and Belgium, it was decided to try to recruit a harbor-traffic controller, or someone else working in the harbormaster's office in Tripoli who would have access to more specific information on the names and whereabouts of ships. Though the Mossad knew the names of the PLO ships, they did not know where they were at any given time.

If you want to sink or apprehend them, you have to find them. That's hard with a ship if you don't know its route or exactly when it sailed. Many of them keep close to shore — the Mossad called it "shore scratching" — and avoid going into open waters where radar can pick them up. It's difficult for radar to locate a ship that's close to shore because the image can be swallowed by the noise of mountains, or a ship may be in one of the many harbors behind the mountains and simply not be seen. Then when it does emerge, its identity may be uncertain. There are a lot of ships on the Mediterranean. The U.S. Sixth Fleet, the Russian fleet, all kinds of ships, including merchant ships from around the world. The Mossad is not free, then, to do anything it wants. All the countries along the Mediterranean have their own radar, so the Mossad has to be very careful what it does there.

Obtaining specific information inside Libya, however, was easier said than done. It was too dangerous to send someone in there to try recruiting, and the Mossad was by now hitting its collective head against a brick wall. At last, someone at the meeting, who had worked as a "reporter" in Tunis and Algiers for *Afrique-Asia*,* a French-language newspaper covering Arab affairs, suggested the best way to begin was simply to telephone Tripoli harbor and find out who had the sort of information they needed. That way, they could at least narrow it down to a specific target.

It was one of those simple ideas that are often overlooked when people become involved in intrigue and complicated operational details. And so, a telephone line was set aside that could be dialed from Tel Aviv but would operate through an office/apartment in Paris, should anyone trace the call. It was attached to an insurance company in France that was owned by a sayan.

Before he called, the katsa had a complete cover built for him as an insurance investigator. He had an office with a secretary. The secretary, a woman, was what is called a *bat leveyha*, which means "escort" (not in the sexual sense). It simply refers to a local woman, not necessarily a Jew, who is recruited as an assistant agent and given a job where a woman is needed. She would be aware that she was working for Israeli intelligence through the local embassy.

---

* See Chapter 3: FRESHMEN

The idea was based on the concept of *mikrim ve tguvot*, Hebrew for "actions and reactions." They already knew the action, but they had to anticipate the reaction. For every possible reaction, another action is planned. It's like a giant chess game, except that you don't plan more than two reactions ahead because it would become too complicated. It's all part of regular operational planning, and it goes into every move made.

In the room with the katsa, and listening with earphones, were Menachem Dorf, head of the Mossad's PLO department, and Gidon Naftaly, the Mossad's chief psychiatrist, whose job was to listen and try immediately to analyze the person answering the phone.

The man who answered first didn't understand French, so he passed the call to someone else. The second man came on the line, gave the name of the man in charge, said he'd be back in half an hour, and immediately hung up.

When the katsa called back, he asked for the harbormaster by name, got him on the line, and identified himself as an insurance investigator with a French underwriting company.

This was their one shot, so it had to work. Not only must the story sound credible, the storyteller must sound as if he believes it, too. And so, the katsa told his listener what business he was in, that they needed to have access to various details about certain ships in the harbors, and that they needed to know who was in charge.

"I'm in charge," the man said. "How can I be of assistance?"

"We know that from time to time ships put in there that their owners claim have been lost or damaged. Now, we're the underwriters, but we can't always check these claims firsthand, so we need to know more."

"What do you need to know?"

"Well, we need to know, for example, if they are being repaired, or if they are loading or unloading. We don't have a representative there, as you know, but we would like to have someone looking after our interests. If you could recommend someone to us, we'd certainly be willing to reimburse him handsomely."

"I think I can help you," the man said. "I have that kind of information, and I don't see any problem with that, as long as we're talking civilian traffic and not military ships."

"We have no interest in your navy," the katsa said. "We're not underwriting its insurance."

The conversation went on for 10 or 15 minutes, during which time the katsa asked about five or six ships. Only one of them, a PLO ship, was there being repaired. He asked for an address where he could send the payment, gave his own address and phone number to the harbormaster, and told him to call anytime he had information he thought would be useful.

Things were going so well, and the target sounded so comfortable, that the katsa felt bold enough to ask the man if he was allowed to accept another job, as an agent for the insurance company, outside his regular work at the harbor.

"I might be able to do some selling," the harbormaster replied, "but only on a part-time basis. At least until I see how it works out."

"Fine. I'll send you a manual and some business cards. When you get a chance to go over that, we'll talk again."

The conversation ended. They now had a paid agent in the harbor, although he didn't know he'd been recruited.

The next task was to summon the business department of Metsada to design the promised insurance manual so that it would make sense *and* allow them to gather the kind of information they wanted. Within a few days, the manual was on its way to Tripoli. Once you commit a telephone and address to someone in a recruitment process, it must be kept alive for at least three years even if stage one in the recruitment process was never passed — unless there had been a confrontation that could expose the katsa, in which case everything would be closed down immediately.

For the next two months or so, the new recruit reported regularly, but during one of the calls he mentioned that he'd read the manual but still wasn't too clear on what being an agent for the company would involve.

"I understand that," the katsa said. "I remember the first

time I saw it, it didn't make a lot of sense to me, either. Listen, when do you have your holidays?"

"In three weeks."

"Great. Rather than trying to sort this out over the phone, why don't you come to France at our expense? I'll send you the tickets. You've already worked out so well for us that we'd love to give you some time in the south of France, and we can combine a little business with pleasure. And I'll be honest with you, it's better for our tax situation for you to come here."

The recruit was thrilled. The Mossad was paying him only about $1,000 a month, while during the time they had him on the string, he made at least three trips to France. He was useful, but he had no real connections beyond his knowledge of the ships in the harbor, so the idea was not to endanger him. After meeting him in person, it seemed the best plan would be to gently drop the attempt to have him do other things, but to continue using him for information on PLO ships.

At first, they asked only about some of the ships entering the harbor, on the pretext that they were the ones being underwritten by their company. Then they devised a plan whereby the harbormaster would provide the full lists of all ships docking. They promised to pay him accordingly. That way, they said, they could supply this information to other insurance underwriters who would be only too happy to pay for the information; they, in turn, could share the proceeds with him.

And so he went happily back to Tripoli where he continued supplying them with information on all harbor traffic. At one point, a ship owned by Abu Nidal, the hated head of the PFLP-GC faction of the PLO, was in the harbor being loaded with military equipment — including shoulder-carried anti-aircraft missiles and many other weapons the Israelis did not want to see ending up in the hands of Palestinian fighters on their borders.

They knew about Nidal's ship through their tie-in with PLO communications, thanks to a slip in Nidal's normally careful speaking habits, and all that remained was to ask their happy harbormaster exactly where the ship was and how long it would be there. He confirmed the vessel's location, along with that of another one also being loaded with equipment destined for Cyprus.

Two Israeli missile boats, SAAR-4 class, appeared to be on regular patrol one warm summer night in 1985, only this time they stopped long enough to unload six commandos in a small, electric-powered submarine with a hood on top, similar in appearance to a World War II fighter plane without the wings — or a long torpedo with a propeller on the back. It was called a wet submarine, and the commandos sat under the hood, dressed for action in their wet suits and oxygen tanks.

After disembarking from the patrol boats, they went quickly to a ship entering the harbor, latched themselves to its hull by magnetic plates, and piggybacked a ride into the harbor itself.

The hood of the submarine provided them with a life-saving protective shield, necessary because the Mossad knew from their conversations with the harbormaster that once every five hours, Libyan security cruised the harbor, tossing hand grenades into the water and creating a tremendous amount of water pressure — enough to finish off any frogman who happened to be in the area. They had discovered this security device one time when the katsa heard explosions in the background and simply asked the harbormaster what was making the noise. It's a routine security measure in most harbors where countries are at war. Syria and Israel both do it, too.

And so, they simply waited in their wet submarine until security made its rounds, then they quietly slipped into the water, carrying their leech mines with them. After attaching them to the two loaded PLO ships, they returned to their submarine. The whole thing took only about two and a half hours. Since they also knew which ships were leaving the harbor that night, they headed for a tanker near the harbor entrance, but decided not to clamp on to it because it would be too difficult to unhook their tiny vessel once the tanker was under full steam.

Unfortunately, they ran out of oxygen in the submarine, and the battery died. There was no point in trying to carry it with them once they were in open waters, so they hooked it on to a buoy where it could be recovered later, attached themselves to one another by rope, and performed what is called a "sunflower." That means putting a blast of air inside their wet suits, which makes them expand like balloons, and allows the frogmen simply to float on top of the water without having to do any work at all to stay afloat. They even took turns sleeping, with one man staying awake on watch at all times. A few hours later, an Israeli patrol boat sneaked in, answering their beeper signals, picked them up, and whisked them off to safety.

At about 6 a.m. that day, there were four large explosions in the harbor, and two PLO ships went down, loaded with millions of dollars worth of military equipment and ammunition.

The katsa assumed that would be it for their harbormaster. Surely the explosions would make him suspicious. Instead, when he called in that day, the man was tremendously excited about it.

"You won't believe what happened!" he said. "They blew up two ships right in the middle of the harbor!"

"Who did?"

"The Israelis, of course," he said. "I don't know how they found the ships, but they did. Fortunately, they weren't any of yours, so you don't have to worry."

The harbormaster went on working for the Mossad for another 18 months or so. He made a lot of money until one day, he just disappeared, leaving a trail of destroyed and captured PLO arms ships in his wake.

17

Beirut

IT WAS NOT Israel's finest hour. In mid-September 1982, images of the massacre were being seen around the world, on television, in newspapers and magazines. There were bodies everywhere. Men, women, children. Even horses had been slaughtered. Some of the victims had been shot point-blank in the head, others had had their throats slashed, some had been castrated; young men in groups of 10 and 20 had been herded together and shot en masse. Almost all of the 800 Palestinians who had died in the two Beirut refugee camps of Sabra and Shatila had been unarmed, innocent civilians caught in a murderous revenge by the Lebanese Christian Phalangists.

Reaction against Israel was unanimous. In Italy, for example, dock workers refused to load Israeli vessels. Britain formally condemned Israel, and Egypt recalled its ambassador. There were mass protests within Israel itself.

* * *

Since the country's beginning, many Israelis have had a dream of being able to live in cooperation with the Arab countries — of becoming part of a world where its people could cross those borders and be greeted as friends. The idea of an open border, such as the much-celebrated U.S.-Canadian border, is still virtually incomprehensible to Israelis.

So it was that in the late 1970s, Admony, then head of liaison for the Mossad, made solid contact through the CIA and his European connections with Lebanese Christian Phalangist Bashir Gemayel, a man as brutal as he was powerful, persuading the Mossad that Lebanon needed their help. The Mossad, in turn, persuaded the Israeli government that Gemayel — a close friend of Salameh, the Red Prince — was sincere. It was a picture they perpetuated for years through the selective distillation of intelligence to the government.

Gemayel was also working for the CIA at the time, but for the Mossad the notion of having a "friend" inside an Arab country — no matter how double-dealing he might be — was exciting. In addition, Israel had never feared Lebanon. The joke was that if the two countries went to war, Israel would send its military orchestra to defeat the Lebanese.

In any case, the Lebanese were too busy fighting among themselves at the time to take on anyone else. The various Muslim and Christian forces were fighting for control, as they still are, and Gemayel, his forces under siege, decided to turn to Israel for help. As an added bonus, the Mossad saw this as a way to get rid of Israel's Public Enemy Number One, the PLO. Throughout the whole period, long after Israel's actions had backfired, the Lebanese connection remained critical for the Mossad, because Admony, its head, was the man who started it all and saw it as his crowning achievement.

In many respects, Lebanon today is like Chicago and New York in the 1920s and 1930s when the various mobs, or mafia families, were openly fighting for control. Both violence and ostentation were the norm, and for a time, government officials seemed unable, or unwilling, to do anything about it.

Lebanon, too, has its families, each with its army or militia loyal to the "don." But religious and family loyalties have long played second fiddle to the power and money of the drug trade and numerous mafia-type activities that feed the engine of Lebanese corruption and maintain the current state of anarchy there.

There are the Druzes, the fourth largest of more than a dozen Lebanese sects, an offshoot of Isma'ili Muslims, with about 250,000 adherents in Lebanon (260,000 in Syria, which backs them, and 40,000 in Israel), headed by Walid Jumblatt.

The governmental system is based on the last census, in 1932, when the Christians still formed a majority. So, the constitution dictates that the president must be Christian, even though there is general acceptance that Muslims now make up about 60 percent of the country's 3.5 million people, and the largest sub-group, about 40 percent, are Shi'ite Muslims, led by Nabih Berri. Another significant fighting force in the early 1980s were the Sunni Muslims, under Rashid Karami.

The Christian forces are divided into two main families, the Gemayel and the Franjieh. Pierre Gemayel founded the Phalangists, and at one time, Suleiman Franjieh was president. When Bashir Gemayel was maneuvering to become president, he eliminated his main rival, Tony Franjieh, in a June 1978 attack on the family's summer villa at Ehden.

His Phalangist soldiers murdered Tony, his wife, their two-year-old daughter, and several bodyguards. Gemayel, the Jesuit-educated thug who would become Israel's "friend" through the efforts of the Mossad, dismissed the attack as a "social revolt against feudalism." In February 1980, a car bomb killed Gemayel's 18-month-old daughter and three bodyguards. In July 1980, Gemayel's troops virtually wiped out the Christian militia of ex-president Camille Chamoun's National Liberation Party.

Gemayel ruled from his family's 300-year-old estate at Bikfaya, in the mountains northeast of Beirut. The family had made untold millions in a scam that began when they won a contract to build a road through the mountainous terrain. The long-term contract also involved regular maintenance fees for upkeep and repairs. The family faithfully collected their money for the road construction and, over the years, for maintenance. The only problem was that they never did build the road. And they argued that they had to keep collecting for maintenance, because if they didn't, someone would come to check and discover the road wasn't there.

In any event, Gemayel was just 35 when he won election by parliament to a six-year term as president in September 1982. He did not live long enough to assume the post, but at the time he was the only candidate. Yet when as few as 56 deputies showed up to vote at the special session to elect him — six short of a quorum — Gemayel's militiamen quickly rounded up six more reluctant deputies and he won the vote 57-0, with five abstentions. Begin sent him a congratulatory telegram that began, "My dear friend."

In addition to the ruling families, there were at the time a host of unaligned gangs, most led by such colorful but brutal characters as Electroman, Toaster, Cowboy, Fireball, and the King. Electroman got his name after being shot through the neck by the Syrians. He was sent to Israel for treatment, where an electronic voice box was installed in his throat. As for Toaster, when he caught someone he didn't like, he'd connect them to high-voltage electricity and literally toast them. Fireball came by his name honestly. He was a pyromaniac, who loved to watch buildings burn. Cowboy looked like something out of a Hollywood western, wearing a cowboy hat and two guns in holsters at his sides. And the King, believe it or not, thought he was Elvis Presley; he had an Elvis hairstyle, tried to speak English with Elvis's twang, and used to serenade his family with off-key Elvis songs.

The gang members drove around in Mercedes and BMWs. Inevitably, they dressed in the finest silk suits from Paris. They always ate well. It wouldn't have mattered if they were under siege for six months, they'd still have had oysters for breakfast. In fact, at the height of the 1982 siege of Beirut, a Lebanese restaurateur tried to buy a scrap German submarine, not to join the war, but to bring fresh food and wine from Europe for his restaurant.

The gangs, in addition to their own criminal activities, often freelanced for the major families, performing such duties as manning roadblocks. For example, to get to the government palace in those days, the president had to pass through two roadblocks and pay twice.

In Beirut, people can live very well, but no one knows for how long. Nowhere today is the end nearer than in Beirut, which explains why those involved in the families and gangs live to the fullest, while they can. At most, they account for 200,000 people living on the fast track, which leaves more than a million Lebanese in and around Beirut trying to live their lives and raise their families under impossible conditions.

In 1978, the baby-faced Bashir Gemayel, with his Mossad connections, had asked for weapons in his ongoing dispute with the Franjieh family. (Tony Franjieh was not on good terms with the Mossad.) The Mossad sold them weapons, bought in a way the Mossad had never seen before.

A group of Phalangists were training in the Haifa military base in 1980, learning, for example, how to operate the small Dabur gunboats manufactured by an Israeli weapons company in, of all places, Beersheba, a city surrounded by desert but halfway between the Mediterranean and the Red Sea. When their training was complete, the head of the Lebanese Christian navy, wearing the customary shiny silk suit, arrived in Haifa by boat along with three bodyguards and three Mossad officials, carrying several suitcases. Gemayel's forces bought five of the boats, at about $6 million (U.S.) each, and they paid for them in U.S currency — cash they had brought with them in the suitcases. They took the gunboats back to Juniyah, the picturesque harbor city on the Mediterranean north of Beirut.

When the suitcases were opened, the Lebanese navy commander asked the senior Mossad official if he wanted to count the money. "No, we'll believe you," he said. "But if you're wrong, you're dead." They counted it later. It was all there.

For the most part, the Phalangists used their "navy" to cruise at five knots — about one mile per hour — offshore, past West Beirut, firing their machine guns at the Muslims: an exercise that killed hundreds of innocent civilians but made little impact on the actual military hostilities.

Because of his Mossad links, strongman Gemayel agreed to allow Israel to set up a naval radar station in Juniyah in 1979, complete with about 30 Israeli navy personnel — the country's first physical structure in Lebanon. That they were there, of course, strengthened the Phalangist hand, since the Muslims — and the Syrians for that matter — were not anxious to tangle with Israel. Many of the negotiating sessions between the Mossad and Gemayel for the radar station took place at his family compound north of Beirut. In return for his trouble, the Mossad was paying Gemayel between $20,000 and $30,000 a month.

At the same time, the Israelis had another friend in southern Lebanon — Major Sa'ad Haddad, a Christian who commanded a militia composed mainly of Shi'ites and who was almost as anxious as the Israelis to get Yassar Arafat's PLO forces out of southern Lebanon. He, too, would prove cooperative when the time came to move against Arafat.

In Beirut, the Mossad station, called "Submarine," was located in the basement of a former government building near the border between Christian-dominated East Beirut and Muslim-dominated West Beirut. At any given time, about 10 people were working in the station, seven or eight of them katsas, with one or two from Unit 504, the Israeli military equivalent of the Mossad, which shared office space with them.

By the early 1980s, the Mossad was deeply involved with several other warring Lebanese families, paying for information, passing it between groups, even paying the gangs and some Palestinians in the refugee camps for intelligence and services. Besides Gemayel, both the Jumblatt and Berri families were on the Mossad payroll.

The situation was what the Israelis called *halemh*, an Arab word meaning "noisy mess." About this time it became even messier, as westerners began to be kidnapped. In July 1982, for example, David S. Dodge, 58, acting president of the American University of Beirut, was kidnapped by four gunmen as he walked from his office to his campus home.

A common way of transporting hostages was called the "mummy transport." That meant wrapping a man tightly, head to toe, with brown plastic tape, usually leaving only an opening at his nose so he could breathe, and sticking the "parcel" in the trunk of a car or under the seat. Several victims were simply left there to die, usually when kidnappers came upon a roadblock set up by a rival group, underscoring a favorite saying in Lebanon that it's only terrible if it happens to you.

* * *

And so it was that, with the Mossad working its various Lebanese connections and Defense Minister Ariel Sharon — described by the Americans as a "hawk among hawks" — itching to get into battle, pressure began building on Begin; at the very least, it was time to wipe the PLO out of southern Lebanon, where they had been using their position to lob shells and stage raids into Israeli villages near the northern border.

Sharon had been hailed by his soldiers after the 1973 Yom Kippur War as "Arik, Arik, King of Israel." The five-foot, six-inch, 235-pound Sharon, frequently called "the bulldozer" because of his shape and style, was only 25 when he led a commando raid that killed scores of innocent Jordanians, forcing Israel's first prime minister, David Ben-Gurion, to make a public apology. Later, Moshe Dayan nearly court-martialed him for defying orders during the 1956 Sinai campaign by staging a paratroop maneuver that cost the lives of dozens of Israeli soldiers.

Months before the Israeli invasion of Lebanon, the PLO had suspected it was coming, and Arafat ordered a halt to the bombardment of Israeli villages. Still, in the spring of 1982, Israel massed its invasion forces near its northern border four times, each time backing off at the last minute, largely because of U.S. pressure. Begin assured the Americans that if Israel ever did attack, its soldiers would go only as far as the Litani River, about 18 miles north of the border, to force the PLO out of the range of Israeli settlements. He did not keep his promise, and considering the speed with which Israeli forces appeared in Beirut, clearly he had not meant to.

On April 25, 1982, Israel withdrew from the last third of the Sinai, which it had occupied since the Six Day War in 1967, fulfilling the 1979 Egyptian-Israeli Camp David accord.

But as Israeli bulldozers were destroying the remains of Jewish settlements in the Sinai, Israel broke a ceasefire along its 63-mile Lebanese border that had been in effect since July 1981. In 1978, Israel had invaded Lebanon with 10,000 men and 200 tanks, but had still failed to dislodge the PLO.

On a sunny Sunday morning in Galilee, June 6, 1982, Begin's cabinet gave Sharon the go-ahead to begin the invasion. That day, Irish Lieutenant General William Callaghan, commander of the United Nations Interim Force in Lebanon (UNIFL), strolled into the forward headquarters of Israel's Northern Command in Zefat to discuss a UN Security Council resolution calling for the end of the PLO-Israeli barrages across the border. Instead of the expected discussion, however, he was told by Israel's chief of staff, Lieutenant General Rafael Eitan, that Israel would invade Lebanon in 28 minutes' time. Sure enough, 60,000 troops and more than 500 tanks were soon sweeping into Lebanon on the ill-fated campaign that would drive some 11,000 PLO fighters out of that country, but tarnish Israel's international image, costing the lives of 462 Israeli soldiers, with another 2,218 wounded.

Within the first 48 hours, much of the PLO strength was wiped out, although they did put up considerable resistance at Sidon, Tyre, and Damur. Begin had responded to two urgent letters from Reagan asking him not to attack Lebanon by saying that Israel wanted only to push the PLO back from its borders. "The bloodthirsty aggressor against us is on our doorstep," he wrote. "Do we not have the inherent right to self-defense?"

While they were attacking the PLO in the south, the Israeli forces joined Gemayel's Christian Phalangists on the outskirts of Beirut. At first, they were hailed as liberators by Christian residents, and showered with rice, flowers, and candy as they entered the city. Before long, they had several thousand PLO commandos sealed off in a siege, along with some 500,000 residents of West Beirut. For the Israeli soldiers, their stay in Lebanon wasn't all war; they'd found a convenient way to make love at the same time in a village just outside Beirut. The place was noteworthy for two things: its beautiful women, and their absent husbands.

But the deadly military bombardment continued, and in August, amid growing domestic and international criticism that they were killing civilians, not warriors, Begin said, "We will do what we have to do. West Beirut is not a city. It's a military target surrounded by civilians."

Finally, after a 10-week siege, the guns fell silent and the PLO commandos evacuated the city, prompting Lebanese Prime Minister Chafik al Wazzan to say, "We have reached the end of our sorrows." He spoke too soon.

In late August, a small U.S.-French-Italian peacekeeping team arrived in Beirut, but the Israelis continued to tighten their grip on the embattled city.

On Tuesday, September 14, 1982, at 4:08 in the afternoon, a 200-pound bomb on the third floor of the Christian Phalange Party headquarters in East Beirut was detonated by remote control, killing president-elect Bashir Gemayel and 25 others as he and about 100 party members were holding their regular weekly meeting. Bashir was replaced by his 40-year-old brother, Amin.

The bombing was traced to Ptabib Chartouny, 26, a member of the Syrian People's Party, rivals of the Phalangists. The operation had been run by Syrian intelligence in Lebanon under Lieutenant Colonel Mohammed G'anen.

Since the CIA had helped put Gemayel together with the Mossad, the United States had an intelligence-sharing agreement with it (this worked largely in the Mossad's favor, since they share very little with any other organization), and because the Mossad saw the CIA as "players who can't play," there is no doubt it was fully aware of the Syrian role in Gemayel's assassination.

But two days after the bombing, Israeli Major General Amir Drori, head of the Northern Command, and several other top Israeli officers had guests at their command post in Beirut port: Lebanese Forces Chief of Staff Fady Frem, and their infamous intelligence chief, Elias Hobeika, a colorful but vicious man who always carried a pistol, a knife, and a hand grenade, and was the most feared Phalangist in Lebanon. He used to kill Syrian soldiers and chop their ears off, stringing them up on a wire in his house. Hobeika was a close associate of Christian General Samir Zaza, and later the two men often alternated as commanders of the Christian army. For the Mossad, however, Hobeika had been an important contact. He had attended the Staff and Command College in Israel. He was the main leader of the force that went into the refugee camps and slaughtered the civilians.

Hobeika, who hated Amin Gemayel and wanted to embarrass him, was involved in a bitter internal power struggle because he was being blamed by some for not having protected Bashir Gemayel.

At 5 p.m. on September 16, Hobeika assembled his forces at Beirut International Airport and moved into the Shatila camp, with the help of flares and, later, tank and mortar fire from the Israeli Defense Force (IDF). At the time, an Israeli cabinet press statement claimed the IDF had "taken positions in West Beirut to prevent the danger of violence, bloodshed, and anarchy."

The next day, Hobeika received Israeli permission to bring two additional battalions into the camps. Israel knew the massacre was taking place. Israeli forces had even set up observation posts on top of several seven-story buildings at the Kuwaiti embassy traffic circle, giving them an unobstructed view of the carnage.

Outraged by this slaughter and by Israel's role in it, the war of words between Reagan and Begin escalated, and by early October, Reagan had sent 1,200 U.S. marines back to Beirut, only 19 days after they had left. They joined 1,560 French paratroopers and 1,200 Italian soldiers in yet another peacekeeping force.

* * *

All this time, the Mossad station in Beirut was busy carrying on its work. One of its informants was a "stinker" — actually also a Yiddish term, used in Israel when referring to an informant (like the English expression "stool pigeon"). The stinker had links with a local garage that specialized in refitting vehicles for smuggling purposes. Many Israeli military people, for example, were smuggling tax-free videos and cigarettes out of Lebanon and turning huge profits in Israel, where the taxes are 100 to 200 percent on such items. The Mossad, in turn, often passed pertinent information along to the Israeli military police, with the result that many smuggling attempts were foiled.

In the summer of 1983, this same informant told the Mossad about a large Mercedes truck that was being fitted by the Shi'ite Muslims with spaces that could hold bombs. He said it had even larger than usual spaces for this, so that whatever it was destined for was going to be a major target. Now, the Mossad knew that, for size, there were only a few logical targets, one of which must be the U.S. compound. The question then was whether or not to warn the Americans to be on particular alert for a truck matching the description.

The decision was too important to be taken in the Beirut station, so it was passed along to Tel Aviv, where Admony, then head of Mossad, decided they would simply give the Americans the usual general warning, a vague notice that they had reason to believe someone might be planning an operation against them. But this was so general, and so commonplace, it was like sending a weather report; unlikely to raise any particular alarm or prompt increased security precautions. In the six months following receipt of this information, for example, there were more than 100 general warnings of car-bomb attacks. One more would not heighten U.S. concerns or surveillance.

Admony, in refusing to give the Americans specific information on the truck, said, "No, we're not there to protect Americans. They're a big country. Send only the regular information."

At the same time, however, all Israeli installations were given the specific details and warned to watch for a truck matching the description of the Mercedes.

At 6:20 a.m. on October 23, 1983, a large Mercedes truck approached the Beirut airport, passing well within sight of Israeli sentries in their nearby base, going through a Lebanese army checkpoint, and turning left into the parking lot. A U.S. Marine guard reported with alarm that the truck was gathering speed, but before he could do anything, the truck roared toward the entrance of the four-story reinforced concrete Aviation Safety Building, used as headquarters for the Eighth Marine Battalion, crashing through a wrought-iron gate, hitting the sand-bagged guard post, smashing through another barrier, and ramming over a wall of sandbags into the lobby, exploding with such a terrific force that the building was instantly reduced to rubble.

A few minutes later, another truck smashed into the French paratroopers' headquarters at Bir Hason, a seafront residential neighborhood just two miles from the U.S. compound, hitting it with such an impact that it moved the entire building 30 feet and killed 58 soldiers.

The loss of 241 U.S. Marines, most of them still sleeping in their cots at the time of the suicide mission, was the highest single-day death toll for the Americans since 246 died throughout Vietnam at the start of the Tet offensive on January 13, 1968.

Within days, the Israelis passed along to the CIA the names of 13 people who they said were connected to the bombing deaths of the U.S. Marines and French paratroopers, a list including Syrian intelligence, Iranians in Damascus, and Shi'ite Mohammed Hussein Fadlallah.

At Mossad headquarters, there was a sigh of relief that it wasn't us who got hit. It was seen as a small incident so far as the Mossad was concerned — that we had stumbled over it and wouldn't tell anybody. The problem was if we had leaked information and it was traced back, our informant would have been killed. The next time, we wouldn't know if *we* were on the hit list.

The general attitude about the Americans was: "Hey, they wanted to stick their nose into this Lebanon thing, let them pay the price."

For me, it was the first time I had received a major rebuke from my Mossad superior, liaison officer Amy Yaar. I said at the time that the American soldiers killed in Beirut would be on our minds longer than our own casualties because they'd come in with good faith, to help us get out of this mess we'd created. I was told: "Just shut up. You're talking out of your league. We're giving the Americans much more than they're giving us." They always said that, but it's not true. So much of Israeli equipment was American, and the Mossad owed them a lot.

During all this time, several westerners continued to be

held captive while others became fresh hostages of the various factions. One day in late March 1984, CIA station head William Buckley, officially listed as a political officer at the U.S. embassy, left his apartment in West Beirut and was abducted at gunpoint by three Shi'ite soldiers. He was subsequently held for 18 months, tortured extensively and, finally, brutally murdered. He could have been saved.

The Mossad, through its extensive network of informants, had a good idea of where many of the hostages were being held, and by whom. Even if you don't know where, it's always crucial to know by whom, otherwise you might find yourself negotiating with someone who doesn't have any hostages. There's the story of the Lebanese who instructed his aide to find someone to negotiate a hostage with. The aide said, "Which country is your hostage from?" The reply: "Find me a country and I'll get the hostage."

Men at Buckley's level are considered of major importance because they have so much knowledge. Forcing information from them can mean a death sentence for many other operatives working around the globe. A group calling itself the Islamic Jihad (Islamic Holy War) claimed responsibility for Buckley's kidnapping. Bill Casey, CIA chief, was so anxious to save Buckley that an expert FBI team specially trained in locating kidnap victims was dispatched to Beirut to find him. But after a month, they'd come up with nothing. Official U.S. policy then prohibited negotiations to ransom hostages, but Casey had authorized considerable sums to pay informants and, if need be, buy Buckley's freedom.

It didn't take the CIA long to turn to the Mossad for help. Shortly after Buckley's kidnapping, the CIA liaison officer in Tel Aviv asked the Mossad for as much information as it could get about Buckley and some of the other hostages.

About 11:30 one morning, an intercom announcement at headquarters asked all personnel to stay off the main floor and the elevator for the next hour because there were guests. Two CIA officials were escorted in and taken to Admony's ninth-floor office. The Mossad head told them he would give them everything the Mossad had, but if they wanted something in particular, they'd have to go through the prime minister, "because he's our boss." In fact, Admony wanted a formal request, so that he could collect on the favor later on, if need be.

In any event, the Americans made a formal request through their ambassador to then prime minister, Shimon Peres. Peres instructed Admony to have the Mossad give the CIA everything it could to help with the U.S. hostage situation. Normally, this sort of request includes limitations — such strictures as "We'll give you whatever information we can, as long as it doesn't harm our personnel" — but in this case, there were no limitations, which was a clear indication of how significant both the United States and Peres considered the hostage issue to be.

Politically, these things can be dynamite. The Reagan administration would remember only too well the irreparable political damage and humiliation Jimmy Carter suffered when Americans were held hostage in Iran following the overthrow of the Shah.

Admony assured Peres that he would do everything he could to help the Americans. "I have a good feeling in this regard," he said. "We might have some information that will help them." In truth, he had no intention of helping them.

Two CIA officials were called in to meet with the *Saifanim* ("goldfish") department, the PLO specialists. The meeting took place at Midrasha, or the Academy. Since Israel considers the PLO its main enemy, the Mossad often calculates that if something can be blamed on the PLO, it has done its job. So they set about attempting to blame the PLO for the kidnappings, even with the knowledge that many of them, including Buckley's, had no PLO connection.

Still, hoping to look as if they were cooperating fully, the Saifanim men plastered maps all over a boardroom wall and offered the Americans a considerable amount of data regarding general locations of hostages; although they were constantly being moved to new locations, the Mossad usually had good general knowledge of where they were. The Mossad left out many of the details they had garnered from their sources, but told the Americans that from the general picture, they could decide if it was worth going further into the specifics. This was all part of an unstated, but very real, system of debt repayment, building Brownie points in return for future favors.

At the end of the meeting, a full report was sent to Admony. For their part, the Americans went back and discussed it with their officials. Two days later, they returned, seeking more specific information on one answer given them in the original briefing. The CIA thought this might prove to be a diamond in the rough, but they wanted to verify the specifics. They asked to speak to the source.

"Forget it," the Mossad man said. "Nobody talks to sources."

"Okay," the CIA man said. "That's fair enough. How about letting us talk to the case officer?"

The Mossad protects katsas' identities vigorously. They simply can't risk letting others see them. After all, who knows when they might be recognized as a result? A katsa in Beirut today could end up working anywhere tomorrow, run into the CIA man, and blow an entire operation. Still, there are many ways of arranging interviews where the two sides don't actually meet. Such methods as speaking behind screens and distorting the voice, or wearing a hood, would have served the purpose. But the Mossad had no intention of being that helpful. Despite direct orders from their "boss," Peres, the Saifanim officials said they'd have to check it with the head of the Mossad.

Word went around headquarters that Admony was having a bad day. His mistress, who was the daughter of the head of Tsomet, had a bad day, too. She was having her period — at least, that was the joke. At lunch in the dining room that day, everybody was talking about the hostage thing. By the time it got down to the dining room, the story may have been slightly exaggerated, but Admony is supposed to have said, "Those fucking Americans. Maybe they want us to get the hostages for them, too. What are they, crazy?"

In any event, the answer was no. The CIA could not see a katsa. Furthermore, they told the Americans that the information they'd been given was outdated and related to a completely different case, so it had nothing to do with the

Buckley case. That wasn't true, but they further embellished their story by asking the Americans to disregard that information in order to save the lives of other hostages. They even promised to double their efforts to help the Americans in return.

Many people in the office said the Mossad were going to regret it someday. But the majority were happy. The attitude was, "Hey, we showed them. We're not going to be kicked around by the Americans. We are the Mossad. We are the best."

* * *

It was just this concern over Buckley and the other hostages that prompted Casey to circumvent the congressional arm of the U.S. system and become involved in the plan to supply Iran with embargoed arms in return for the safety of American hostages, culminating in the Iran-Contra scandal. Had the Mossad been more helpful initially, it not only could have saved Buckley and others, it might also have averted this major U.S. political scandal. Peres had clearly seen it as being in Israel's interest to cooperate, but the Mossad — Admony in particular — had other interests and pursued them relentlessly.

The final tragedy of Israel's Mossad-led involvement in Lebanon was that when their station "Submarine" was closed, a lot of agents were left behind, and their entire network collapsed. Many agents were killed. Others were smuggled out successfully.

Israel didn't start the war and they didn't end it. It's like playing blackjack in a casino. You don't start the game, and you don't end it. But you're there. Israel just didn't hit any jackpots.

During this period, Peres's "adviser on terrorism" was a man named Amiram Nir. When Peres suspected the Mossad wasn't being as helpful as it might have been with the Americans, he decided to use Nir as his personal liaison between the two countries, a move that brought Nir into contact with U.S. Lieutenant Colonel Oliver North, a central figure in the subsequent Iran-Contra scandal. Nir's position in the scheme of things was such that he carried the famous Bible auto-graphed by Ronald Reagan when North and former United States national-security adviser Robert McFarlane — using false Irish passports — secretly visited Iran in May 1986 to sell arms. Money from that sale was used to buy arms for the U.S.-backed Contras in Nicaragua.

Nir was definitely a man with connections and inside knowledge. He had played a major role in capturing the hijackers of the cruise ship *Achille Lauro* in 1985, and he briefed then U.S. vice-president (and former CIA director) George Bush on the Iran arms negotiations.

Nir was on record as saying that he and North supervised several counter-terrorist operations in 1985 and 1986, authorized by a secret U.S.-Israel agreement. In November 1985, North credited Nir with the idea of generating profits from arms sales to Iran to pay for other covert operations.

Nir's involvement in all this becomes even more intriguing because of his relationship with a shadowy Iran-based businessman called Manucher Ghorbanifar. CIA chief Bill Casey eventually warned North that Ghorbanifar was almost certainly an Israeli intelligence agent. Still, Ghorbanifar and Nir did successfully arrange for Iranian help in the July 29, 1986, release of the Reverend Lawrence Jenco, an American hostage held by Lebanese extremists. Within days of Jenco's release, Nir briefed George Bush on the need to respond by shipping arms to Iran.

Ghorbinafar had been a CIA source since 1974, the man who planted rumors in 1981 about Libyan hit teams being sent to the United States to kill Reagan. Two years later, after determining the rumor was fabricated, the CIA ended his relationship as a source, and in 1984 issued a formal "burn notice" warning that Ghorbinafar was a "talented fabricator."

Even so, it was Ghorbinafar who produced a bridge loan of $5 million from Saudi Arabian billionaire Adnan Khashoggi to overcome distrust between Iran and Israel in the arms deal. Khashoggi himself had been recruited years earlier as an agent by the Mossad. Indeed, his spectacular personal jet, about which much has been written, was fitted in Israel. Khashoggi was not getting a base salary from the Mossad the way regular agents do, but he was using Mossad money for many of his exploits. He got loans whenever he needed money to tide him over, and considerable sums of Mossad money were funneled through Khashoggi's companies, much of it originating with Ovadia Gaon, a French-based Jewish multimillionaire of Moroccan background who was often called upon when large amounts of money were needed.

In any event, Iran didn't want to pay until it had the weapons in hand, and Israel didn't want to send the 508 TOW missiles until it had the money, so the bridge loan through Khashoggi was critical in completing the transaction. Shortly after that deal, another American hostage, the Reverend Benjamin Weir, was released, further convincing the Americans that despite his talents as a liar, Ghorbanifar could still deliver hostages through his contacts in Iran. At the same time, Israel was secretly selling about $500 million worth of arms to Iran's Ayatollah Khomeini, so there is little doubt that Ghorbanifar and his associate, Nir, used this leverage to wrangle deals over American hostages.

On July 29, 1986, Nir met with Bush at the King David Hotel in Jerusalem. Details of the meeting were recorded in a top-secret three-page memo written by Craig Fuller, Bush's chief of staff. It quotes Nir as telling Bush of the Israeli involvement, "We are dealing with the most radical elements [in Iran because] we've learned they can deliver and the moderates can't." Reagan had consistently claimed he was dealing with Iranian "moderates" in sending weapons to Iran. Nir told Bush the Israelis "activated the channel. We gave a front to the operation, provided a physical base, provided aircraft."

Nir was scheduled to be a key witness in the 1989 trial of North over the Iran-Contra scandal, particularly since he had claimed that counter-terrorist activities he and North supervised during 1985 and 1986 were authorized by a secret U.S.-Israeli agreement. His testimony could have been highly embarrassing, not only to the Reagan administration, but also in outlining just how large a role the Israelis played in this whole affair.

However, on November 30, 1988, while flying in a Cessna

T210 over a ranch 110 miles west of Mexico City, Nir was reportedly killed along with the pilot when the plane crashed. The other three passengers, all slightly injured, included Canadian Adriana Stanton, 25, of Toronto, who claimed to have no connection with Nir. However, the Mexicans described her as his "secretary" and his "guide," and she did work with a firm with which Nir was connected. She refused further comment.

Nir had been in Mexico to discuss marketing avocados. On November 29, he had visited an avocado-packing plant in the western Mexican state of Michoacán. He held a large financial interest in the plant. He chartered a light plane the next day for a flight to Mexico City, using the alias Pat Weber and, according to officials, was killed when it crashed. However, his "body" was identified by a mysterious Argentine, Pedro Cruchet, who worked for Nir and was in Mexico illegally. He told police he had lost his ID at a bullfight, but even without it, he managed to obtain custody of Nir's remains.

In addition, original reports from the state attorney general's office confirmed both Nir and Stanton, while supposedly on legitimate business, were traveling under assumed names. Later, an inspector at the departure airport said that wasn't true, although the error was never explained.

More than 1,000 people came to Nir's funeral in Israel and Defense Minister Yitzhak Rabin spoke of his "mission to as-yet-unrevealed destinations on secret assignment and to secrets which he kept locked in his heart."

At the time of Nir's accident, one unnamed intelligence official was quoted in the *Toronto Star* as saying that he did not believe Nir was dead. Rather, he said that Nir had likely got his face surgically altered in Geneva, "where the clinics are very good, very private, and very discreet."

Whatever happened to Nir, we can only speculate on how much damage to the Reagan administration and the Israeli government his testimony could have done in the subsequent Iran-Contra hearings and criminal trials.

But during the U.S. Senate Select Committee investigations in July 1987, a memo written by North to former national-security adviser, Vice Admiral John Poindexter, dated September 15, 1986, and censored for security reasons, recommended that Poindexter first discuss the arms deal with Casey and then brief President Reagan.

Poindexter was the only one of seven people convicted in the scandal who had to go to jail. On June 11, 1990, he received a six-month sentence and a stern lecture from U.S. District Court Judge Harold Greene, who said Poindexter deserved incarceration as the "decision-making head of the Iran-Contra operation."

On March 3, 1989, Robert McFarlane was fined $20,000 and given two years' probation after pleading guilty to four misdemeanor counts of withholding information from Congress. On July 6, 1989, following the sensational Washington trial, Oliver North was fined $150,000 and ordered to do 1,200 hours of community service. He had been found guilty by a jury on May 4 on three of 12 counts. North also received a three-year suspended sentence, plus two years' probation.

North's memo to Poindexter underscores the importance of Nir's role in this scandal in a section that reads: "Amiram Nir, the special assistant to Prime Minister (Shimon) Peres on counter-terrorism, had indicated that during the 15-minute private discussion with the president, Peres is likely to raise several sensitive issues."

By then, three American hostages had been released in connection with the arms sales. They were Jenco, Weir, and David Jacobsen.

Under the heading "hostages," the memo said: "Several weeks ago, Peres expressed concern that the United States may be contemplating termination of current efforts with Iran. The Israelis view the hostage issue as a hurdle which must be crossed en route to a broadened strategic relationship with the Iranian government.

"It is likely that Peres will seek assurances that the United States will indeed continue with the current 'joint initiative' in that neither Weir nor Jenco would be free today without Israeli help . . . it would be helpful if the president would simply thank Peres for their discreet assistance."

Apparently, Reagan did. And it's highly likely that Peres returned the thanks, at least in part, by arranging for Nir's convenient "death" to avoid his testifying in public.

It is difficult to be certain, but given the questionable circumstances — plus the fact that Israeli arms dealers were funneling weapons and training through the Caribbean to Colombian drug lords at the time — it is unlikely that Nir is dead.

We may never know for sure. But we do know that, had the Mossad been more forthcoming with intelligence concerning American and other western hostages, the entire Iran-Contra affair might never have happened.

Epilogue

On DECEMBER 8, 1987, an Israeli army truck collided with several vans in Gaza, killing four Arabs and injuring 17 others. The incident sparked widespread protests the next day, particularly as rumor spread that the accident had been a deliberate reprisal for the December 6 stabbing death of an Israeli statesman in Gaza.

The next day, Gazon protesters blocked roads with barricades of burning tires. They threw stones, Molotov cocktails, and iron rods at Israeli troops. On December 10, the rioting spread to the Balata refugee camp near the West Bank city of Neblus.

On December 16, special Israeli anti-riot forces used water cannon for the first time against protesters, and great numbers of Israeli soldiers were sent to the Gaza Strip, attempting to quell the growing unrest.

Two days later, after Friday prayers, Palestinian youths rushed out of Gaza's mosques, confronting Israeli troops in running street battles. Three more Arabs were shot to death. Afterward, Israeli troops stormed Gaza's Shifa Hospital, arresting dozens of wounded Arabs, and beating doctors and nurses who tried to protect their patients.

The *intifada* had begun.

On May 16, 1990, a 1,000-page report sponsored by the Swedish branch of the Save The Children Fund, and financed by the Ford Foundation, accused Israel of "severe, indiscriminate, and recurring" violence against Palestinian children. It estimated that between 50,000 and 63,000 children had been treated for injuries, including at least 6,500 wounded by gunfire. It said most of the children killed had not been participating in stone-throwing when they were shot, and one-fifth of the cases it examined showed that the victims were shot either at home or within 30 feet of their homes.

The intifada still rages, with no end in sight. By July 1990, according to Associated Press, 722 Palestinians were killed by Israelis, and 230 more by Palestinian radicals; at least 45 Israelis have died.

During 1989, Israel sent a peak of 10,000 soldiers into Gaza and the West Bank to try to keep order. By April 1990, that had fallen to about 5,000 troops.

On February 13, 1990, the *Wall Street Journal* reported that an Israeli bank study had estimated that the first two years of the uprising had cost Israel $1 billion in lost growth and production. In addition, it had cost that country $600 million for the army to suppress the intifada.

There are more than 600,000 Palestinians crammed into the Gaza Strip's 146 square miles. About 60,000 of them travel into Israel to work each day, toiling primarily in low-paying menial jobs, returning home each night because they are forbidden to stay there overnight.

On March 16, 1990, Israel's Knesset defeated the government of Prime Minister Yitzhak Shamir by a vote of 60 to 55, the first time an Israeli government had fallen on a non-confidence vote. It came after Shamir refused to accept a U.S. plan for beginning Israeli-Palestinian peace talks.

On June 7, Shamir and his right-wing Likud Party formed a coalition with some splinter parties, giving them a two-seat edge in the Knesset in what most observers saw as the most extreme right-wing government in Israeli history, allowing Shamir to continue his policies of promoting settlements in the disputed territories and refusing to talk to the Palestinians.

On November 15, 1988, at the climax of a four-day meeting in Algiers, the Palestinian National Council, considered by the PLO to be its parliament in exile, had proclaimed the establishment of an independent Palestinian state, and voted for the first time to accept key UN resolutions that implicitly recognize Israel's right to exist.

* * *

During this prolonged period of unrest, Israel's image abroad has suffered serious harm. Despite increasing efforts by Israeli officials to muzzle the reporting of West Bank and Gaza unrest, the images of armed troops beating and shooting unarmed Palestinian youths have begun to upset even some of Israel's staunchest allies.

Three days after Shamir lost in the non-confidence vote, former U.S. president Jimmy Carter, on a tour of the region, said the revolt was "being perpetuated partially by the abuse of the Palestinians" by Israeli soldiers, including unjustified killings, house demolitions, and detention without trial.

"There is hardly a family that lives in the West Bank that has not had one of its male members actually incarcerated by military authorities," said Carter.

Israeli army figures show that between 15,000 and 20,000 Palestinians have been wounded and up to 50,000 arrested. About 13,000 of them remain in jail.

In what seemed a deliberate attempt to provoke the Christian community, on April 12, 1990, during Easter week, a group of 150 ardent Jewish nationalists moved into a vacant, four-building, 72-room complex known as St. John's Hospice, in the heart of Jerusalem's Christian quarter. The hospice is within yards of the Church of the Holy Sepulcher, revered by Christians as the traditional site of the tomb of Jesus Christ.

For 10 days, the Israeli government denied any role in the event. Finally, it admitted that it had secretly funneled $1.8 million to the group, 40 percent of the cost of subletting the complex.

U.S. Senator Robert Dole, during an interview while he toured Israel, suggested that the United States should consider cutting its massive aid package to Israel to free up funds for emerging democracies in Eastern Europe and Latin America.

On March 1, 1990, U.S. Secretary of State James Baker said that the Bush administration was willing to consider "shaving" foreign aid to Israel and other countries to help emerging democracies. Baker outraged Shamir by linking an Israeli request for a $400 million loan guarantee to a freeze on new settlements in the occupied territories.

Perhaps the best illustration of the prevailing mood of the right wing in Israel is the celebrated case of Rabbi Moshe Levinger, leader of the far-right Jewish Settlers' Movement. In June 1990, he was sentenced to six months in jail for negligence: he had shot and killed an Arab.

Levinger had been driving his car in Hebron on October 7, 1988, when someone threw a stone at it. He jumped out and began firing his gun, killing an Arab who was standing in his own barber shop. During one court appearance, Levinger approached the court waving his gun over his head and saying he had been "privileged" to have shot an Arab. After he was sentenced, he was carried off to jail on the shoulders of a cheering throng.

Rabbi Moshe Tsvy Neriah, head of the famous B'Nai Akiva Yasheeva (religious school), said during a lecture on Levinger's behalf, "It's not time to think, but it's time to shoot right and left."

Justice Heim Cohen, a retired judge of Israel's supreme court, said, "The way the situation is going now, I would be afraid to say where we are going. I never heard of anybody who was tried for negligence after shooting somebody in cold blood. I'm probably getting old."

* * *

The intifada and resultant breakdown of moral order and humanity are a direct result of the kind of megalomania that characterizes the operation of the Mossad. That's where it all begins. This feeling that you can do anything you want to whomever you want for as long as you want because you have the power.

Israel is facing its biggest threat ever. This thing is uncontrollable. In Israel, they're still beating Palestinians, and

Shamir says, "They're making us become cruel. They're forcing us to hit children. Aren't they terrible?" This is what happens after years and years of secrecy; of "we're right, let's be right, no matter what"; of keeping the officials deliberately misinformed; of justifying violence and inhumanity through deceit, or, as the Mossad logo says: "by way of deception."

It's a disease that began with the Mossad and has spread through government and down through much of Israeli society. There are large elements inside Israel who are protesting this slide, but their voices are not being heard. And with each step down, it gets easier to repeat, and more difficult to stop.

The strongest curse inside the Mossad that one katsa can throw at another is the simple wish: "May I read about you in the paper."

It might be the only way to turn things around.

Appendix I

Organizational Charts and Documents

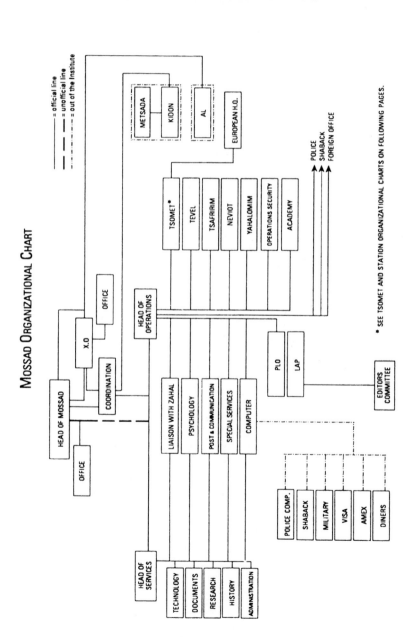

MOSSAD ORGANIZATIONAL CHART

= official line
= unofficial line
= out of the Institute

HEAD OF MOSSAD

OFFICE

COORDINATION

X.O

OFFICE

HEAD OF OPERATIONS

TSOMET*

TEVEL

TSAFRIRIM

NEVIOT

YAHALOMIM

OPERATIONS SECURITY

ACADEMY

METSADA

KIDON

AL

EUROPEAN H.Q.

POLICE
SHABACK
FOREIGN OFFICE

HEAD OF SERVICES

TECHNOLOGY

DOCUMENTS

RESEARCH

HISTORY

ADMINISTRATION

LIAISON WITH ZAHAL

PSYCHOLOGY

POST & COMMUNICATION

SPECIAL SERVICES

COMPUTER

PLO

LAP

EDITORS COMMITTEE

POLICE COMP.

SHABACK

MILITARY

VISA

AMEX

DINERS

* SEE TSOMET AND STATION ORGANIZATIONAL CHARTS ON FOLLOWING PAGES.

Tsomet Organizational Chart

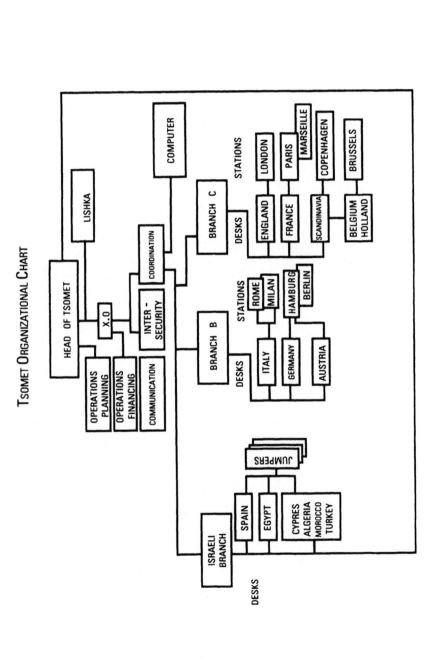

OFFICIAL FLOW OF INTELLIGENCE

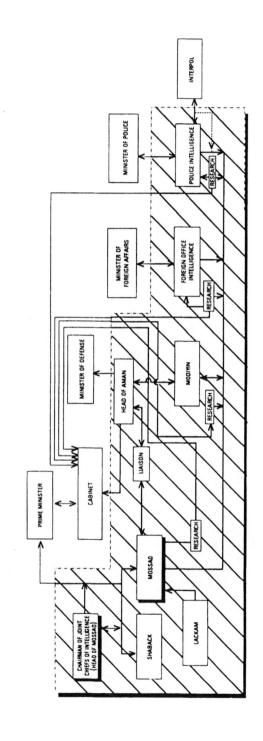

◫◫◫ = INTELLIGENCE COMMUNITY

PRIME MINISTER

CABINET

CHAIRMAN OF JOINT CHIEFS OF INTELLIGENCE (HEAD OF MOSSAD)

SHABACK

LACKAM

MOSSAD

RESEARCH

LIAISON

MINISTER OF DEFENSE

HEAD OF AMAN

MODIYIN

RESEARCH

MINISTER OF FOREIGN AFFAIRS

FOREIGN OFFICE INTELLIGENCE

RESEARCH

MINISTER OF POLICE

POLICE INTELLIGENCE

RESEARCH

INTERPOL

ORGANIZATION OF A STATION

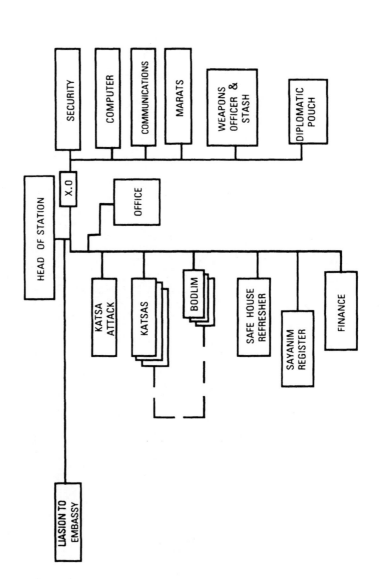

ACTUAL FLOW OF INTELLIGENCE

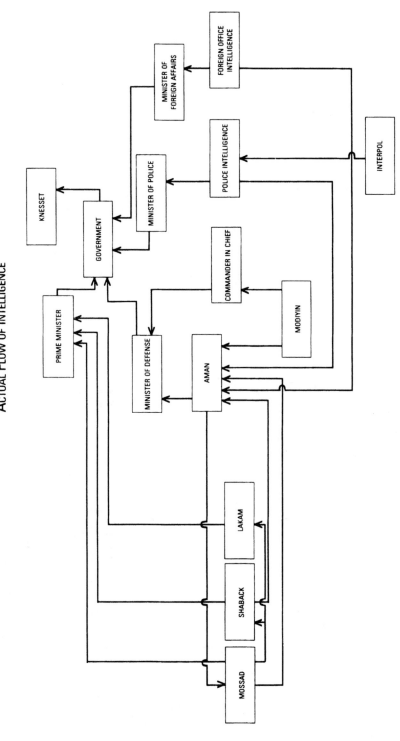

Layout of the Mossad Academy

Main Floor

1 SECRETARY OF COMMANDER
2 OFFICE OF COMMANDER
3 OFFICE OF X.O
4 OFFICE OF RUTY KIMELLY
5 OFFICE OF COURSE COMMANDER
6 SAFE ROOM
7 WASHROOM
8 KITCHEN
9 OPEN YARD

10 PING PONG ROOM
11 CLASSROOM
12 STUDY ROOM
13 INDOOR GARDEN
14 TELEPHONE
15 CONFERENCE AND GUEST ROOM
16 CONFERENCE ROOM
17 CONFERENCE ROOM
18 CONFERENCE ROOM
19 GUEST PARKING

Second Floor

TV STUDIO

CONFERENCE HALL

HEDER HAKHASH

OPEN ROOF

WASHROOMS

CLASSROOM

CLASSROOM

CLASSROOM

Mossad Pay Sheet Indicating Monthly Salary Paid to Victor Ostrovsky

(The form indicates its origins in the Office of the Prime Minister)

PROTECTIVE ROUTE:
METHODS OF DEALING WITH DANGEROUS AGENTS

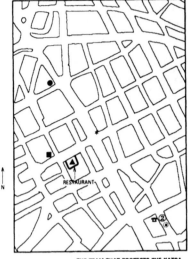

THE TEAM THAT PROTECTS THE KATSA

	THE TEAM THAT PROTECTS THE KATSA
●	HEAD OF TEAM
▲	NO 2
■	NO 3
✳	NO 4
✖	NO 5
◉	KATSA
⊗	SUBJECT
①	CAR NO 1
②	CAR NO 2
☎	TELEPHONE

THE TEAM THAT PROTECTS THE KATSA
IN STAGE ONE, EVERYBODY GETS INTO POSITION

1. #2 waits inside the restaurant. (Restaurant has already been determined "clean"; it was under surveillance before its address was passed to the subject so that he could not have staked it out.)

2. #3 is across the street, watching the entrance, ready to follow subject.

3. #4 is in position to watch and follow.

4. car #1 is in position.

5. Katsa is in car #2, well out of the way and waiting. Car will be positioned near a pay phone so katsa can call subject and give instructions.

6. #5 is in car #1, following subject's cab.

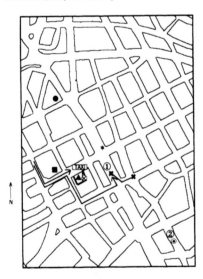

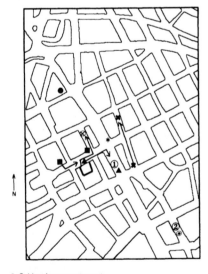

1. All in position as subject arrives in cab.

2. #5 will get out of car #1 and signal the katsa in car #2 to phone the subject in the restaurant.

3. When the call has been made, car #2 will flash its lights to signal this to car #1 from which signals will go to #4 (etc) that subject has received instructions.

4. Subject leaves restaurant.

5. #3 follows subject and receives signal from #2 that subject made no phone calls while in restaurant (if he <u>had</u>, operation would be called off, with everyone leaving area by car).

6. #2 then walks to car #1 and waits (because he was with the subject in the restaurant, he is now out of the picture).

7. #5 advances to the pick-up point (or "take" point).

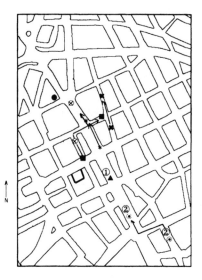
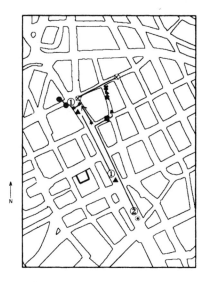

8. Subject continues along as instructed.
9. #3 leaves subject to #4, signaling that he is clean.
10. #4 takes over subject.
11. Car #2 with katsa gets into position 2.
12. #5 gets into position and will close.

13. Subject continues.
14. #5 takes subject.
15. #4 gets to corner and signals head of team and #4.
16. Car #1 advances and picks up head of team and #4.
17. Car #2 advances and picks up #3.

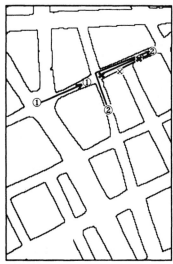
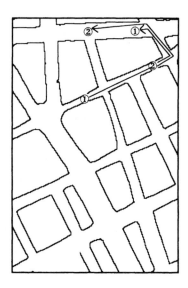

18. At this point, #5 closes on the subject.
19. Car #2 converges on subject.
20. The katsa opens the back door, while the subject is helped in by #5 who frisks him.
21. Car #2 comes in closer to follow and protect.

22. They disperse.

Appendix II

Mossad Reports on the Structure of Danish Security Services

*[Translation of a Mossad computer printout
describing Danish intelligence.]*

Country 4647 1985

reprint
copy for country

Regular — 1536 13 June 1985

To: Mashove

From: Country

SECRET — 4647

Purple A — Danish Civil Security Service (DCSS)

1. The Danish Civil Security Service is an integral part of the police. It is a subordinate of the justice department.

2. The police provide the service with manpower and logistical support; the justice department supervises the activities of the service. That supervision includes the approval of operational activities, with each one considered according to the target in question.

3. Under the head of the service and his second-in-command are three legal advisers who act as liaison of the command to the field level. Each of the three works with several units.

4. The main objectives of the service are counterespionage and counter terrorism. The service is also responsible for safeguarding Danish installations and foreign embassies. Its obligations to Israel include maintaining a constant observation of the Palestinian community in Denmark — numbering about 500 people.

5. There is suspicion and hostility toward any operational activity of the DCSS. This limits its capabilities.

   The service is also overseen by the judicial establishment, limiting its activities. The service is obligated to explain, analyze, and justify every action it wants to take, especially where individual freedoms are involved.

   Since the service is headed by legal people, it is virtually paralyzed.

6. Meetings with Purple are frequent. Should we need clarification of operational subjects we can organize a meeting within several hours.

   Once every three years there is a PAHA seminar. The last one took place last month.

7. There is very close cooperation with Purple A. The relationship is good and intimate.

   One of our listening people [marats] sits in the Purples' listening department, acting as an adviser to them on PAHA.

   The Purples do and will consult us regarding targets for mayanot [code for listening locations; literal translation is "fountain" or "source"].

   The highlight of the cooperation is operation "friendship" [the interrogation of a Palestinian pilot in a hospital in Denmark by someone from HQ in Tel Aviv. The code used for Tel Aviv HQ is HA-Y-HAL or "palace"]. In this operation to recruit an Iraqi pilot, the Purples have taken great risks, and the whole operation is only for our benefit.

   In the past we began an operation with "Shosanimo" and "Abu el Phida" that was supposed to take place in Denmark. It was not carried out because of an operational decision on our part.

8. The information we get from the mayanot gives us a full and comprehensive picture of the Palestinian community in Denmark and some material on PLO political activities.

9. There is a good dialogue on the above subjects.

10. On the subject of mahol [literally "dance" — referring to mutual recruitment operations] there is total cooperation when and as we call for it.

11. <u>Central Figures</u>

    A. Henning Fode — head of the service. Appointed November 1984.

    B. Michael Lyngbo — second-in-command from August 1983. Has no experience in intelligence and yet he is in charge of counterespionage.

    C. Paul Moza Hanson — legal adviser to the head of the service, he is our contact man with the Purples. His main activity is counter terrorism. He is about to finish his term. Hanson took part in the last PAHA seminar in Israel.

    D. Halburt Winter Hinagay — head of the anti terrorism and subversive activity department, participated in the last PAHA seminar in Israel.

Regular — 1024 14 June 1985

To: Mashove Regular

From: Country

SECRET — 4648

Purple B — Danish "Mossad" (Danish Defense Intelligence Service, DDIS)

1. General

The Danish "Mossad" is the intelligence arm of the Danish military. It is directly subordinate to the army chief and the minister of defense. Head of the DDIS is a department head in the army.

2. "Mossad" Structure

The DDIS is comprised of four units.

A. Administration.

B. Listening (8200).

C. Research.

D. Gathering.

3. DDIS Responsibilities

A. For NATO:

(1) Covering Poland and East Germany.

(2) Covering East Bloc ship movements in the Baltic, using a very powerful and highly sophisticated unit.

B. Internally:

(1) Political and military research.

(2) Positive gathering inside Denmark.

(3) Liaison with the foreign services.

(4) Providing the government with national evaluations. [In general the main subject of interest to the DDIS is the East Bloc.]

C. There is a new function in the making, that will cover the Middle East. At first it will be covered by one person one day a week. The objective is to gather intelligence information from Danish trade and businessmen who come in contact with the Middle East, as we have recommended in the PAHA conference.

4. Material we receive from DDIS is mainly on the subject of East Bloc, e.g. Soviet land, sea, and air activity. They specialize in photographing Soviet aircraft.

There has been special emphasis on installation of new antennas on the aircraft.

The Purples are the first service to pass to us photos of the SSC-3 system.

5. As of the visit of their air research branch head to Israel and their navy research head to Haifa, there has been an awakening of the relations with the DDIS.

There will be a combined military meet in Israel in August.

6. Central Figures

   A. Mogens Telling. Head of the service from 1976: visited Israel 1980.

   B. Ib Bangsbore. Head of humant gathering department from 1982. Plans to leave 1986.

Appendix III

AMAN Questionnaire on Syrian Military Preparedness

*[This is a translation of an actual document
given to a high-ranking Syrian agent prior
to his departure from Europe back to Syria.]*

The following is a military information briefing for a subject who is going down to a target country. It is set up in descending order of importance. Use your own judgment in dropping subjects that you think the source will not be capable of answering.

STATE OF ALERT READINESS AND WARNINGS

1. How is each state of readiness defined in the Syrian ground forces and how is it apparent in the following:

   a) The presence of soldiers in the bases;

   b) Training routines;

   c) Operational fitness of equipment;

   d) Quantity of armaments and ammunition.

2. What is the present readiness of the Syrian army for war based on the following criteria:

   a) Manpower status in the units;

   b) The level of equipment fitness;

   c) Levels of stock, ammunition, other equipment (quartermaster);

   d) Training that various units have received;

   e) Strategic stock levels in Syria — food, gasoline.

3. How many battalions constitute the following brigades:

   a) Armored Brigade 60;

   b) Armored Brigade 67;

   c) Mechanized Brigade 87 from the 11th Armored Division;

   d) The 14th "Special Forces" Division.

TRAINING PROGRAM FOR 1985

4. What are the Syrian goals within the training framework of 1985?

5. Which units at the brigade or division level are expected to exercise this year in full mobilization and when?

6. Which exercises are expected at the top command staff/corps/division/ and what is the timetable?

7. What are the lessons the Syrian army has taken from the 1984 training year?

8. Which units in particular excelled in this training year and what objectives were achieved?

SPECIFIC SUBJECTS FOR CHECKING

9. What techniques were tested in offensive exercises?

10. How long does the management of a battle take in the various training levels?

11. What part of this training is done at night?

12. What exercises have been carried out by Armored Division N. 11 and its various units?

13. Were there exercises this year that involved SSM [surface- to-surface missile] units?

14. Which commando units trained during 84 and at what levels?

15. What are the lessons learned by Syrians from the Galily peace move in the following subjects:

   a) Armored units;

   b) Commando units;

   c) Artillery and anti-aircraft units;

   d) Command and control.

   e) How far have the Syrians gone in finding answers to the various lessons?

THE THEORY OF BATTLE [Teaching of War]

16. The Syrian battle theory in terms of breaking through a fortified space such as the Golan Heights:

   a) How do the Syrians regard the Israeli fortifications and how do they think it's composed from the engineering aspect?

   b) What do the Syrians possess to overcome those obstacles?

   c) Do the Syrians have models of the Israeli line?

   d) What is the battle theory the Syrians have developed to overcome the Israeli fortifications?

e) Which units are designated for the breakthrough? What means will be allotted to them for that particular job during the war and what means do they have today?

f) How well trained are they as units in fulfilling their job?

SYRIAN COMMANDOS

17. How will "Special Forces" Division No. 14 operate as an airborne division as the "source" says if (as he says) the Syrians have a limited helicopter transport capability?

18. Are commandos equipped with armored troop carriers or will they be in future? If so, for what purpose?

19. Will they create more "Special Forces" divisions? If so, what is the time-table?

20. a) Do the Syrians plan to land commandos on the front line fortifications?

b) Do the Syrians plan to land commandos on Tel Abu Nida?

c) Do the Syrians plan to land commandos on Tel El Hantsir?

d) Do the Syrians plan to land commandos on Tiel Pars?

e) Do the Syrians plan to land commandos on the Bukata Ridge?

f) Will they land commandos on intersections?

g) Will they land commandos to try and take command posts?

21. What is the exact technique the Syrians plan to use to land commandos?

FUNDAMENTALS

22. What is the force the Syrians estimate they will need to achieve strategic balance with Israel?

a) How many divisions and corps do the Syrians assume they need to achieve this goal?

b) How many tanks, armored personnel carriers, and artillery do they think they need to achieve this goal?

c) How many special means (see itemization below) do they need to achieve this goal?

1. Bridge and minefield penetrators.

2. SSMs.

3. Capability for operating chemical warfare.

d) What troop helicopter transport capacity is the Syrian army striving for?

e) How many anti-tank helicopters should there be in the Syrian army within this framework?

23. What is the essence of the multi-year growth plan? (See itemization.)

   a) Was the growth plan completed over 84? If yes:

      1) What were the original targets?

      2) How many did they achieve?

      3) Do they think they have completed the task and to what degree of success?

   b) What are the goals of the present growth program?

      1) The number of units/regiments that are going to be formed or re-formed?

      2) What is the quantity goal of the plan regarding tanks, ATC, artillery, anti-aircraft, and engineering?

      3) What is the process that the army has to go through according to the plan?

      4) What is the timetable for every phase of the plan? When is the process expected to be completed?

24. The structure of the defense company today.

   a) What units are included in "Defense Company"?

   b) What is the hierarchy among the defense companies?

   c) What units were transferred from the defense company to Siroko?

   d) Were there signs of revolt on the grounds of transferring soldiers from the defense companies to other units?

   e) What are the operational objectives of the defense companies today?

25. "Special Forces" Division No. 14.

   a) What units are incorporated today within the division?

   b) Are there plans to create more logistical support units to be subordinated to the division command?

26. The Guard of the Republic.

   a) What secondary units are included in the Guard today and what are their weapons?

   b) Are there plans to expand this unit?

27. Reserve units in the Syrian army.

   a) Are there (outside of recruiting reserves to fill in gaps for casualties of war) such reserves organically extant?

   b) What units are they and what is their deployment?

   c) What type of training do they receive and what is the level of their readiness?

ARMORED DIVISION NO. 11

28. More itemization in all that regards the sub units of the division (organic battalions of the brigades, battalions of the artillery batteries, and battalions subordinated directly to the division command). The armaments and supplies in the various units; officers and manpower in Division 11; present deployment, training and alert status of the division.

29. The tasks and objectives of Division 11. Will the division act as general staff reserves for deployment in the rear or will it be part of a new corps?

30. What type of tanks are there in every brigade of Division 11? And what is the quantity per brigade through to November 84?

31. Brigade 87 and Brigade 60. Itemize their sub units, their numbers, weapons and equipment, manpower and officers, present deployment, training and alert.

MOUNTAIN BRIGADE 120

32. a) To whom is Brigade 120 subordinate today?

b) Where is it deployed today?

c) Where are its permanent bases?

33. Itemize the units subordinate to Brigade 120, weaponry and equipment, manpower and officers, training.

34. Goals and objectives of the brigade. Where will it be deployed in an emergency and who will it belong to?

TERRITORIAL COMMANDS IN THE SYRIAN ARMY

35. Itemize the various territorial commands and which operational units are under their command.

36. Officers and manpower in the various commands.

37. The duties of the various commands during peace and war.

38. Military camps and installations in the various commands.

CORPS IN THE SYRIAN ARMY

39. Are there plans to create more corps in the S.A.? If so, itemize and provide timetable.

40. If such corps are created, will there still be general command reserves?

FIELD FORCES GENERAL COMMAND

41. At what stage is the creation of the field forces general command?

42. What units will be subordinate to such a command?

43. Officers and manpower in the command?

44. Deployment of units and command posts during emergency and routine?

45. Objective of such command?

GENERAL STAFF ANTI-TANK

46. Give list of the general staff command anti-tank units, their numbers, and officer staff.

47. Their present deployment.

48. Objectives and targets.

49. The standard weapons of a unit.

PURCHASING AIM

50. Itemize the purchasing contracts with the Soviet Union since Assad's visit to Moscow, October 84, with emphasis on advanced weapons systems (type, quantity, time of arrival, method of payment).

51. Which units will be first to receive the advanced weapons systems (improved T-72 tanks, armored troop carriers BMP.1, anti-tank systems, tank assistance systems and artillery) that are planned to arrive this year?

52. Contacts and contracts with western European countries in the last year and in the near future, with the emphasis on advanced weapons systems (tanks, ATC, mobile artillery, assistance equipment).

STORAGE FACILITIES

53. Itemize the storage facilities for new purchases and old equipment in the S.A. Capacity, subordination, objective.

54. Specify the contents of each storage area.

NIGHT VISION EQUIPMENT

55. Is there an interest in the S.A. in purchasing such equipment and for what use? Where are such purchases taking place? It sounds strange that the "source" does not know about the use of such equipment in the S.A.

ANTI-TANK

56. On what does the subject base his determination that the anti-tank fodge will not be turned into anti-tank brigades? [A "fodge" is a unit smaller than a brigade; relevant to Arab armies.]

57. What is the difference between an anti-tank fodge and an anti-tank brigade?

SPECIAL FORCES

58. On what does the source base his determination that the commando fodge will not be turned into commando battalions?

59. What is the difference between a commando fodge and a commando battalion?

OFFICERS AND MANPOWER

60. List the new appointments and expulsions according to the bulletin expected Jan. 85.

61. The changes among the command staff after the return of Rifad Assad and after the Baath Convention expected soon.

62. Why is Halmat Shaby absent from military formalities that normally call for the participation of the chief of staff? Are there any changes expected in his status as chief of staff?

63. Are the rumors that Ebrahm Tsafi from Division No. 1 is expected to be appointed second-in-command to chief of staff after the appointment of Ali Atslan to chief of staff, instead of Shaby correct?

64. Are there any changes expected to the placements of Ali Duba and his second-in-command, Magid Said? If so, where will they be appointed and who will replace them?

65. Are there any changes expected in the responsibility and objectives of the body to be headed by Rifat Assad? According to the "source," Rifat will replace Ahamed Diab as head of the office for national security.

66. New appointments in Division 569.

67. The structure of the Syrian defense department.

68. Specify the training programs for cadets in the military academy at Homs.

69. What is the size of the new cadet course that is supposed to start training in 1985 in the military academy in Timz?

70. What is the system by which they give out the advance serial numbers to the cadets in the military academy in Homs? Explain in detail.

71. Quantity of manpower in S.A. compared to status allotment, specifically in the divisions.

72. Lists of officers for as many units as possible in the S.A.

73. The codes of the reserve reservoir according to professions or per specific units.

74. Places of storage of the above?(73 x 73)

75. How often do those codes change?

76. Specify the expected recruitment class expected for 84-85 based on education structure.

Glossary of Terms

ACADEMY — (*Midrasha*) Officially called the prime minister's summer residence, it is the Mossad training school north of Tel Aviv.

AGENT — A widely misused term. It is a recruit, not a domestic employee of an intelligence agency. The Mossad has about 35,000 in the world, 20,000 of them operational and 15,000 sleepers. "Black" agents are Arabs, while "white" agents are non-Arabs. "Warning" agents are strategic agents used to warn of war preparations, e.g., a doctor in a Syrian hospital who notices a large new supply of drugs and medicines arriving; a harbor employee who spots increased activity of war ships.

AL — A secret unit of experienced katsas working under deep cover in the United States.

AMAN — Military intelligence.

APAM — (*Avtahat Paylut Modienit*) Intelligence operational security.

BABLAT — "Mixing up the balls" or *bilbul baitsin*, talking nonsense.

BALDAR — Courier.

BASE COUNTRY — Western Europe, United States, Canada: wherever the Mossad has bases.

BAT LEVEYHA — Female escorts, not for sex; usually local women, not necessarily Jews, hired as assistant agents.

BENELUX — The Belgian/Holland/Luxembourg desk at Mossad headquarters.

BODEL — (*bodlim,* plural) Or *lehavdil.* Go-between, messenger between safe houses and embassies or between various safe houses.

CASE OFFICER — In most intelligence services, the name used instead of the Mossad's *katsa.* In the Mossad, case officers are the people in Metsada who handle the combatants.

COMBATANTS — The real "spies": Israelis sent to Arab countries to work under cover.

DARDASIM (Smerfs) — A sub-department within Kaisarut; they work in China, Africa, and the Far East establishing relations.

DAYLIGHT — Highest state of alert of a Mossad station.

DEVELOPMENT — Tied in to military unit 8520; they manufacture special locks, suitcases with false bottoms, etc.

DIAMOND (*yahalomim*) — A unit in the Mossad that handles communications to agents in target countries.

DIRECT INTELLIGENCE — Actual physical movements or activities that can be observed; e.g., movements of arms or troops, or readiness of hospitals or harbors for war.

DUVSHANIN — Usually UN peacekeeping troops paid to transport messages and packages back and forth across Israeli-Arab borders.

EXPERTS WITH HANDLES — Term used to describe a professional in a field outside of espionage and/or intelligence who is taken on missions to identify documentation or equipment in his area of expertise. "With handles" is a metaphor for a parcel, i.e., he is carried in by the Mossad team.

FALACH — Arab peasant farmers in Lebanon, often recruited by Israeli military as low-grade agents.

FIBER INTELLIGENCE — Observations that are not physical, such as economic indicators, rumors, morale, general feelings.

FRAMES (*Misgarot*) — Jewish self-protection units set up all over the world.

GADNA — Israeli para-military youth brigades.

HETS VA-KESHET (bow and arrow) — The emblem and summer training camp of Gadna.

HORSE (*sus*) — A higher-ranking person who helps you up the ladder.

HUMANT — The collection of information from human beings, i.e., agents of all types.

INSTITUTE — The formal name of the Mossad. In Hebrew, Mossad is *Ha Mossad, le Modiyn ve le Tafkidim Mayuhadim*, or in English, the Institute for Intelligence and Special Operations.

JUMBO — Personal information beyond official intelligence, gathered by Mossad liaison officers from foreign intelligence liaison officers, e.g., CIA.

JUMPERS — Katsas stationed in Israel who jump into various countries on a short-term basis, as opposed to katsas actually stationed abroad.

KAISARUT (originally *Tevel*) — Liaison at Israeli embassies; known as intelligence officers by local authorities.

KATSA — "Gathering officer" or "case officer." Mossad has only about 35 in operations recruiting enemy agents worldwide, compared with many thousands for KGB and CIA.

KESHET — (Later *neviot*) "Bow." Gathering information from still objects, e.g. break-ins, installing listening devices.

KIDON — "Bayonet." Operational arm of Metsada responsible for executions and kidnappings.

KOMEMIUTE — See *Metsada*.

KSHARIM — "Knots." Computer records of who is tied in with whom.

LAKAM — (*Lishka le Kishrei Mada*) Israeli prime minister's scientific affairs liaison bureau.

LAP — (*Lohamah Pscichlogit*) or psychological warfare.

LEAD — Recruiting one person to get at another.

MABUAH — Someone who brings information from a source of information rather than directly.

MALAT — Branch in liaison dealing with South America.

MARATS — Listeners.

MASLUH — "Route." a system used for self-protection, to know if you're being tailed or not.

MAULTER — Hebrew word meaning simply "unplanned." Used to describe unplanned or improvised security route.

MELUCKHA — Originally *Tsomet*, meaning "kingdom." Recruiting department that handles katsas.

METSADA — (Later *Komemiute*) Highly secret, like a mini-Mossad within the Mossad; operates combatants.

MISGAROT — See "frames."

MISHLASHIM — "Triplers." Drops and dead-letter boxes.

MOLICH — "Walker." Like a seeing-eye dog; one recruited not for himself, but to lead someone else.

NAKA — Uniform Mossad writing system for operation and information reports.

NATIV — Collects information re Soviet Union; helps create escape routes for Eastern Bloc Jews.

NEVIOT — See *Keshet.*

OTER — An Arab paid to help make contact with other Arabs, often used in recruitment process, usually paid $3,000 to $5,000 a month, plus expenses.

PAHA — (*paylut hablanit oyenet*) Hostile sabotage activities, e.g., PLO.

ROUTE — See *maslut.*

SAFE HOUSE — Actually called "operational apartments" by Mossad; apartments or houses owned or rented for secret meetings and as operations bases.

SAIFANIM — "Goldfish," the department within the Mossad that deals with the PLO.

SAYAN — (*Sayanim*, plural) Volunteer Jewish helpers outside Israel.

SEVEN STAR — Small, leather-bound daybook carried by katsas, containing phone numbers and contacts in code.

SHABACK — The Israeli equivalent of the FBI; the internal security force.

SHICKLUT — The department handling listening personnel, i.e. *marats.*

SHIN BET — Former name for Shaback.

SLICK — Hiding place for documents, weapons, etc.

TACHLESS — Getting to the point.

TARGET COUNTRY — Any Arab country.

TAYESET — Code name for training department.

TEUD — "Documents" — manufacturing documents, e.g. passports.

TEVEL — See *Kaisarut*.

TSAFRIRIM — "Morning breeze" in English. Organizes Jewish communities outside Israel; helps set up frames.

TSIACH — (*Tsorech Yediot Hasuvot*). Annual meeting of military and civilian Israeli intelligence organizations; also name of document describing intelligence requirements for the next year, listed in descending order of importance.

TSOMET — See *Meluckha*.

UNIT 504 — A mini-Mossad; intelligence-gathering unit in military for cross-border intelligence.

UNIT 8200 — A military unit that handles all communication intercepts for Israeli intelligence.

UNIT 8513 — A branch in military intelligence that is in charge of photography.

YARID — "Country fair." Teams in charge of European security.

Index

LaVergne, TN USA
04 March 2011
218890LV00001B/37/A